SACRED SOUND AND SOCIAL CHANGE:
LITURGICAL MUSIC IN JEWISH
AND CHRISTIAN EXPERIENCE

TWO LITURGICAL TRADITIONS

Volume 3

Sacred Sound
and Social Change:

Liturgical Music in Jewish and Christian Experience

Edited by

LAWRENCE A. HOFFMAN

and

JANET R. WALTON

University of Notre Dame Press

Notre Dame   London

Manufactured in the United States of America

Library of Congress Cataloging-in-Publication Data

Sacred sound and social change: liturgical music in Jewish and Christian experience / edited by Lawrence A. Hoffman and Janet R. Walton
    p.   cm. — (Two liturgical traditions ; v. 3)
    Took its origin from a conference held in oct. 1986 at Hebrew Union College-Jewish Institute of Religion
    Includes bibliographical references and index.
    ISBN 0-268-01745-X
    1. Church music. 2. Music—Religious aspects—Christianity. 3. Synagogue music—History and criticism. 4. Jews—Music—History and criticism. I. Hoffman, Lawrence A., 1942– II. Walton, Janet Roland. III Series.
ML2900.S2 1992
782.3—dc20   91–51120
                                                    CIP

Contents

Introduction

North American Culture
and Its Challenges to Sacred Sound

What do we sing in a time when nations battle, when cultures clash, when races are at odds, when sexes struggle in the courts (and out of them), when religions revert to factitious "holy wars"? Can we really be so bold as still to sing, "God's covenant lasts forever"?

Over the centuries, liturgical music in synagogue and church has shaped communities' faith. More persuasively than words alone, music expresses what we believe about God. It proclaims the terms of our relationships with each other. It connects our faith to the tangible concerns that confound our world.

Poignant illustrations of the power of music are strikingly exemplified in communities where those tangible concerns mean nothing less than the work of human survival. Jews on the brink of extinction in Nazi death camps are reported nonetheless to have sung *Ani ma'amin*, "I believe with perfect faith in the coming of the Messiah," just as their forebears in eleventh-century Rhineland communities sang *Alenu leshabe'ach*, "It is our lot to praise the Eternal One," even as Crusaders were burning them alive.[1] No evidence assured them that their song

1

could change their circumstances. Yet they persisted in singing.
Song offered not only a public witness but also strength one
to another.

Similarly, blacks in the midst of slavery sang,

> My burden's so heavy, I can't hardly see,
> Seems like everybody is down on me,
> An' that's all right, I don't worry,
> Oh, there will be a better day.[2]

The "blues" style of this song—both its music and its text—
gave voice to the reality of utter pain but "a refusal to be conquered by it."[3] In their singing, blacks identified and solidified
their determination. Their color would not destine them to be
demeaned forever. "There will be a better day."

Music's capacity to express emotion as well as conceptual
insight makes it a primary vehicle for the worshiper to identify
with the deepest core of his or her faith. When a community
or an individual sings about suffering, joy, or determination,
what might otherwise be perceived as experience inchoate
receives a name, and then can be shared in both heart and mind.
In that sharing is power, participation in the "fresh stuff of
faith"[4] that makes belief matter.

Liturgical music has always functioned this way, linking
experience to faith in an atmosphere of emotional commitment.
But standing now at the close of the twentieth century, we find
religious communities asking new questions of their worship.
Knowing that a succession of wars, economic upheavals, and
the denial of basic human rights mark their world, people are
demanding liturgical experiences that enable them to make their
faith matter, in the sense that it will carry over to the ordinary
and the not-so-ordinary choices that contemporary circumstances
foist upon them. Such an expectation challenges all liturgical
leaders, but invites composers and performing musicians in a
special way. The rapidly changing—some would even say,
deteriorating—situations featured on the nightly news quickly
make yesterday's worship appear utterly irrelevant. Old texts
and sounds come under attack as thoughtful and committed
people ask, "What does it mean to sing 'God's covenant lasts

forever' in the face of senseless deaths, pervasive violence, differences settled only by war? What sounds and words do we use to call upon God? What are the terms of this covenant?'' As traditional music is thus subjected to careful scrutiny, new music is emerging to express a spectrum of responses. ''Never in the history of the church,'' says Robin Leaver, ''have so many new hymnals been published within such a short time. Never has there been more activity in the writing of new texts and tunes.'' Leaver is quite correct! He estimates that between 1984 and 1994, forty-five new hymnals will be produced, thirty as official hymnals for church denominations.[5]

Driving this unprecedented musical output are both theological and sociological developments. Theologically speaking, we have come to recognize what ought surely to have been evident long before: as a cursory glance at religious history discloses, a human understanding of the nature of God is uncontainable in any single set of metaphors. No words identify God adequately. No image suits every generation equally. Each age seeks knowledge of God through its own favored tropes that emerge as privileged because they make God real in the light of the circumstances that each age faces. Particularly now, therefore, as we recognize God's uncapturable essence, we find ourselves engaged in continuous attempts to identify the many manifestations of God's unfolding among us. Our search opens up aspects of God that have been lost or overlooked for centuries, even entire eras! Such metaphors as God as *mother* or *lover,* for example, correct the tradition that has excluded all but patriarchal divine/human expressions. We find ourselves probing the entire gamut of human experience to discover where God is present, thereby to name God differently from what we might otherwise have imagined, were we to limit our religious vocabulary to the set of divine imagery most familiar to us.

The issues of consequence occasioned by our world crisis fuel our theological search; we discover the inadequacy of the conventional set of texts and sounds to express the terms of the covenant as that covenant unfolds in our day. What promise of faith should guide our choices about life and death? How does covenantal awareness affect our responsibility to care for the earth, to feed the millions of people dying from hunger, to eliminate illiteracy, to narrow the gap between rich and poor?

Surely the challenges implicit in social change are not entirely new as critical factors shaping sacred sound. Perhaps what is different, however, is a sociological phenomenon: the growing self-empowerment of congregations—at least in some denominations—whereby congregants themselves wish to decide what they will sing. The "right" hymns, songs, and chants are no longer merely "givens" dictated by authorities. Exposed to a broad spectrum of musical styles, both within and beyond church and synagogue, worshiping communities have a sense of what they find banal and what they find compelling. They know what moves them beyond themselves as well as into solidarity with each other. No longer is the choice of music the sole responsibility of professional musicians or liturgists. Professional musicians play the essential roles of exposing worshipers to the breadth of musical possibilities and of insuring qualitatively good performances, but congregations are becoming active partners in the final selection of what will or will not be sung.

We have discovered also that worshiping communities are not monochromatic; nor do they all have similar socioeconomic, class, or cultural backgrounds. Barriers that isolated whites from blacks, Europeans from Asians and Africans, rich from poor are dissolving. In a world where planetary and human survival depends on the collaboration and talents of all cultures, the singing of hymns that reflect only, or even primarily, the white Anglo-Saxon perspective is at best inadequate and more often demeaning. Far more appropriate—indeed, even mandatory—is a broad repertory with a variety of texts, tunes, and instrumental accompaniments that represent a number of cultural expressions. Such diversity is critical because music interprets our faith through culturally conditioned symbols. To sing or hear music that reflects the reality of particular cultures acknowledges the theological claim that God's activity is known more accurately through many voices and symbols, rather than through one or only a few.

Congregations should expect sacred music to be visionary as well. They want music that asks something of them even beyond what they can anticipate; their music should invite them to experience the extraordinary capacities of God's ways. "We need a language that is both contemplative and prophetic," says Gustavo Gutiérrez, "contemplative because it ponders a God who is love, prophetic because it talks about a liberator God."[6] What is required is music that frees congregations to encounter God—a constantly unfolding deity mysteriously known both beyond the confines of human limitations and through them.

A favorite Christian hymn, heard often during the Easter season, is "The Strife Is O'er, the Battle Won." Most often sung to a sixteenth-century melody by Palestrina, this hymn expresses a sense of victorious completion, telling of a God who has conquered death forever. Robert McAfee Brown, however, comments:

> In heaven, perhaps; on earth, never. Never, as long as history lasts, will our program notes be enough, never will the script come to the last page, never will good emerge a permanent victor over evil, never will the resolution be achieved, never will the curtain come down in conclusion.
>
> There is no conclusion. The curtain stays up and the play goes on. And we are on stage.[7]

Sacred music reminds us of the ever-ongoing script and of our participation in it. The sobering realities of our world put into question the traditional notion of an omnipotent, victorious God who wills the events of this world into being and then controls them ever after. Rather, what we know is a God who is incarnate in our attempts toward honesty, justice, kindness, and compassion. Thus, successful liturgies for today's evolving congregations feature sacred music that constitutes a source of insight into the human struggle to be godly, and an experience of support, hope, and sustenance for the journey toward that end.

Through its extraordinary range of symbols, liturgy has the power to shape experiences that make God's presence accessible. Worship in community invites engagement with an elusive, unrelenting God represented in the community of disparate persons and cultures who have come together in their common human condition. What Henri Nouwen says about liberation theologians is true also about liturgical communities: "They live themselves into a new way of thinking."[8] In the best of circumstances, liturgy embodies a new way of being and an invitation to "live into" it. Music is an indispensable resource of this power.

Recognizing the theological and sociological challenges of our time, and the indispensable need for sacred music to help congregations "live into a new way of thinking," a symposium on "Sacred Sound and Social Change" was sponsored jointly by three institutions dedicated to education and to faith—the School of Sacred Music at Hebrew Union College–Jewish Institute of Religion (in New York), Union Theological Seminary (in New York), and the Institute for Sacred Music at Yale University (in New Haven). Held at Hebrew Union College–Jewish Institute of Religion in October 1986, the symposium addressed several questions: How are alterations in social structure reflected culturally in the public liturgies of society's religions? Can Christians and Jews expect their worship and especially their music to reflect the social upheavals of their time? How does music meet the needs of congregations for transcendence, community, transformation? Musicologists, composers, leaders, and members of Jewish and Christian congregations discussed a wide and rich range of responses to all these questions.

This book took its origin from the conference. A few chapters were first presented as lectures there. Others were solicited subsequently in order to provide a more complete exposition of the topic; among these are the first and third chapters of part 1, which trace the origins and evolution of Jewish and Christian music. As one might expect, an examination of music in ancient Jewish and Christian liturgical communities offers insight about current liturgical practices, not the least of which are psalmody and the role of the choir in church and synagogue. The long-cherished tradition of having a trained group of singers has its own story, a cycle of both good and bad use. At its best, the choir offered a broad repertory that enriched immeasurably a worshiping community's experience. At its worst, it took over the role of the congregation and the congregation stopped singing.

Chapters 2 and 4 in part 1 continue the effort to reconstruct our musical past by addressing moments in history that may serve as models for the present. The nineteenth century (for Jews) and the Protestant Reformation (for Christians) present parallel eras when social change altered musical practice. These chapters lead to part 2, where three prominent composers and theorists describe the situation of sacred music for Roman Catholics, Reformed Protestants, and Reform Jews in our time. Their essays reveal the extent to which the musical challenges facing contemporary communities evoke dissatisfaction in some worshipers, enthusiasm in others.

Case studies mentioned in this book offer insights for North American congregations. They point to the growing proliferation of musical styles, increasing complexity in making musical choices, and the expansion of the musical canon to reflect the changing complexion and needs of the worshiping community. They indicate as well the complication involved in change, but also the still untapped resources available to congregations for the enrichment of public prayer. The potential of music as an agent of liberation and transformation has never yet been fully unleashed.

Part 3 presents what is perhaps the unique contribution of this book: the inclusion of four newly composed musical pieces commissioned for the conference. Each composer was invited to set Psalm 136, newly translated and with inclusive language. Its repetitive phrase, ''God's covenant lasts forever,'' presented them with particular theological, musical, and pastoral challenges. What sounds would express the emerging under-standing of God's covenant with humankind? Should the style resonate with the long tradition of singing the psalms? What would an entirely new sound be like? What music shapes the faith of the diverse liturgical traditions represented by the various composers? In addition to their music, the composers were asked to reflect on the process by which their work came into being, and what they hoped to accomplish, musically and liturgically.

The comments by our four composers, representative of four diverse traditions, are followed in part 4 by three more general perspectives on the dilemmas faced by musicians and liturgists in our eclectic and fast-paced age. They raise concerns about distinctive claims that social change is now making on the development of sacred sound. And finally, we offer some concluding thoughts that arise out of the book as a whole.

The text of Psalm 136 expresses well the purpose of this book. Christians and Jews share the belief that God's covenant will last forever, that God will be always present to humankind, participating fully in our pain and delight with a promise of a better day. Liturgy celebrates that promise, even as it sharpens our awareness of the harsher realities that typify life as it must be lived until the promise is realized. The authors engage us in a provocative dialogue on the potential of sacred sound to accomplish this liturgical task.

NOTES

1. See liturgical passage attesting to the *Alenu* replicated in Chaim Stern, ed., *Gates of Repentance* (New York, 1978), p. 434; drawn from several medieval documents discussed in Lawrence A. Hoffman, *Gates of Understanding,* vol. 2 (New York, 1984), p. 221.

2. James H. Cone, *The Spirituals and the Blues* (New York, 1972), p. 141.

3. Ibid., p. 140.

4. May Sarton, "Greeting: New Year's Eve, 1937," in Serena Sue Hilsinger and Lois Byrnes, eds., *Selected Poems* (New York, 1978).

5. Robin Leaver, "Music for Worship," in Robin Leaver, ed., *Church Music: The Future* (Princeton, N.J., 1990), p. 17.

6. Gustavo Gutiérrez, "Reflections from a Latin American Perspective: Finding Our Way to Talk About God," in Virginia Fabella and Sergio Torres, eds., *Irruption of the Third World: Challenge to Theology* (Maryknoll, N.Y., 1983), p. 232.

7. Robert McAfee Brown, *Gustavo Gutiérrez: An Introduction to Liberation Theology* (Maryknoll, N.Y., 1990), p. 184.

8. Henri Nouwen, *Gracias* (New York, 1983), p. 159.

Reconstructing the Past: Sacred Sound from the Bible to Reform

Introduction

Our musical challenges of the present arise out of the interface and, to some extent, the conflict between, on the one hand, age-old musical traditions having a cultural life of their own and, on the other hand, the contemporary realities of North American culture. Part 1 establishes the nature of our musical traditions by summarizing the development of what has classically been considered "sacred sound" in synagogues (in the first two essays) and churches (in the third and fourth essays). At the same time, the authors explore the impact of social change in eras past, demonstrating that neither Jewish nor Christian liturgical music is homogeneous.

Eliyahu Schleifer, noted Jewish musicologist, teaches liturgical music history at the Hebrew Union College–Jewish Institute of Religion in Jerusalem. His article, the first historical study in the book, is actually two essays in one. It begins with a detailed synopsis of presynagogue music, that is, music from the cult of the First and Second Temples. Since these institutions are the background out of which many later musical traditions arose, or to which they were retroactively linked, we have included the lengthy discussion of Temple music as a preamble for the entire historical discussion of part 1. The second half of the article chronicles the history of synagogue music from its inception until the rise of Reform Judaism in the nineteenth century.

Later, in the third essay, Margot Fassler and Peter Jeffery provide a parallel survey for Christian music up to the Protestant Reformation. Both authors are researchers in the field of medieval liturgical music. Fassler teaches the history of music

at Brandeis University. Jeffery is currently on leave from the
University of Delaware, with a John D. and Catherine T.Mac-
Arthur Fellowship.

We have chosen two chronologically disparate but functionally
similar points at which to break up the essays in part 1. Following the suggestion in volume 2 of this series (and the order
of volume 1), we see the Protestant Reformation of the sixteenth
century and the rise of Reform Judaism three centuries later
as parallel phenomena, two instances in which social change
disrupted medieval traditions and successfully questioned each
tradition's continuity in the single authoritative form with which
it had presented itself. With the thought that these two events
might prove paradigmatic for our own age—which volume 2
suggests, in fact, is a "second reformation"—we asked the
authors of our first and third essays to conclude their accounts
at the point where the reformation relevant to their own tradition occurs.

To take our narrative through the reformation periods in question, we turned to Geoffrey Goldberg (for the second essay of
the book) and Robin A. Leaver (for the fourth and final essay
in part 1). Both a rabbi and a cantor, Goldberg is currently a
faculty member of the School of Sacred Music, Hebrew Union
College–Jewish Institute of Religion, New York, specializing
particularly in the music of nineteenth-century Reform Judaism.
Leaver, who teaches at both Westminster Choir College and
Drew University, is known for his research in the music and
liturgy of the Reformation. Each in his own way, Goldberg and
Leaver explore the impact of social change on sacred sound
during another era: the birth of Reform Judaism, for Jews, and
the Protestant Reformation, for Christians.

Jewish Liturgical Music from the Bible to Hasidism

ELIYAHU SCHLEIFER

This survey summarizes three millennia of Jewish liturgical music, from countries as diverse as Yemen and Germany, and is influenced by musicological trends that go back to the father of Jewish musicology, Abraham Zvi Idelsohn (1882–1938).[1] Idelsohn can now be criticized for his overzealous attempts to trace different musical traditions back to a common layer as early as the Second Temple and before. Moreover, much of his masterwork, *Jewish Music in Its Historical Development*,[2] including his theory of the modes, needs a thorough revision. Yet even with these shortcomings, he remains today the exemplary scholar in the field. His *Thesaurus of Hebrew Oriental Melodies*[3] is still the most important anthology of Jewish chants and songs.

Evident also is the influence of my own teachers and colleagues, such as Edith Gerson-Kiwi, Hanoch Avenary, and the members of the Jewish Music Research Center in Jerusalem. It may also reflect the biased view of the author as a practicing Ashkenazi[4] cantor, and the pedagogical habits of a teacher who is constantly forced to simplify (perhaps oversimplify) the issues for his students. The survey is confined to the musical practices of "rabbinic" Judaism. It does not include Samaritan, Karaite, and Ethiopian liturgical music because these traditions require special studies of their own.

A firm foundation to the present study and to Jewish liturgical music itself is to be found, of course, in the Bible.

13

MUSIC IN BIBLICAL TIMES

It is doubtful whether the early periods of the Bible, before the establishment of the Temple worship, have any influence on our liturgical music today. Nevertheless, some early biblical references allude to the liturgical music of ancient ceremonies.

The Bible presents severe problems for the student of Israel's ancient liturgical music,[5] not the least of which is the fact that we can only guess what biblical music sounded lilke. No precise musical notation indicated melody and rhythm until the thirteenth century. Moreover, music is far from the Bible's center of interest, so descriptions of music are scanty; allusions to instruments, obscure. To some extent, we interpret scriptural information from traditional interpretations of the text and the reappearance of the Bible's musical terms in later sources. Such later sources, however, are insufficient and, at times, even misleading.[6] We prefer, therefore, to apply historical and etymological analyses derived from comparisons of ancient translations, such as the Aramaic *targum* or the Greek Septuagint, or evidence from archeological findings. Alternatively, we consult ancient Christian sources and ethnomusicological studies of the living Semitic cultures of the Middle East, such as that of the Bedouins of the Negev and Sinai deserts.[7]

Ceremonial Music in the Patriarchal Period

The Bible's description of the patriarchal period mentions no liturgical music at all. Instead, music is either connected to family and folk celebrations or described as a means to invoke divine inspiration. Genesis 31:26, for instance, records Laban's protest to Jacob that had he known that Jacob was intent on leaving him, he would have sent him on his way with songs and instrumental music. The text alludes to a farewell ceremony which was probably common among the ancient nomadic tribes. Laban mentions two musical instruments: *tof* (probably a kind of tambourine similar to the Arabic *daf*) and *kinnor* (probably a kind of lyre). These, together with the *ugav* (perhaps an ancient reed instrument such as the Greek *aulos*), constituted the main musical instruments of the patriarchal period. The *kinnor* and the *ugav* were associated with Jubal, the mythical father of music (Gen. 4:21), and were perhaps considered men's instruments. The *tof,* on the other hand, was associated with women's dance songs (*mecholot*), such as Miriam's song at the Red Sea (Exod. 15:20).[8]

The Period of Settlement

The sojourn in Egypt and contact with Egyptian culture may have influenced the music of the Israelites. The silver trumpets of the tabernacle were probably similar to those found in Egyptian tombs; other instruments were perhaps imported from Egypt, especially during the reign of King Solomon.[9] Egyptian songs, too, may have influenced those of the Israelites, and the worship at the Shiloh Temple may have borrowed musical practices from Egyptian or Canaanite worship. That none of this is mentioned in the books of Joshua and Judges is perhaps due to internal censorship that reflects the Bible's rejection of these other cultures.

The book of Joshua is little concerned about music. Despite the story of the fall of Jericho (Josh. 6), the sound of the shofar, the ram's horn, was never considered music; rather, it was, and still is, regarded as a sacred signal of alarm and remembrance. Only two poetic lines appear in the book (Josh. 10:12–13), and they quote the lost "Book of Yashar," which may have been a compilation of ancient poems or ballads, including a longer version of David's lament over Saul and Jonathan (see 2 Sam. 1:18). In the ancient world, such poetry was usually sung or chanted during civil or religious ceremonies.

The books of Judges and Samuel contain a few references to music and dance. Women welcome victorious leaders with song and dance (Judg. 11:34; 1 Sam. 18:6; and Deborah's song, Judg. 5); young women dance in vineyards at Shiloh during the festival celebrations (Judg. 21:19–23); a "company of prophets" descends from the sacred shrine prophesying to the accompaniment of a *nevel* (a stringed instrument of uncertain identification), *tof, chalil* (the pipe), and *kinnor;* a musical boy,

David, plays the *kinnor* before Saul to relieve the king from his melancholy (1 Sam. 16:23); leaders and prophets recite (probably chant) political speeches and moralizing fables (Judg. 9:7–20, 1 Sam. 15:22–23, 2 Sam. 12:1–4); people sing laments over the death of their heroes (2 Sam. 1:17–27 and 3:33–34).

Secular Music in the Kingdoms of Judea and Israel

The Bible's few allusions to secular music comment with reproach. But even these scanty references indicate that the people, especially the upper classes, had a vivid musical culture. Amos (ch. 6) describes what was perhaps a typical feast of the rich people of Samaria, with fat food, wine, rich ointment, song, and instrumental music. Isaiah (5:11–12) relates a similar scene in Judea. Later still, Job depicts the wicked as playing the *tof, kinnor,* and *ugav.* Instrumental music is also associated with mourning; Jeremiah (48:36) uses the sound of pipes (*chalils*) as a simile of his mocking lamentation of the fate of Moab.

Generally the prophets associate music with the general corruption of the rich; Isaiah (23:15–16) even connects it with harlotry. Perhaps the only verses that show a positive attitude towards secular music are Jeremiah 31:4 and 13, which foresee the restoration of song and dance as part of the future redemption of Israel. We know little for sure about the relationship between sacred and secular music in ancient Israel, but I think that the two did not differ much in ancient times and that they strongly influenced each other.

Sacred Music in the First Temple

Sacred music first receives an important role with the biblical narration of King David's life. Music as part of the regular worship is not mentioned in the Bible before David. Earlier descriptions of the divine worship mention only the blowing of the shofar and trumpets over the sacrifices, but these were nonmusical, priestly functions. The story relating the transfer of the holy ark to Jerusalem (2 Sam. 6, 1 Chron. 6:16–17), however, describes music for the first time as an integral part of the worship. Some discrepancy exists between the two versions of the story, yet both suggest the use of string, wind, and percussion instruments along with singing and dancing.

1. Dí-xit Dóminus Dómino mé-   o : * Séde a déxtris mé-   is.

or : mé-   is.   or : mé- is.   or : mé-   is.   or : mé-   is.

or : mé-   is.   or : mé-   is.   or : mé-   is.   or : mé-   is.

2. Donec pónam inimícos túos, * scabéllum pé*dum tu*órum.
3. Vírgam virtútis túae emíttet Dóminus ex Síon : * domináre in médio inimic*órum tu*órum.
4. Técum princípium in díe virtútis túae in splendóribus sanctórum : * ex útero ante lucíferum *génui* te.
5. Jurávit Dóminus, et non paenitébit éum : * Tu es sacérdos in aetérnum secúndum órdi*nem Me*l*chi*sedech. (D² : *Me*l*chi*sedech.)
6. Dóminus a déxtris túis, * confrégit in díe írae *súae* réges.
7. Judicábit in natiónibus, implébit ruínas : * conquassábit cápita in térra mu*l*tórum.
8. De torrénte in vía bibet : * proptérea exal*tábit* cáput.
9. Glória Pátri, et Fílio, * et Spirí*tui* Sáncto.
10. Sicut érat in princípio, et núne, et sémper, * et in saécula saecu*lórum*. Amen.

Example 1. Roman Catholic psalmody. Ps. 109 (=110):1, according to the *Liber Usualis* (Tournai and New York, 1962), p. 128.

Jewish psalmodic formulas vary from one community to another, and they are in general more complicated than their Roman Catholic counterparts. Usually, two recitation tones are used, a higher one for the first hemistich and a lower one for the second. These tones are frequently embellished with many other auxiliary notes (see example 2).

Schema:

Example 2. Jewish psalmody. Ps. 92:13–14, chant from Bagdad, according to Edith Gerson-Kiwi, "Justus ut Palma," in *Festschrift Bruno Stäblein* (Kassel, 1967), pp. 64–73 (ex. 8).

It is quite difficult to ascertain from the current Jewish and Christian examples how the original psalmodies sounded. Nevertheless, the structure of the text and the need for a simple formula for the execution of many verses of a similar structure may assure us that the psalmody of the Temple was at least in principle very similar to some current formulas. Many scholars believe that the medieval Jewish and Christian formulas branched off from the ancient patterns of the Temple. Yet it is also possible that the formulas that we can hear now in synagogues and churches developed independently. The similarity of the structure might testify, not to the migration of the ancient chants, but to the structural strength of the psalm verses themselves. In other words, if you would have to invent a melodic pattern to fit the numerous psalm verses that have to be chanted in the liturgy, you would have no choice but to create a psalmody that in principle would closely resemble existing Jewish or Christian formulas.

While we may have some idea about the singing of the psalms, we have very little knowledge of the musical instruments in the Temple and their function. The Book of Psalms contains many obscure terms, either in the psalm titles or in the psalms themselves. Of these, some may refer to instruments or to instrumental music. Thus, for instance, the term *asor* (Ps. 92:4), or *nevel asor* (Pss. 33:3 and 144:2) may mean a ten-string harp or *kithara,* whereas the term *sheminit* (Pss. 6:1 and 12:1) may again mean an eight-string instrument of the same family; but we are unable now to describe the instrument or its musical qualities.

Some terms present special problems of interpretation. Jewish tradition understands the word *selah* as "forever." Yet the Septuagint translated it as *diapsalma,* that is, a sort of instrumental interlude between verses or a postlude for the entire psalm; and some medieval Jewish commentators concur.[10]

Interestingly enough, dancing is not mentioned as part of the worship in the First Temple. King David's dance before the ark (2 Sam. 6 and 1 Chr. 16) is an exception rather than a precedent.

Sacred music was also used outside of the Temple, in coronation ceremonies and in wars. Thus Jehoshaphat is reported using Levite singers in his war against the Ammonites (2 Chr. 20). The singers lead the army into battle and head up a victory procession into Jerusalem with the regular Temple instruments. Temple music, similar to that of Jerusalem, may have existed in other centers of worship such as Beth El and Dan, or even in less important "high places."

As is suggested by Psalm 137, the "Song of Zion," must have been famous even beyond the Land of Israel. But contrary to what could be deduced from the same psalm, the exiled Levites by the rivers of Babylon did sing the Lord's song on foreign soil; or at least they transmitted it in other ways to later generations who restored it to Second-Temple worship. The same returning generations may also have heard the rich music of the Babylonian temples and been influenced by it, just as they borrowed also the new Assyrian script and the Babylonian calendar.

One hundred twenty-eight Levite singers, "the sons of Asaph," are said to have returned from the Babylonian exile (Ezra 12:41). Moreover, during the inauguration of the rebuilt Temple, the priests blew the trumpets and the Levites played the cymbals and sang King David's Psalms (Ezra 3:10–13). Nehemiah (12:27–43) describes in detail the inauguration of the wall of Jerusalem with a grand processional of two groups

of priests and Levites who marched in opposite directions on
the wide wall, blowing the trumpets, singing and playing the
cymbals, and plucking their *nevels* and *kinnors.*

Music in the Second Temple

Rabbinic literature recalls worship at the Second Temple,
especially after its reconstruction by King Herod. To the extent
that these recollections are valid, we can say that the Temple
choir consisted of at least twelve Levites "and their number
could be increased without end." Young Levites could serve
as choir boys "to add sweetness to the melody" (M. Arak.
2:3–6). The psalms were still the main hymns and were probably still sung antiphonally, responsorially, or as a litany (B.
Suk. 38b). Each day is said to have had a psalm of its own (M.
Tamid 5:4):

Day	*Psalm*
Sunday	24
Monday	48
Tuesday	82
Wednesday	94
Thursday	81
Friday	93
Saturday	92

The Levites are credited also with developing various techniques of virtuoso singing. It was said of Hugras the Levite that
when he sang his virtuoso passages he inserted his thumb into
his mouth and placed his index finger under his nose, and that
by this means he was able to produce unusual tones that used
to astonish the attending priests.[11]

The instrumental music at the Second Temple seems to have
been richer than that of the First Temple. The orchestra consisted of two to six *nevels* (probably *kitharas*), nine or more
kinnors (lyres; the maximum number was limitless), two to
twelve *chalils* (pipes, perhaps shawms of the *aulos* type), and
one cymbal. The priests blew the shofar and at least two trum-

pets. They also sounded the *magrefah* (the rake used for clearing the ashes of the altar) by throwing it forcefully on the ground in order to signal the beginning of the Temple worship.[12]

Summarizing the Mishnah, Idelsohn describes the main musical worship, which—as in the First Temple—was part of the morning sacrifice. "After the priests on duty had recited a benediction, the Ten Commandments, the *Shema* (Deut. 6:4–9), the priestly benediction (Num. 6:22–26), and three other benedictions, they proceeded to the offerings," after which, "one of them sounded the *Magrefah,* . . . the signal for the priests to enter the Temple to prostrate themselves, whereas for the Levites that sound marked the beginning of the musical performance. Two priests took their stand at the altar immediately and started to blow the trumpets. . . . After this performance, they approached Ben Arza, the cymbal player, and took their stand beside him, one at his right and the other at his left side. Whereupon, at a given sign with a flag by the superintendent, this Levite sounded his cymbal, and all the Levites began to sing a part of the daily Psalm. Whenever they finished a part they stopped, and the priests repeated their blowing of the trumpets and the people present prostrated themselves.[13]

Usually, during the sacrifices and in some festive processions, only the trumpets were blown; but on New Year's Day and on fast days, the shofar was sounded together with the trumpets (M. RH 3:3–4) in very stylized manner, utilizing two particular sounds: *tekiyah,* a plain sustained sound, and *teruah,* a trill or a tremolo.[14] On weekdays seven rounds of this order were performed by the trumpeters: one for the opening of the Temple gates at dawn, three at the morning sacrifice, and three at the afternoon sacrifice. On Sabbaths, New Moons and festivals three rounds were added at the additional sacrifices. On Friday afternoons, two special rounds were sounded to announce the beginning of the Sabbath (M. Suk. 5:5).

The best time to hear the music of the Temple was probably during the celebrations of the water libation at the festival of Sukkot. The festivities took place at night and included singing and dancing of all assembled (the only occasion when dancing in the Temple is mentioned in the sources), as well as acrobatic feats performed with torches. The Levites formed a huge choir and orchestra "with innumerable musical instruments" that stood on the fifteen steps that led from the men's section to the women's. They sang psalms of praise, perhaps the fifteen Psalms of Ascent, Psalms 121–135 (M. Suk. 5:4).

The postbiblical sources tell us little about the role of music in domestic sacred ceremonies. Singing and dancing is mentioned here and there but no details are given. The most frequently mentioned musical instrument is the *chalil*, a reed instrument of the *aulos* family which was used at weddings and funerals (M. B.M. 4:1; Matt. 9:23 and 11:17; Luke 7:32). It was held that "even the poorest of Israel should hire not less than two *chalils* and one wailing woman" for his wife's funeral.[15]

THE RISE OF THE SYNAGOGUE,
THE CHAZZAN, AND EARLY CHANT

Even before the Temple was destroyed, synagogues were active throughout the country and in the Diaspora. The worship at the synagogue differed considerably from that of the Temple. Instead of a sacrificial focus synagogue liturgy centered on the reading of Scripture and on prayer, and the officiants were not the priests but the laity.

Halakhic Prohibitions

The simplicity of the music in the early synagogue was influenced by the halakhic prohibitions against playing musical instruments, or, under certain circumstances, even singing. These prohibitions stem from three different sources: rules of Sabbath observance; the mourning over the destruction of the Temple; and the struggle against what the Rabbis took to be promiscuity.[16]

Musical instruments and the shofar were considered inseparable parts of the Sabbath service in the Temple; rabbinic law could do nothing regarding their presence there. But the Rabbis could and did prohibit them outside the Temple for fear that playing an instrument on the Sabbath, a permissible act in and of itself, might lead inadvertently to the musician's tuning it, mending it, or carrying it from one public place to another— all of these being forbidden acts of work. Since the main synagogue service took place on Sabbath mornings, no musical instrument could become an integral component thereof. Even the shofar could not be blown, if Rosh Hashanah occurred on the Sabbath.

Mourning over the destruction of the Second Temple led to a rabbinic ban on all secular songs and instrumental music. Quoting Hosea (9:1), "Do not rejoice, O Israel, with merriments like the nations," the Rabbis declared: "An ear listening to songs will surely be cut off. . . . A song in the house means destruction is at its threshold" (Sotah 48a). Concessions were made permitting music, even instrumental music, for the sake of a religious obligation, such as rejoicing with groom and bride; but the Sabbath ban remained, and, in general, music was not favored.

The only instrument allowed in the synagogue, precisely because of its nonmusical significance, the shofar was blown mainly on Rosh Hashanah, to fulfill the biblical obligation as stated in Leviticus 24:29 and Numbers 29:1. The instrument is also sounded at the end of the concluding service (Ne'illah) on Yom Kippur and after the weekday morning services during Elul, the month preceding Rosh Hashanah. In the Sephardic and Yemenite rites,[17] the penitential services clustered around the High Holy Day season (selichot) feature many shofars blown simultaneously when the thirteen attributes of God (Exod. 34:5–7) are chanted. The awesome sound of the shofar served also to create a mournful atmosphere in services of public fasts, and even to invoke a sense of dread during ceremonies of excommunication.

Behind both Sabbath regulations and the desire to mourn for the Temple, however, we see the Rabbis' puritanical ethic, with its fight against real or imagined promiscuity, as evident in the extremist talmudic maxim: "A woman's voice is indecency" (Ber. 24a). In the Temple, and later in the synagogue, men and women were separated and only the men sang. In spite of a unique testimony to the contrary among the Therapeutae,[18] the antiphonal singing of men and women became unacceptable in rabbinic worship. "Men singing and women answering is promiscuity; women singing and men answering is like fire set to chaff" (Sotah 48a).[19]

Three Genres of Chant

Early synagogue music consisted of three genres of chant: psalmody, cantillation of Scripture, and the liturgical chant in which the statutory prayers were recited by a local worship leader (generally not a Rabbi) who functioned in many different roles in the early synagogue and was known as the chazzan (a word now reserved for, and translated as, "cantor"). Psalmody, particularly popular in the ancient Palestinian rite, though considerably restricted in the Babylonian rite whence most Western liturgies are derived, was adopted from the Temple and probably was performed in a similar manner. Cantillation of Scripture, a focus of worship on Mondays and Thursdays (the market days), Sabbaths, New Moons, holy days, and fast days, featured the chanting of a verse, followed by its translation into the vernacular and (perhaps) its immediate exegesis to the public. Both the verse and its translation were probably chanted to a simple psalmodic formula. This could have been the origin of the tradition, that later became the norm, of dividing all verses, even the prose ones, into half-verses. Remnants of the early psalmodic concept of cantillation can still be heard in the Torah reading of the Yemenite and some other Middle Eastern Jewish communities.[20] Some Yemenite congregations still retain the custom of reading and translating. Each verse is read once in Hebrew, by an adult, and a second time in Aramaic, by a child. The readers use different psalmodic formulas to differentiate the source from the translation.

Current practice in both Jewish and Christian worship and the structure of liturgical texts suggest that liturgical chant consisted of simple melodies that were constructed as patchworks of traditional musical motives. Two of the three genres, namely, psalmody and centonization (melodic patchwork), had their

counterparts in the early Christian church and became permanent elements in the chants of the Eastern and Western
churches.[21]

The Tiberias System of Cantillation

All ancient cultures, rabbinic Judaism among them, preferred
to chant their sacred texts rather than to recite them. Talmudic
tradition (Meg. 3a, P.T. Meg. 4a) holds that the cantillation
of the Pentateuch was practiced even in the Second Temple.
But various cantillation methods were crystallized only slowly,
during a period of over eight hundred years.

The liturgical recitation of Scripture in the synagogue service demanded the setting of norms for the proper chanting of
the text. The scrolls used for liturgical reading contained only
an unpunctuated and unvocalized text, so that the slightest change
of a vowel or a misunderstanding of the proper division of the
verse could introduce a new and unwelcome meaning to the
reading. On the other hand, marking the scrolls with any additional signs was forbidden. Thus the right interpretation of the
text had to be transmitted orally for many centuries.

The invention of the codex, the bound book, introduced a
change, in that it became permissible to copy the sacred text
into the codex with additional signs to aid the reader. One could
not chant from the codex in public, but one could study the
proper interpretation of the text from the bound book and
memorize the signs in the codex before chanting from the scroll
during services.[22]

From the seventh to the ninth century C.E., various schools
of grammarians in Babylonia and Palestine attempted to build
a coherent system of symbols for the entire text of the Bible.
These attempts culminated during the ninth century in the
development of the most sophisticated system by the Massoretic
school of Tiberias.[23]

The grammarians of this school defined four objectives for
their system: (1) to provide the text with proper vocalization;
(2) to indicate to the reader what syllable to accentuate; (3) to
divide and subdivide the verses according to syntactical and
grammatical considerations; (4) to indicate the desired musical

patterns of the traditional chant. These goals were achieved by
furnishing the biblical text with the double system of *nikkud*
and *te'amim*. The *nikkud* signs were written above, below, and
inside the letters to indicate the vowels and the special pronunciation of some consonants. The *te'amim* signs were usually
placed above or below the accented syllables, and they further
divided and subdivided the verses, indicating the desired musical
motives to which the text was to be chanted. The names and
some of the graphical shapes of the *te'amim* were derived from
hand motions (known as chironomy) which were used by
prompters to remind the reader of the appropriate musical
patterns. The original Tiberias signs have been preserved in
a few excellent manuscript codices of the tenth and eleventh
centuries,[24] whence new editions of the Hebrew Bible are
derived.

The Tiberias Massoretic system was universally accepted by
all Jewish communities; but different musical interpretations
of the *te'amim* developed through the ages. No community can
claim today that it has preserved the ancient melodic patterns
that were practiced by the Tiberian grammarians.[25] Eight
different regional traditions of cantillation coexist now.[26] Some
of them, like the Yemenite tradition, antedate the Tiberias system
and ignore some of its components; others, such as the eastern
European Ashkenazi tradition, follow the signs meticulously.
This, however, does not mean that all the Ashkenazi musical
patterns emerged the minute the theory of the *te'amim* was
accepted by Europeans. On the contrary, some of their musical
patterns developed much later, during the past four centuries.[27]

Within the eight regional traditions one can further identify
more specific local styles of cantillation belonging to the various
countries or districts of the region. In addition, each of these
traditions uses different musical systems for the various books
of the Bible. Thus, for instance, the eastern European Ashkenazi
tradition, which is practiced in most synagogues in the United
States, consists of six different musical systems: (1) regular
reading of the Pentateuch; (2) High Holy Day reading of the
Pentateuch; (3) the Prophets; (4) the scroll of Esther; (5) the
scrolls of Ruth, Song of Songs, and Ecclesiastes; (6) the scroll
of Lamentations (see examples 3a and 3b).

Examples 3a and 3b. Two cantillation patterns in the six eastern European systems, according to A. W. Binder, *Biblical Chant* (New York, 1959), p. 117.

Since the liturgical reading of Scripture requires much knowledge and preparation, it is relegated in most Jewish communities to a professional reader called a *ba'al keriah* (literally, master of reading). Some communities of North Africa, Yemen, and Italy still follow the custom of using an assistant (*somekh*), whose hand motions prompt the reader.

The Chazzan and the Liturgical Recitative

The early synagogue developed the role of prayer leader, or precentor, a knowledgeable man who was conceptualized theologically as serving as the "agent of the congregation" (*sheliach tsibbur*) in voicing the statutory liturgy before God. Though not necessarily possessing the most beautiful voice, the precentor was to be a paragon of learning and piety. Moreover, since prayer texts were transmitted orally until the fourth or the fifth century, precentors had to possess a strong memory for mandatory texts and an ability to improvise musical settings for them. The precentor chanted the prayers to simple traditional melodic patterns that developed locally but were then disseminated among other communities by wandering cantors.

We think today of the chazzan (the cantor) as the precentor. But in the early synagogue the chazzan functioned in many roles before specializing as the leader of prayer. When the professional cantor emerged as primarily a singer is not clear, though the rise of the specialized *piyyut* (see below) may have been the primary factor, in that the *piyyut*, being complex poetry, required specialized education on the part of anyone charged with chanting it.[29] Then again, distinctions in musical ability have always been the norm. Various passages of the Talmud require two precentors for the morning services, and it seems that the second one was usually the better singer. Placing the better singer after a nonprofessional remains the custom today in most traditional Jewish communities, which still differentiate the lay precentor (*ba'al hatefillah*, master of prayer) from a professional or semiprofessional cantor (chazzan).

Whenever it was that the post of cantor developed into a primarily musical role, good cantors were in great demand, and they went from community to community, shaping regional repertories of melodies and melodic fragments that eventually crystallized into fixed patterns that individual communities viewed as sacred and obligatory. Early forms of such chants were preserved in all Jewish communities, but we can never be certain about the antiquity of any particular chant. Simple melodies based on one or two tetrachords may date back to the early Middle Ages or before, but their simplicity may deceive us. Simple tunes may be ancient, or they may be later simplifications of more complicated chants.

The synagogal chant repertories are known as the collective noun, *nusach*. It serves today as the entire repertory for the lay precentor, but as the mere basis for the liturgical recitative of the professional cantor, whose liturgical art is called *chazzanut*. It makes use of the traditional melodic patterns—some of them fixed, others flexible or modular—in order to create an artistic musical expression of the form or content of the prayer. Particularly prominent in the Ashkenazi tradition, liturgical recitative involves some improvisation and artistic freedom; yet at its best, it is firmly bound to the traditional melodic formulas that in turn are connected to the liturgical function of the prayer and its calendrical setting.

In the Sephardi tradition, cantors tended to emphasize diction and accurate Hebrew pronunciation, rather than vocal embellishment. Where such ornamentation developed into chazzanut, however, as in the Ashkenazi synagogue, ambivalent feelings developed towards cantorial artistry. At its best, chazzanut expresses sublimely religious sensitivity, even if the style is suspected of deteriorating into a display of cantorial vanity and of opening the back door through which foreign melodies may infiltrate sacred worship. Severe criticisms of chazzanut abound in the rabbinic literature of many countries and various periods from the ninth century to this day.[30]

THE INFLUENCE OF THE PIYYUT

As synagogues grew in importance, their services tended gradually toward greater fixity, under the standardizing principles espoused by the Rabbis. Though no uniform text was universally accepted by all Jews, local customs emerged at least by the fifth century C.E.[31] Simultaneously, however, increasingly complex poetry was devised either as artistic additions to the fixed prayers or, on some occasions, actually as substitutes for portions of them. Precentors thus composed and sang new poems, called *piyyutim,* which combined references to the occasions on which they were sung, the relevant liturgical rubric in which they were placed, and the homiletic interpretation of the lectionary. Some of the poems had short refrains for congregational singing; others had more complicated responsive texts that were probably sung by a small choir.[32] The insertion of these poems into the prayers raised heated rabbinic debates;[33] yet the people loved this new art and cherished its singer-composers, the *payyetanim.*

The early "preclassical" *piyyut* was built of lines containing two or three words each, or of lines combining two- and three-word segments. The number of syllables and the meter were not fixed; they often changed from one line to the next. The music was probably built up from melodic formulas with fixed motives for the stressed syllables and flexible auxiliary notes to accommodate the varying number of unstressed syllables. Such melodies are still used for these poems. That any melodies are the original ones is, however, highly doubtful.

The classical *piyyut* of poets like Eleazar Kallir (c. sixth-seventh centuries) is built around new principles of rhyming and strophe, while the variable number of syllables within the lines remained. Musically, this structure called for a long melody to accommodate one strophe and perhaps another melody for a refrain, when needed. Since the poems were sung by the professional *payyetan,* it is safe to assume on the basis of common Middle Eastern practices that each strophe was sung to an embellished variation of the melody. The refrain sung by the congregation or the choir had a fixed melody. However, a common feature of refrains of this sort is that they are sung in heterophony; that is to say, the congregation never sings in exact unison, but different members of the congregation sing their own private versions of the melody, which together form

a simultaneous rhythmical cloud of variations. Again, melodies
to classical *piyyutim* exist in various Jewish communities, yet
none can be identified as the original tune of a specific poem.

We do, however, have some evidence of what such early
music may have sounded like, the best-known example being
a melody found in a Genizah fragment of the twelfth century.[34]
The text is a *piyyut* for Shavuot or Simchat Torah by an unknown
poet named Amar, with music notated in old, nonstaved neumes
by Obadiah, an Italian priest who converted to Judaism at the
beginning of the century and lived in Egypt after 1121 (see
example 4).

Example 4. Obadiah the Proselyte, *Mi 'al har horev,* according to Hanoch
Avenary, *Hebrew Hymn Tunes* (Tel Aviv, 1971), pp. 12–13.

This melody and another one notated by the same hand[35] have
been the subjects of scholarly debate since their discovery.
Possibly the melodies are original compositions by Obadiah and
were perhaps influenced, like the notation itself, by Gregorian
chant; yet they may be transcriptions of Jewish melodies that
Obadiah heard in the East.[36]

SEPHARDI CULTURE (SPAIN AND
PORTUGAL) AND ISLAMIC INFLUENCE

It is convenient to distinguish two liturgical-musical traditions in Jewish culture. Ashkenazi Jews (see below) hailed

largely from Italy and began settling the Rhineland by the ninth century. By the eleventh century, they had already established their cultural hegemony there, whence they spread north and west to France and England, south and east to other German-speaking lands, and to Poland, Russia, and the various territories that constituted the Hapsburg Empire. By contrast, the Sephardi community was established in Spain, where it enjoyed cultural efflorescence first under Moslems and then again, after the reconquest, under Christians. The expulsion of Jews from Spain in 1492 resulted in Sephardi culture being carried elsewhere, to some extent northward to other parts of the Spanish Empire, where it was practiced secretly until it could resurface—in the Protestant Netherlands, for instance—but primarily eastward throughout the Mediterranean world, where it eventually adapted to various Islamic cultural patterns. We have already mentioned this or that aspect of both Ashkenazi and Sephardi music. This section and the next trace these two major cultures in more detail.

Arabic Musical and Poetic Patterns

Arabic culture made an indelible impression on Jewish poetry and music. Initially, the influence was felt in Jewish theoretical treatises on music, as, for example, the last chapter of Saadiah Gaon's *Sefer Emunot Vedeot (Book of Beliefs and Opinions,* 933 C.E.), which deals with the eight rhythmical modes according to the Hellenized Arabic theory of the time. Later, during the eleventh and twelfth centuries in Spain and elsewhere, Hebrew poetry was written according to Arabic patterns and was structured after the Arabic *qasida* or *muwashah* forms. Poets like Solomon Ibn Gabirol, Abraham Ibn Ezra, and Yehudah Halevi wrote secular and sacred poetry according to the new patterns established by Dunash Ibn Labrat (tenth century). These patterns were based on a Hebrew adaptation of the Arabic principle of differentiating short from long syllables,[37] a consideration that now had to be added to such older factors as rhyming patterns, acrostic signatures, and the requisite allusions to biblical verses. The secular poems were recited or sung at social events; the sacred ones, chanted or sung during religious services. In the synagogue as at home, the poems were sung to Arabic musical patterns.

As the new poetic beauty captured the public, Sephardi prayer books blossomed with sacred poems which are sung even today with great enthusiasm by all the Sephardi, North African, Yemenite, and Middle Eastern communities. Long-lost original melodies have been replaced by locally popular substitutes, some of which adhere strictly to the rhythmical patterns of the poems, others of which do not.[38] Sephardi communities thus established congregational singing as a major characteristic of their services. By contrast, in the Ashkenazi communities, where this poetry was unknown, cantorial recitative thrived while congregational singing was minimal until the late nineteenth century.

Nuba and Bakkashot

After their expulsion from Spain in 1492, Sephardi Jews remained faithful to some features of Arabic–Andalusian music and poetry. Hebrew poetry and synagogue melodies were constructed according to the Andalusian *nuba,* an extended suite form, unified by specific melodic modes and rhythmic patterns, and using both songs and instrumental pieces, except in certain circumstances—e.g., on Shabbat, when (as we saw) instruments are not permitted—when vocal imitations of instruments occurs.[39] Such songs are still created by the Jews of Morocco and are sung at the Friday night *Bakkashot* services (a Sephardi liturgical practice derived from Kabbalistic theory, featuring the stylized singing of *piyyutim* in the hours after midnight). A "neo-*nuba*" style was created during this century in Morocco and Israel by the *payyetan* R. David Bouzaglo and his disciples.[40]

As the popularity of the *Bakkashot* service indicates, Arabic influence reemerged in the last decades of the sixteenth century in Palestine and Syria, under the influence of the Lurianic school of Kabbalah in Safed. Among other things, an attempt was made to modernize Hebrew poetry by using the old Arabic meters and combining them with the rhythm and style of popular Arabic tunes of the day. Poets such as Menachem Lonzano (1550– before 1624) and Israel Najara (1555?–1625?) provided new sacred Hebrew poems to well-known Arabic and Turkish tunes.

These were sung as ceremonial Sabbath table songs and they even penetrated the synagogue services.[41] The trend still continues. In the *Bakkashot* services of the Aleppo Jews in Jerusalem, New York, and elsewhere, sacred poems are sung to the latest tunes of Arabic popular singers as heard on radio and television.[42]

Paraliturgical Compositions

In Yemen, the favored form of paraliturgical songs is the Arabic-inspired sequence of *Nashid, Shirah, and Hallel.* The sequence begins with a free and florid solo recitative; continues with a strict rhythmical song in Arabic meter, sung and danced to by a small group of men; and concludes with a florid heterophonic recitation of sacred verses by all the male participants.[43] Also in Yemen, as in other Arabic countries, Jewish women adopted songs of non-Jewish women, or improvised Judeo-Arabic folk poems to rural Arabic tunes, using these in women's life-cycle ceremonies, such as the *chinnah* ceremony preceding the wedding, a Sephardi custom in which female friends and relatives of the bride meet to paint her hands with red henna as a means of warding off the evil eye.

The Maqam

Arabic art music, and especially the modal system of the *maqam* with its numerous scales and melodic patterns penetrated every musical activity of the Jews in the Moslem countries, so much so that special synagogue calendars were constructed to enable the cantors to sing their services each Sabbath according to a different *maqam.* The system has even taken over the cantillation of the Pentateuch, in that Jews who hail from Moslem lands chant the *te'amim* according to melodic patterns of a *maqam* called *siga.*[44]

Judeo-Spanish Songs

The coexistence of Jews and Gentiles in the Diaspora, even in times of persecution, enriched both cultures. Medieval Spain was a special case in point. Under the Moslem rulers, the Jews developed the rich, new poetry that was influenced by the Arabic poetic concept; under the Christian rulers, they developed a rich treasury of songs in the Judeo-Spanish dialect sometimes called *Judeo-Español* or *Ladino*. Many of these songs originated in the Christian kingdoms of Castile, Leon, or Aragon and were originally gentile folk songs and ballads. Both the gentile and Jewish songs were preserved by the Jews, mostly by Jewish women, in the various countries where they lived after their expulsion from Spain. Many more songs were created in the new countries, especially in the Balkans, in Turkey, and in Morocco. The new creations were also in the ancient Spanish dialect with a mixture of words in the local languages.

A rich and beautiful melodic heritage has been transmitted with these Judeo-Spanish songs.[45] The melodies range from the simplest rhythmical dance songs to the most sophisticated recitative-like love songs. Scholars tend to doubt whether this melodic treasure represents the preexpulsion musical heritage in all its purity.[46] In all probability, the Judeo-Spanish melodic repertory is rich precisely because it was able to absorb many local idioms that developed in various countries after 1492.

Research has not yet exhausted the repertory's many forms, but four main genres are discernible thus far:

1. *romances:* narrative, sometimes epic, ballads based on medieval knightly tales and sung to repeated four-line musical stanzas
2. *complas:* songs for the celebration of the Jewish holidays, or songs that accompany important life-cycle events, consisting of long, asymmetrical stanzas
3. *canticas:* life-cycle songs in simple, popular style and short stanzas, sometimes with a refrain, sung to lively, rhythmical melodies and at times accompanied by a tambourine
4. *endechas:* dirges and other songs of mourning

Melodies of the last three genres were easily adapted for liturgical use: *complas* are reserved largely for paraliturgical functions like Sabbath meals, and a limited number of synagogue services, such as the reading of the scroll of Esther on Purim; *cantica* melodies are adapted to the texts of Sabbath and festival hymns, such as *Adon Olam, Yigdal,* and *El Adon,* or even to the Kaddish: *endecha* patterns lend themselves during the Ninth of Av services and in the story of the binding of Isaac that is chanted before the shofar blowing on Rosh Hashanah.

The Sacred and the Secular

Sephardi music is thus characterized by the absence of a sharp dividing line between the secular and the sacred. The practice of adopting secular melodies to synagogue use is so widespread that research into Sephardi sacred song often begins by locating secular Judeo-Spanish sources first, and only secondarily discovering how they have been adapted for sacred use.

DEVELOPMENTS IN ASHKENAZ
(NORTHERN AND EASTERN EUROPE)

During the early Middle Ages, the Jews of Ashkenaz[47] developed their own distinguishable culture. The most prominent group among them spoke the Middle High German that later developed into Yiddish. Wherever they migrated, they retained special dialects of the old German language mingled with Hebrew and local vernacular words; a distinctive pronunciation of Hebrew; and their own religious music and customs, often carried far afield by traveling rabbis who also served as cantors. The most venerated authority in this regard came to be R. Jacob Levi Moellin, known as the Maharil (c. 1356–1427), who served in the double capacity of rabbi and cantor in various German and Bohemian communities, and whose rulings are still considered obligatory for the Orthodox Ashkenazim.[48]

By the end of the fifteenth century, Ashkenazi Jewry can be subdivided into two cultural segments: western Europe (*Minhag Ashkenaz* proper, sometimes known also as *Minhag Rinus,* or the Rhineland rite) and eastern Europe (*Minhag Polin,* or the Polish rite). Both branches shared the main features of the liturgy and the old Ashkenazi *piyyutim,* and they retained similar basic prayer chants and cantillation motives. Gradually, each branch developed independent cultural and musical characteristics, but various melodies traveled from one branch to the other, thanks to migrating cantors and wandering rabbinical emissaries who crossed cultural borders.

The mass immigration of European Jews from the second half of the nineteenth century and the destruction of the Jewish communities of Europe in the Holocaust transplanted the Ashkenazi tradition to Palestine, Australia, South Africa, and America. Though here and there the western tradition was retained or even prevailed (e.g., among nineteenth- and early twentieth-century American Reform Jews, or in pockets where German subculture is still venerated, as in New York City's Washington Heights),[49] in most places, the eastern liturgical and musical tradition came eventually to dominate.

Ashkenazi Liturgical Chants

The traditional synagogue chant of the Ashkenazi Jews, both east and west, consists of four interacting layers, each of which emerged in a different time: (1) cantillation of Scripture (2) *nusach* (3) *misinai* melodies and (4) cantorial improvisation.

The earliest layer is probably the musical motifs used for the cantillation of Scripture. When they are first heard, the eastern European cantillation motives seem very different from their older western European counterparts. But both stem from a common origin. We do not know when the proto-Ashkenazi motifs emerged and how they are related to the ninth-century Tiberian chants, since no early musical transcriptions of *te'amim* exist.[50] Nevertheless, they show some agreement with early verbal descriptions of the old motifs and therefore it seems plausible that they were already in use during the eleventh or early twelfth centuries.

The second layer, the simple prayer chants known as *nusach,* developed simultaneously with, or slightly later than, basic melodic patterns of the *te'amim.* Usually sung by lay precentors, these chants consist of simple psalmodic formulas for the opening morning prayers and psalms (*pesukei dezimrah*) and patchwork melodies for more complex texts, such as the weekday benedictions of the *Tefillah*. Some of these chant patterns are related to cantillation motifs.[51]

A third layer, *misinai* tunes, are sung on solemn occasions, especially the High Holy Days. They are common to both eastern and western Ashkenazim who revere them highly. We do not know when the term *misinai* (literally, from Sinai) was first coined, but cantors of the past two or three centuries have believed that the tunes were very old, perhaps revealed like the Torah itself to Moses on Sinai and, therefore, equally unalterable. Even less naive people use the term to distinguish the old, obligatory tunes from the new, fashionable ones.

In all probability, *misinai* melodies date back to Germany or northern France at various times between the twelfth and the sixteenth centuries. In 1926, Idelsohn linked *misinai* tunes to the melodies of the medieval German minnesinger and concluded that the tunes combine oriental Jewish and German elements. Continuing Idelsohn's line of thought, Eric Werner compared the great *Alenu,* one of the most sacred *misinai* tunes, to the Gregorian Sanctus and Agnus Dei of the ninth Mass.[52]

The most famous *misinai* tune is the one used for Yom Kippur eve's *Kol Nidre* and is considered by many to be the crown of Jewish liturgical chant. In a brilliant article, Idelsohn concluded that the tune was compounded from melodic patterns of various sources; that some important patterns were derived from the western Ashkenazi cantillation of the Prophets; and that the tune showed clear influence of German minnesinger melodies. The tune was probably composed in southern Germany in "the later part of the Period of the Minnesong," namely the end of the fifteenth or the beginning of the sixteenth century.[53] Unfortunately, no extant transcriptions of the *Kol Nidre* tune predate the eighteenth century, by which time it was already outfitted with many late cantorial embellishments (see example 5).[54]

Example 5. Aron Beer's version of *Kol Nidre,* according to Abraham Zvi Idelsohn, *Thesaurus of Hebrew Oriental Melodies,* vol. 6, pp. 187–88.

Two *misinai* tunes became famous in non-Jewish circles after they were arranged by great gentile composers. The Kaddish by Maurice Ravel is an imaginative arrangement of a faithful transcription of the *misinai* Kaddish melody that introduces the High Holy Day period's *Selichot* and *Musaf* services.[55] One of the many versions of the *Kol Nidre* tune has become famous in Max Bruch's setting for cello and orchestra.[56]

The fourth layer of Ashkenazi liturgical music consists of cantorial improvisations. These are built on tunes and motifs of the previous layers with the addition of musical elements that are borrowed from vocal and instrumental music of the day.[57] During the eighteenth century, musical idioms were borrowed from European baroque and early classic styles; during the nineteenth and twentieth centuries, the idioms of Italian opera penetrated cantorial improvisations.

The traditional improvisations are based on special modes called (in Yiddish) *shtayger*s (German: *Steiger*).[58] A *shtayger* is a musical corpus of melodic patterns that are related to a scale and are associated with particular prayers, functions, and services. Unlike the European scales, *shtayger* modes contain different sequences of tone and semitone in different octaves. The *shtayger*s are said to be connected to certain notions of ethos or emotional contexts, but how much so is disputed among scholars. Cantors recognize three main *shtayger*s and a few auxiliary ones, and name them by the prayers with which they are most often sung. The three main *shtayger*s are these: *Adonay malakh* (whose scale, in the main octave only, resembles the Mixolydian mode), *Magen avot* (similar to natural minor mode but with many additional features), and *Ahavah rabbah* (with a tone-and-a-half step between the second and the third degrees of the scale). The last *shtayger,* which is common to many eastern European, Jewish and non-Jewish folk tunes (e.g., the famous *Havah Nagillah*), has become the symbol of Jewish music, although it is by no means the characteristic mode of all, or even a majority, of the Jewish tunes.[59]

The scales of the *shtayger* need not contain the same accidentals in all octaves; on the contrary, one of the salient characteristics of some *shtayger*s is the variety of tone and semitone series in the different octaves. The melodic patterns of some *shtaygers* help cantors modulate from one *shtayger* to another and back again. All have clear formulas for the beginning of a piece or a section and for cadencing at the end of a piece, and other melodic gestures for various musical functions. However, all of the patterns are flexible enough to allow for regional and personal stylistic differences. In this respect they resemble jazz patterns which good musicians play with as if they were musical toys.

At its best, cantorial improvisation seeks to highlight the text of the prayers by means of musical interpretation. The cantor tries to convey the emotional contents of the prayer or to depict in sound some of its visual images. At its worst, it deteriorates into a vain display of vocal tirade. The art of cantorial improvisation developed into virtuoso style in eastern Europe during the nineteenth and early twentieth centuries. Some of the improvisations by cantors such as Ephraim Zalman Razumni, Pinchas Segal "Pinchik," Joseph Rosenblatt, and Leib Glantz were of sublime beauty. After long developmental and incubational periods, some of these great improvisations were finally transcribed into musical notation or recorded by their creators. Once published, they became part of the common stock of cantorial art that many cantors sang as classical pieces.

The Introduction of Polyphony

Folk polyphony is common to many non-European cultures. Jews, too, have practiced such unlearned polyphonic devices as drones, simple two-part singing, and the like.[60] Simple drones may even have been used in the Second Temple. A particularly interesting form of polyphony, practiced by Yemenite Jews, consists of the congregation forming parallel lines of heterophonic singing at the intervals of perfect fourths and fifths. This remarkable phenomenon is redolent of medieval European organum as described in theoretical treatises of the tenth and eleventh centuries, and it can be called heterophonic organum.[61] However, it seems that European polyphonic art music was introduced into the synagogue only at the end of the sixteenth or the beginning of the seventeenth century.

Simple European polyphony seems to have been sung by a small group of singers in some Ashkenazi (Tedeschi) synagogues in northern Italy around the year 1600. It is possible that this kind of polyphony was related to the practice of the vocal trio of cantor, bass, and boy singer that was common in Ashkenazi synagogues until the nineteenth century. Most of the singing by this trio was done from memory or by extemporization, and melodic accompaniment followed well-known conventions of droning and responding to solos with a word or two in simple chords. Some of these conventions are still heard in choirs of Orthodox synagogues.[62]

The first musician to introduce composed polyphony into the synagogue music was Salomone di Rossi of Mantua (c. 1565?– after 1628). In 1622, he published his compositions in a set of part books printed in Venice under the title *Hashirim asher Lishlomoh (The Songs of Solomon)*. The books were intended to provide polyphonic substitutes for the cantor's part in some services, as well as choral settings of some psalms and *piyyutim*.[63] Although the publication of Rossi's compositions was warmly supported by one of the greatest rabbinical figures of the time, Yehudah Arieh (Leone) di Modena, it found no immediate followers. Nevertheless, during the second half of the seventeenth century, the Jews of Italy introduced baroque cantatas into some ceremonies of the synagogue. The favored ceremonies were connected with the inauguration of new synagogues and celebrations of pious societies, especially on the last intermediary day of Sukkot (Hoshanah Rabbah). Frequently, non-Jewish composers were commissioned to set ancient and newly invented Hebrew texts.[64]

During the eighteenth century, cantatas were composed and sung in various communities of Europe, such as Comtat Venaisin in southern France and the Portuguese synagogue in Amsterdam. When rabbinic law permitted it, instrumental music, too, was used in a few synagogues. In some towns, welcoming the Sabbath (*Kabbalat Shabbat*) was celebrated on Friday afternoons with instrumental music, and some synagogues even introduced the organ. In Prague, for instance, the three main synagogues— namely, the Pinkas-Schul, Altneuschul, and Meisel-Schul—all possessed portable organs and celebrated *Kabbalat Shabbat* with organ and other instrumental accompaniment until the end of the eighteenth century.[65] New trends of polyphonic music were introduced into the European synagogues during the nineteenth century, and these are treated elsewhere in this volume.[66]

MYSTICAL TRADITIONS:
KABBALAH AND HASIDISM

The Influence of Kabbalah

As we saw above, rabbinic Judaism deemphasized the role of music, seeing in it a potential source of disrespect for the memory of Jerusalem and even a cause of what they considered promiscuity. Thus even though all Jewish communities sang, danced, and played musical instruments whenever possible, no theoretical support for such activities was offered by rabbinical texts. This changed in the sixteenth century, with the popularization of several forms of mysticism generally subsumed in the title, *Kabbalah*. Convinced that music possessed the power to lift the human soul to the Eternal,[67] or even to attain prophecy,[68] early Kabbalists explored music's magical and theurgical powers. But Kabbalistic literature was originally the province of the elite. Only with the rise of Kabbalistic adepts in sixteenth-century Safed (in Israel's eastern Galilee) did its mystical doctrines penetrate every aspect of Jewish life to the point where unlearned Jews practiced Kabbalism without even knowing that they did so.

The Kabbalah of Isaac Luria (1534–1572), the central figure in Safed Kabbalism, and his disciples revolved around the central idea of *tikkun*, i.e., mending the catastrophic break within the divine emanation. The Kabbalistic myth of creation held that in the process of divine emanation whence the universe came into being, the divine light had become embroiled with *kelipot* (shards of evil), such that the created cosmos abounds with evil too. *Tikkun*, "reparation," will return the sparks to their pristine state, redeeming both Creator and created simultaneously. Performing *mitzvot* (acts commanded by God) accomplishes *tikkun olam*, "the reparation of the cosmos."

The Kabbalists viewed music too as having fallen into the realm of evil, on account of human sin. It was therefore necessary to find a *tikkun* for music, so as to lift it up towards its divine source. The *tikkun* for music was to sing it in sacred circumstances, such as during the Sabbath meal or with the holy words of prayer. For centuries, Jews had been borrowing secular and non-Jewish tunes for their worship, but without theoretical support for what was merely an instance of a universal pattern known to all cultures. Now, however, the practice was outfitted with a theological rationale. A direct and immediate result of the new freedom to recast secular melodies as sacred entities were the *piyyutim* of Israel Najara, which were based on Arabic and Turkish sounds. Najara used to sit in Arabic coffee houses in order to learn new tunes (and was severely criticized for this, even in Kabbalistic circles). The idea of *tikkun* also inspired European Jews to introduce baroque music into the synagogue, and the same idea inspired eastern European Hasidim to adopt foreign tunes and "Judaize" them.

Kabbalistic theology postulated also that the various stages of emanation could be conceptualized as Sefirot, or spheres of light, that came into being at intervals of time different from the moment when the light was set loose from its source until it eventuated in the final act of bringing an actual world into being. In the idealized state of divine wholeness, nothing had separated one Sefirah from another, but now, the Godhead itself was in disarray. This was particularly so because one Sefirah contains the feminine principle, while another holds the masculine principle, such that masculine and feminine exist in disharmonious separation from each other, a condition mirrored by earthly travail as well—the exile of Israel from the Holy Land, for instance, which is an earthly reflection of the exile of the divine feminine power from its masculine counterpart. *Tikkun olam* leads to the Messianic era when God's male and female powers will be reunited for good and Israel will return to its country.

To foster this reunion, the Kabbalists established private devo-

tions known as *tikkun chatsot,* a midnight vigil of penitential
prayers to be chanted on weekdays, when the exile of the
feminine principle is particularly evident. By contrast, temporary
union occurs every Sabbath, which is known as a "taste of the
world to come." Kabbalist liturgy thus fostered rituals designed
to celebrate the divine reunion of male and female, most notably,
the Kabbalat Shabbat service that actually welcomes the Sabbath queen and bride as the sun sets on Friday evening. By the
seventeenth century, this service had become an integral part
of the liturgy in every community, even non-Kabbalistic ones
which accepted the new ritual for its beauty, without perhaps
even knowing its Kabbalistic rationale. The central *piyyut* of
this service is *Lekhah Dodi* by Solomon Halevi Alkabetz, who
embedded in its lyrics many allusions to the divine reunion.
The poem attracted hundreds of tunes all over the Diaspora.

The same Kabbalistic ideas led to the establishment of other
Friday night ceremonies too: a Sabbath Eve meal with after-
dinner singing (as if one is attending the divine marriage); and
Bakkashot services in Syrian and Moroccan communities on
Friday nights in winter after midnight (see above), where to
this day, the best Middle Eastern cantorial singing can still be
heard.

The Hasidic Niggun

Eighteenth-century European pietism led to eastern European
Hasidism, which borrowed directly the motifs of Lurianic
Kabbalah. Its founders, Israel Baal Shem Tov and his disciples,
were convinced that God was best worshiped out of a sense
of great joy. Music and dance were the most important means
for releasing the soul from the influence of the shards of evil.[69]

The Hasidic theory of the *niggun*—a melody without lyrics—
maintained that melodies, too, contain divine sparks, so that
defiled melodies can be redeemed by being sung in sanctity.
Further, melodies, like souls, are of divine origin, yet not all
are equal. There therefore exists a hierarchy among the various
kinds of *niggun.* The lowest melodic form is simply an expression of joy. Higher up are liturgical songs that express the inward

meaning of the prayers. But the highest melodies are those created by the *tzaddikim,* Hasidic leaders and saints; the musical patterns of their songs were believed to express secret Kabbalistic ideas.

A melody's place in the musical hierarchy varied also with its relationship to a text, in that melodies with texts are like souls with bodies, whereas melodies without texts are like pure souls. Therefore the Hasidim composed many melodies with any text and sang them with nonsense syllables such as *ya-ba-bam* or *doy-doy-doy* and the like (see example 6).

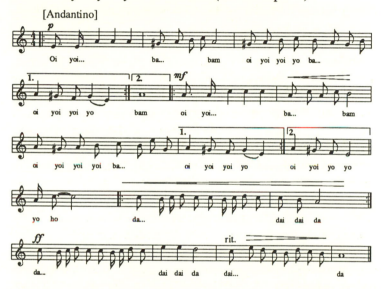

Example 6. Hasidic meditative *niggun,* according to Chemjo Vinaver, *Anthology of Hasidic Music,* Eliyahu Schleifer, ed., p. 232.

At times, such wordless *niggunim* served as substitute prayers: a long wordless melody would be followed by a hasty recitation of the corresponding prayer.

Hasidic leaders, some of whom were themselves gifted musicians, encouraged the creation of new *niggunim.* They or their followers composed melodies for statutory worship and for distinctive Hasidic rituals like the ceremonial meal known as a *Tisch.* Other leaders employed court composers, whose musical output was carefully scrutinized. It was not uncommon in the middle of the nineteenth century for Hasidic masters to employ their own chazzan, along with choirs of *meshorerim* charged with the task of disseminating new melodies by teaching them to the pilgrims who flocked to the *tzaddik*'s court during the Holy Day seasons. Thus different melodies and different performance practices developed under the various Hasidic dynasties. Until recently, all the melodies were considered *torah shebe'al peh* (oral law) not to be written, but in the last four decades some Hasidic authorities have begun permitting, and even encouraging, the notation of their *niggunim* as a means of preservation and proliferation.

Among the many genres of *niggunim,* the most important are short dance melodies; melodies used in services, either as introductions to prayers or as substitutes for them; and long meditative melodies called *dveikes* and used in important gatherings at the *tzaddik*'s table. Most melodies contain two to four sections, but some may have as many as thirty-six! The sections are said to represent stages of ecstasy or cleavage to God.

Nowadays, Hasidic music is well and thriving. New melodies for many occasions are composed by the various courts, and these regularly replace old ones. The influence of Hasidic music is felt even in the liturgical music of non-Hasidic Jews. Genuine Hasidic melodies have penetrated Orthodox, Conservative, and Reform services alike. Furthermore, imitations of Hasidic music are quite fashionable in wide circles, even among pop composers, whose work is highlighted in an annual Israeli "Festival of Hasidic Music," whence it travels to non-Hasidic services worldwide. Even the Reform movement, which arose as a bastion of anti-Hasidic sentiment, now features services that claim to have been composed in Hasidic style, though most of the imitations are much-simplified versions of the real thing.

TRADITION AND CHANGE

At the beginning of this century, scholars of Jewish music, including Idelsohn, believed that some Jewish communities, such as the Yemenite or Babylonian Jews, preserved their ancient musical traditions in pristine purity. Proof of the antiquity of their chants was to a great measure the simplicity of the melodies. This innocent belief became a major factor in the rebuilding of Jewish musical culture, especially in its old-new homeland. But the more we study Jewish musical traditions, the more we are aware of the changes that took place in each tradition throughout the ages. Recent studies, especially those by Amnon Shiloah,[70] have tried to understand the dynamics of change that influenced the traditional oriental chants during their encounter with the new cultural milieu of modern Israel. Similar changes, though not at as fast a pace, must have been the norm all along and need now to be documented.

We no longer can believe that some Jewish communities were so secluded that they never were influenced by others. The essence of the Jewish experience with history has been that Jews have moved like peddlers from community to community, carrying their musical merchandise with them. Some rabbis and cantors traveled to distant places expressly intending to transplant their liturgical chants to the cultural soil of foreign Jewish communities. Thus, for instance, modern studies should inquire whether the resemblance of the Amsterdam Portuguese chants to their Moroccan counterparts is related to the fact that both communities are descendents of the Sephardim of Spain, or whether other factors were involved. Perhaps the Moroccan chant was imported to Holland by Moroccan rabbis and cantors such as Isaac Uziel of Fez, an authoritative rabbi and excellent musician who was invited by the Dutch community in around 1610 to lead the congregation there.[71] Neither can we subscribe to the idea that the simpler the melody, the more ancient. Liturgical melodies may have developed from the simplest patterns to the most complex ones; or they may have shrunk from highly developed forms into simple patterns. Indeed, melodies have a tendency to undergo various changes through the ages, especially if they are transmitted orally.[72]

The study of change in Jewish liturgical music must take into account the major historical factors that were presented in this survey: the destruction of the Temple and rise of the synagogue;

the development of the cantillation of Scripture; the ascent of the *piyyut;* the influence of Arabic culture; the infiltration of non-Jewish melodies during the Middle Ages and later; the changing nature of the cantorate in different places and times; the introduction of polyphony into the services; and finally, the influence of Kabbalah and Hasidism.

NOTES

1. See *Yuval* 5 (1986), the Abraham Zvi Idelsohn memorial volume, especially Eliyahu Schleifer, "Idelsohn's Scholarly and Literary Publications: An Annotated Bibliography," pp. 53–180.

2. *Jewish Music in Its Historical Development* (New York, 1929; 1967).

3. Published between 1914 and 1933, in German as *Hebräisch-orientalischer Melodienschatz.* A Hebrew version covers vols. 1–5, and the English version all but vols. 3–5. Details in Schleifer, "Idelsohn's Publications," pp. 63–92.

4. In general, Ashkenazi Jews trace their cultural roots to Germany, while Sephardi Jews hark back to Spain. See below for fuller definitions.

5. See Alfred Sendrey, *Music in Ancient Israel* (New York, 1969).

6. Modern Hebrew usage is especially misleading: e.g., *kinnor,* "violin."

7. For a masterful study of this kind, see Bathja Bayer, "The Biblical Nebel," *Yuval* 1 (1968): 89–131.

8. Possibly, however, *machol,* which appears together with *tof,* indicated some kind of flute. *Tuppim umecholot* (Exod. 15:20) would then mean tambourines and flutes, perhaps similar to the ancient "tabor and pipe."

9. Under the directorship of Moshe Gorali, an attempt was made by the Haifa Music Museum and Amli Library to reconstruct the trumpets and other biblical instruments. See the catalogue, *Music in the Ancient World* (The Haifa Museum of Ancient Art, Spring 1971). These reconstructions, however, cannot be considered final and authoritative. Moreover, at best, all we can reconstruct is the instrument, not the sounds that were produced by the ancients.

10. On other related problems, see Bathja Bayer, "The Titles of

the Psalms: A Renewed Investigation of an Old Problem,'' *Yuval* 4 (1982): 29–123, and the vast bibliography there.

11. Midrash Shir Hashirim Rabbah, ch. 3.

12. The *magrefah* was erroneously identified in ancient sources and modern interpretations as an organ of the Roman *hydraulos* type. See Bathja Bayer, *Encyclopedia Judaica* (Jerusalem, 1971), vol. 12, cols. 1452–53. In an unpublished article read at the Tenth Congress of Jewish Studies, August 1989, Bayer sums up the evidence showing that the *magrefah* was nothing but the rake, and that the term could not have been used for an organ of any type.

13. Idelsohn, *Jewish Music,* pp. 18–19.

14. A third sound, *shevarim,* was probably added after the destruction of the Temple.

15. M. Ket. 4:4. See Hanoch Avenary, "'Flutes for a Bride or a Dead Man': The Symbolism of the Flute According to Hebrew Sources,'' *Orbis Musicae* 1/1 (August 1971): 11–24.

16. Cf. Aharon Kahn, "Music in Halakhic Perspective (Part I),'' *Journal of Jewish Music and Liturgy* 9 (1986–1987): 55–72.

17. See n. 4, above. The Ashkenazi/Sephardi cultural differentiation can be further broken down into smaller, more precise categories, often identical with a geographical taxonomy (see Lawrence A. Hoffman, *Beyond the Text: A Holistic Approach to Liturgy,* Jewish Literature and Culture [Bloomington, Ind., 1987], pp. 46–59). The Yemenite rite is thus a subsection of Sephardi culture.

18. *De vita comtemplativa,* on the Therapeutae sect.

19. On subsequent halakhic rulings, see Baruch David Schreiber "The Woman's Voice in the Synagogue,'' *Journal of Jewish Music and Liturgy* 7 (1984–1985): 27–32. The Christian dictum, *Mulier taceat in ecclesia* ("Let woman be silent in church''), may have had a similar effect in the medieval church worship; but its original source and meaning were different. It is based on 1 Cor. 14:34, and is related not to eroticism in the female voice but to the duty of women to obey men and not to speak up in public meetings. See Gedaliah Elkoshi, *Thesaurus of Latin Proverbs and Idioms [With Hebrew Translations and Annotations]* (Jerusalem, 1981), p. 286.

20. On the Yemenite cantillation of the Pentateuch, see Uri Sharvit, "The Realization of Biblical Cantillation Symbols (*Te'amim*) in the Jewish Yemenite Tradition,'' *Yuval* 4 (1982): 179–210.

21. On the liturgical and musical relations between the synagogue and the church, see, e.g., Eric Werner's *The Sacred Bridge,* vol. 1 (New York, 1959); and *The Sacred Bridge: The Interdependence of*

Liturgy and Music in Synagogue and Church during the First Millenium, vol. 2 (New York, 1984). While Werner's ideas are intriguing and thought provoking, his syntheses are speculative. See Peter Jeffrey, "Werner's *The Sacred Bridge, Volume 2:* A Review Essay," *The Jewish Quarterly Review* 77/4 (April 1987): 283–98. For a more modest, but more successful reconstruction, see Hanoch Avenary, "Contacts between Church and Synagogue Music," *Proceedings of the World Jewish Congress on Jewish Music (Jerusalem 1978)* (Tel Aviv, 1982), pp. 89–107.

22. This is still the custom today. The Pentateuchal reading, though prepared from a printed Bible, is chanted from the scroll. Other readings (generally the prophetic lection) are permitted from printed volumes. At specified holiday periods, Song of Songs, Ruth, Lamentations, Ecclesiastes, and Esther (known to Jewish tradition as the *five scrolls* are read from scrolls which, however, are differentiated visually from Torah scrolls in that they are constructed differently.

23. The most exhaustive studies of the Tiberias system in English are still William Wickes's books *Ta'amei Kaf Alef Sefarim [The Accents of the Twenty One Books]* and *Ta'amei Emet [The Accents of the Poetic Books]* (Oxford, 1887 and 1881); reprinted together, with a new prolegomenon by Aron Dotan (New York, 1970). The best new study is Mordecai Breuer, *Ta'amei Hamikra Bekhaf Alef Sefarim Uvesifrei Emet* (Jerusalem, 1989).

24. The best known are the Aleppo "Crown," c. 920 C.E. (now in the Jewish National Library in Jerusalem) and the Leningrad Codex, C. 1010 C.E.

25. For a recent speculative, but highly intriguing, attempt to reconstruct the original musical patterns of the Tiberias system, see Dalia Cohen and Daniel Weil, "Progress in Deductive Research on the Original Performance of the Tiberian Accents," *Proceedings of the Ninth World Congress of Jewish Studies* (Jerusalem, 1986), pp. 265–86. See also their forthcoming article, "The Scale System of the Tiberian Masoretic Accents," *Orbis Musicae* 10 (in preparation).

26. See the present writer's classification in "Cantillation," *Encyclopedia of Judaism* (Jerusalem, 1989), pp. 148–49. A different classification into five regions is suggested by Avigdor Herzog in "Masoretic Accents (Musical Rendition)," *Encyclopedia Judaica* (Jerusalem, 1971), vol. 11, cols. 1098–1111.

27. See Hanoch Avenary, *The Ashkenazi Tradition of Biblical Chant between 1500 and 1900: Documentation and Musical Analysis, Documentation, and Studies, no. 2* (Tel Aviv, 1978).

28. For a detailed description of the musical systems (according to one interpretation) see A. W. Binder, *Biblical Chant* (New York, 1959). For one Ashkenazi system, see Solomon Rosowsky, *The Cantillation of the Bible: The Five Books of Moses* (New York, 1957).

29. Cf. Idelsohn, *Jewish Music,* pp. 108–9; Eric Werner, *A Voice Still Heard: The Sacred Song of the Ashkenazi Jews* (University Park and London, 1976), pp. 9–13.

30. For rabbinic writings on chazzanut, see Israel Adler, ed., *Hebrew Writings Concerning Music in Manuscripts and Printed Books from Geonic Times up to 1800* (Munich, 1975).

31. For process of liturgical standardization, which continued until the eleventh century, cf. Joseph Heinemann, *Prayer in the Talmud* (Berlin and New York, 1977); Lawrence A. Hoffman, *The Canonization of the Synagogue Service* (Notre Dame, 1979), especially ch. 11; and most recently, the summary essay by Stefan Reif, "The Early History of Jewish Worship," in the first volume of this series, Paul Bradshaw and Lawrence A. Hoffman, eds., *The Making of Jewish and Christian Worship, Two Liturgical Traditions, Vol. 1* (Notre Dame, 1990).

32. For the standard account of the development of the art of the *piyyut,* see Ezra Fleischer, *Shirat Hakodesh Ha'ivrit Bimei Habeinayim* (Jerusalem, 1975). But see also Alfred Sendrey, *Music of the Jews in the Diaspora (up to 1800)* (New York, 1970), pp. 150–65.

33. See, e.g., Hoffman, *Canonization,* ch. 4.

34. JTS, Adler Collection, ms 4096b.

35. Cambridge TS K5/41.

36. The melodic structure of *Mi al har horev,* for instance, is indeed such as one would expect from a classic *piyyut* setting (see example 4). See also Idelsohn, *Jewish Music,* ch. 7, where some melodies deviate from the poetic rhythms or contradict them. See Israel Adler's musical transcription in *Ariel* 15 (1966): 32–33. A performance of this version is included in the recording *Synagogal Art Music XIIth–XVIIIth Centuries, Anthology of Musical Traditions in Israel* (Jerusalem, 1979), AMTI 7901. A different musical transcription has been suggested by Hanoch Avenary, *Hebrew Hymn Tunes: The Rise and Development of a Musical Tradition* (Tel Aviv, 1971), pp. 12–17.

37. Syllables with the semivowel *sheva,* or with its compounds (*chataf*) were considered short; those with any other vowel were deemed long.

38. Bouzaglo's singing is recorded in the album *Chants hébreux*

de la tradition des Juifs marocains (Tel Aviv, 1984), RCA RL90034.

39. On the *nuba,* see the classic work, Alexis Chottin, *Tableau de la musique morocaine* (Paris, 1939); and, more recently, Peter Schuyler, "Andalusian Music of Morocco," *The World of Music* 21 (1978): 33–46. On the influence of the *nuba* on Jewish music, see Amnon Shiloah, "La nuba et la célébration des bakkashot au Maroc," in M. Abitbul, ed., *Judaisme d'Afrique du Nord* (Jerusalem, 1980), pp. 108–13. See also Abraham Eilam-Amzallag, *Modal Aspects of the Singing of Supplications (Bakashot) among Moroccan Jews* (Ph.D. Diss., Jerusalem: The Hebrew University, 1986), 2 vols. (in Hebrew, with an English summary).

40. Bouzaglo's singing is recorded in the album *Chants hébreux de la tradition des Juifs marocains* (Tel Aviv, 1984), RCA RL90034.

41. The most famous song of this kind is Najara's *Yah ribon olam,* which is modeled on a popular Arabic love song and has become a universally popular Sabbath table song. The original melody of the song is lost.

42. See Ruth Katz, "The Singing of *Baqqashot* by Aleppo Jews: A Study in Musical Acculturation," *Acta Musicologica* 40 (1968): 65–85. *Bakkashot* songs from a Syrian-Jewish community in Brooklyn are available on the record album *Pizmon: Syrian-Jewish Religious and Social Song,* Kay Kaufman Shelemay and Sarah Weiss, eds. (Ho-Ho-Kus, N.J.: 1985), Meadowlark 105.

43. See Yehiel Adaki and Uri Sharvit, eds., *A Treasury of Yemenite Jewish Chants* (Jerusalem, 1981), especially nos. 68–83. For studio recordings of Yemenite paraliturgical songs, with explanations and transcriptions, see Naomi and Avner Bahat, eds., *Jewish Yemenite Songs from the Diwan: Anthology of Musical Traditions in Israel* (Jerusalem, 1982), AMTI 8201.

44. On the *Maqam* in general, see Amnon Shiloah, "Arab Music," in the *New Grove Dictionary of Music and Musicians* (London, 1980), vol. 1, pp. 514–39; see also Shiloah's article, "The Arabic Concept of Mode," *Journal of the American Musicological Society* 34 (1981): 19–42. For the influence of the *maqam* on Jewish music, see Abraham Zvi Idelsohn, *Thesaurus of Hebrew Oriental Melodies,* vol. 4 (1932), and preface to the German and Hebrew eds., ch. 4. The latest contribution to the field is Edwin Seroussi, "The Turkish *Makam* in the Musical Culture of the Ottoman Jews: Sources and Examples," *Israel Studies in Musicology* 5 (1990): 43–68.

45. See Israel J. Katz, *Judaeo-Spanish Traditional Ballads Collected in Jerusalem: An Ethnomusicological Study,* 2 vols. (Los

Angeles, 1967). Susana Weich-Shahak, *Sephardic Songs from the Balkans: Anthology of Musical Traditions in Israel,* AMTI 8001 (Jerusalem, 1980), contains original recordings of secular songs and examples of their adaptation to sacred texts. The most recent publication in the field is Weich-Shahak's *Judeo-Spanish Moroccan Songs for the Life Cycle: Recordings, Transcriptions, and Annotations* (Jerusalem, 1989).

46. See, for example, Israel J. Katz, "The 'Myth' of the Sephardic Legacy from Spain," *Proceedings of the Fifth World Congress of Jewish Studies* (Jerusalem, 1973), pp. 237–43.

47. The Lotharingian part of the Carolingian Empire, including the Rhineland, some northern parts of France, and Flanders.

48. His dicta on liturgical customs and chants were collected by his disciple, Zalman of St. Goar, and were published in 1556 as *Sefer Minhagei Maharil.*

49. For synagogue music in the United States, see Mark Slobin, *Chosen Voices: The Story of the American Cantorate* (Urbana and Chicago, 1989).

50. The western Ashkenazi motifs were first transcribed into European renaissance notation by non-Jewish humanist scholars of the sixteenth century. The earliest published transcription, by Johannes Boeschenstein, was printed in Johannes Reuchlin's Hebrew grammar, *De Accentibus et orthographia linguae Hebraicae* (Hagenau, 1518). To suit the taste of the time, the melodic patterns were set in four parts (SATB), the tenor part containing the original melody. Needless to say, the reading of Scripture was never chanted in polyphony. On other early transcriptions, see Avenary, *Biblical Chant,* pp. 10–16.

51. An excellent *nusach* collection (mostly west European) is Abraham Baer, *Ba'al T'fillah oder "Der practische Vorbeter"* (Göthenburg, 1877). The second edition (1883) was reprinted as vol. 1 of the series, Out of Print Classics of Synagogue Music (New York, 1953). For a recent scholarly exposition of simple weekday *nusach* patterns, see Brian J. Mayer, "The Origins and Identification of the *Nusach lechol* of Frankfurt am Main," *Journal of Synagogue Music* 19/1 (July, 1989): 6–55.

52. Idelsohn's original article, "Der Missinai-Gesang in der deutschen Synagog," appeared in *Zeitschrift für Musikwissenschaft* 8/8 (May, 1926): 449–72, and was revised for his *Thesaurus of Hebrew Oriental Melodies,* vol. 7 (1932), ch. 5 of the introductory section. Eric Werner treats *misinai* tunes in *A Voice Still Heard,* pp. 27–45.

53. "The *Kol Nidre* Tune," *Hebrew Union College Annual* 8/9 (1931–1932): 493–509.

54. The earliest extant transcription is a manuscript (Mus. 102a) notated between 1765 and 1783 by Aron Beer (1738–1821), in the Birnbaum Collection, Hebrew Union College, Cincinnati. Beer's version was published by Idelsohn in his *Thesaurus,* vol. 6 (1932), no. 1. For this and other early transcriptions, see Israel Adler, *Hebrew Notated Manuscript Sources up to Circa 1840,* (Munich, 1989). See also Werner, *A Voice Still Heard,* pp. 35–38, who tries, in an oversimplified way, however—especially on p. 36—to reconstruct the original.

55. Ravel includes only the cantor's part, not the congregational response.

56. Only the beginning and the end of the composition come from the original *Kol Nidre* tune; the rest is borrowed from an unrelated nineteenth-century source.

57. See, for instance, improvisations that embellished the *misinai* tune of *Alenu* and similar chants, in Hanoch Avenary, "The Cantorial Fantasia of the Eighteenth and Nineteenth Centuries," *Yuval* 1 (1968): 65–88.

58. For a survey of the literature on the modes, see Max Wohlberg, "The History of the Musical Modes of the Ashkenazic Synagogue and Their Usage," *Journal of Synagogue Music* 4/1–2 (April, 1972): 46–61. Baruch S. Cohon maps out all the Ashkenazi *shtaygers* in "The Structure of the Synagogue Prayer-Chant," *Journal of the American Musicological Society* 2 (1950): 17–31. See also Hanoch Avenary, "The Concept of Mode in European Synagogue Chant," *Yuval* 2 (1971): 11–21; his "Second Thoughts about the Configuration of a Synagogue Mode," *Orbis Musicae* 9 (1986): 11–16; and Joseph A. Levine, "Toward Defining the Jewish Prayer Modes with Particular Emphasis on the *Adonay Malakh* Mode," *Musica Judaica* 3/1 (1980–1981): 13–41.

59. Idelsohn (*Jewish Music,* pp. 84–89) traced this mode to Mongolian or Tartarian music.

60. See Edith Gerson-Kiwi, "Vocal Folk-Polyphonies of the Western Orient in Jewish Tradition," *Yuval* 1 (1968): 169–193.

61. For European organum, see Richard H. Hoppin, *Medieval Music* (New York, 1978), pp. 178–98. Simha Arom and Uri Sharvit, who are now studying the Yemenite phenomenon, call it "Yemenite Plurivocality." For their findings, see forthcoming in *Yuval* 6.

62. Indications for the bass and boy singers occur already in some

eighteenth-century manuscripts. See Adler, *Hebrew Notated Manuscript Sources,* Index I4a, pp. 799–802.

63. A "modernized" version of Rossi's *Hashirim* was published by Samuel Naumbourg as *Cantiques de Salomon Rossi hebreo* (Paris, 1877) reprint ed. (New York, 1954). A better, scholarly edition in three volumes was published by Fritz Rikko (New York, 1967–1973). A new critical edition by Don Harran of Jerusalem is planned as part of the publication of Rossi's collected works. On Rossi's innovation and its background, see Israel Adler, "The Rise of Art Music in the Italian Ghetto," in A. Altmann, ed., *Jewish Medieval and Renaissance Studies,* (Cambridge, Mass., 1967), pp. 321–64; and Don Harran, "Tradition and Innovation in Jewish Music of the Later Renaissance," *Journal of Musicology* 7/1 (Winter 1989): 107–30.

64. Various cantatas of this sort were discovered and published by Israel Adler through the Israel Music Publications, Jerusalem.

65. See Alfred Sendrey, *The Music of the Jews in the Diaspora* (New York, 1970), pp. 348–56.

66. See below, Geoffrey Goldberg, "Jewish Liturgical Music in the Wake of Nineteenth-Century Reform."

67. See Amnon Shiloah, "The Symbolism of Music in the Kabbalistic Tradition," *The World of Music* 20 (1978): 56–69.

68. See Moshe Idel, "Music and Prophetic Kabbalah," *Yuval* 4 (1971): 150–78; and his Hebrew article in the Hebrew section of the same volume.

69. See Idelsohn, *Jewish Music,* ch. 19. The best early collection of Hasidic melodies is Idelsohn's *Thesaurus,* vol. 10 (1932). A rich collection of melodies is Velvel Pasternak's *Songs of the Chassidim* (Cedarhurst, N.Y., 1971). For explanations of Hasidic melodies, see Chemjo Vinaver, *Anthology of Chasidic Music,* Eliyahu Schleifer, ed. (Jerusalem, 1985). See also Andre Hajdu and Yaacov Mazor, "The Musical Traditions of Hasidism," *Encyclopedia Judaica* (Jerusalem, 1971), vol. 7, cols. 1421–32; and the extensive Mazor-Hajdu article, "The Hasidic Dance-Niggun: A Study Collection and Its Classificatory Analysis," *Yuval* 3 (1974): 136–265. Some of Hajdu-Mazor's authentic recordings were included in *Hasidic Tunes of Dancing and Rejoicing: Anthology of Musical Traditions in Israel* (Jerusalem, 1976), RCA (n.n.).

70. See, for instance, Amnon Shiloah and Eric Cohen, "The Dynamics of Change in Jewish Oriental Ethnic Music in Israel," *Ethnomusicology* 27 (1983): 227–51.

71. See Edith Gerson-Kiwi's preface to David Ricardo, ed.,

Selected Tunes from the Portuguese Jews' Congregation, Rishon Le-Zion [Private publication, 1975]; and Israel Adler, *Musical Life and Traditions of the Portuguese Jewish Community of Amsterdam in the XVIIIth Century,* Yuval Monograph Series, no. 1 (Jerusalem, 1974), pp. 11, 93.

72. See Hanoch Avenary, "The Aspect of Time and Environment in Jewish Traditional Music," *Israel Studies in Musicology* 4 (1987): 93–112.

Jewish Liturgical Music in the Wake of Nineteenth-Century Reform

GEOFFREY GOLDBERG

Background for Change:
Music and Emancipation

The music of the synagogue is inseparable from the Jewish community's struggle for emancipation.[1] This chapter focuses particularly on developments in the German-speaking states of central Europe. However, the pace of modernization was by no means uniform with respect to social class, time, or place.[2] In eastern Europe, for instance, emancipation came a full century later than it did in the west, bringing with it its own unique religious musical genre: the Hasidic *niggun* (wordless melody). This largely, though not exclusively, extrasynagogal chant that expressed several mystical concepts, flourished at exactly the same time as the first musical changes were occurring in synagogues in the west. The development of the *niggun,* however, was motivated by an apolitical ideology, whereas the musical developments of the western Jews can be understood only within a wider political framework. Moreover, the western musical accommodation threatened the loss of authentic Jewish liturgical music as the price to be paid for social acceptance and equality.

This danger was most acute during the early, radical phase of the movement for reform. The aesthetics of premodern Jewish worship were measured against the modern standards of the non-Jewish world and found wanting. The following description from before c. 1775 of such a premodern Ashkenazi synagogue, this one in Amsterdam, would still have been applicable a few decades later:

At my first entrance, one of the priests [sic]³ was chanting part of the service in a kind of ancient *canto firmo,* and responses were made by the congregation, in a manner which resembled the hum of bees. After this, three of the sweet singers of Israel, which [sic] it seems are famous here . . . began singing a kind of jolly modern melody, sometimes in unison, and sometimes in parts, to a kind of *tol de rol,* instead of words, which to me, seemed very farcical. One of these voices was a falset, more like the upper part of a *vox humana* stop in an organ, than a natural voice. . . . The second of these voices was a very vulgar tenor, and the third was a *baritono.* The last imitated, in his accompaniment of the falset, a bad bassoon. . . . At the end of each strain, the whole congregation set up such a kind of cry, as a pack of hounds when a fox breaks cover. It was a confused clamour, and riotous noise, more than song or prayer. . . . I shall only say, that it was very unlike what we Christians are used to in divine service.⁴

This mode of worship was deemed unacceptable by Jews who had moved beyond the parameters of a closed Jewish society and sought instead a religious ambience of order, beauty, and decorum—all three characteristics as defined by western, non-Jewish cultural and aesthetic standards.

Early Reforms in Westphalia, Berlin, and Hamburg

The first opportunity to introduce modern European aesthetics occurred in 1809 in the Kingdom of Westphalia, established by Napoleon two years earlier. In the consistorial—i.e., the state-supervised—school in Cassel (1809), and then in the new temple in Seesen (completed in 1810), a number of musical innovations were introduced by Israel Jacobson (1768–1828). These changes, promulgated from above and by no means enjoying very wide popular support, received government backing in the form of a *Synagogenordnung.*⁵ Protestantism provided the aesthetic norms: German prayers, an organ, and hymns. Biblical lections and prayers were read, not chanted, as the traditional sing-song chants were deemed too oriental for modern use. Jewish hymn texts were sung to music taken from non-Jewish sources.⁶

With the Kingdom of Westphalia's demise in 1813, Jacobson moved to Berlin where Reform services were held in his private synagogue in the spring of 1815. Between 1817 and 1823 somewhat less radical services were convened also in the home of Jacob Herz Beer (1769–1825), father of the composer Meyerbeer. Halakhic (legal) support for the innovations, especially for the use of the organ, came in the form of four rabbinic responsa entitled *Nogah Hatsedek* (*The Radiance of Light*), published in Dessau in 1818. The leading respondent was Aaron Chorin (1766–1844), rabbi of Arad, Hungary. But controversy within the community forced the government to close the private synagogue. The community synagogue remained unchanged, however, leaving unsatisfied a generation of culturally sophisticated Jews. An unyielding rabbinate, a cantor barely possessing western musical skills,[7] and a repressive government thus combined to prevent any further substantive musical reforms in Berlin until the 1840s.[8]

In Hamburg a temple was dedicated in 1817, followed two years later by a new prayer book containing theological modifications that incurred the wrath of rabbinical authorities throughout Europe. The Bible was merely declaimed and German hymns sung, as in Seesen; and a Sephardi cantor was installed, primarily because the music of Sephardi culture and its distinctive Hebraic pronunciation were considered more cultured than their Ashkenazi equivalents.[9] A few of the hymn tunes were based on traditional Jewish melodies, but the majority were commissioned from gentile composers of little talent.[10] The ensuing result was "a strange combination of Sephardi modes in the Hebrew together with the contemporary style of church music in the German hymns."[11]

Salomon Sulzer

This loss of Jewish musical distinctiveness nearly occurred in Vienna, too, where an appeal was made in 1819 by some fifty "tolerated" Jews for reforms according to the Berlin and Hamburg models.[12] In 1821, Isaac Noah Mannheimer (1793–1865) was appointed preacher—the government prohibited the title *rabbi*. Though originally a radical reformer, Mannheimer came to fear that too much change would destroy communal unity. He was persuaded, however, to initiate moderate reform, by a new and youthful chazzan of remarkable musical and vocal ability, namely, Salomon Sulzer (1804–1890), who was appointed in 1826 to lead the services in the new Seitengaße Synagogue.

Together, Sulzer and Mannheimer established a form of service known as the Vienna rite, which became a model of moderation and beauty. This dignified service had an enormous impact throughout central Europe, even among many acculturated Orthodox synagogues, and in eastern Europe as well.

What is remarkable is that Sulzer's assumption of the Vienna cantorate coincided with two decades of decline in musical taste and performance standards following the deaths of Beethoven (1827) and Schubert (1828). Gentile visitors were deeply impressed by the music they heard in the Vienna synagogue. Following his visits there between 1826 and 1828 the German-born music critic, Joseph Mainzer, expressed:

> To whatever religion one may happen to belong, I declare that it is impossible to bear witness without emotion, and even not to be actually edified by the conduct of the service which is so simple, so noble, so elevated, and purified from all vain display by a reform in accordance with the times in which we live. . . . This Temple shines in new glory and can serve for a second time as a model for the Christian churches.[13]

Mainzer also declared that "never, except for the Sistine Chapel, has art given me higher joy than in that synagogue."[14] Other gentile visitors included Franz Liszt; the critic Eduard Hanslick, who was of Jewish descent; and Frances Trollope, the writer of romantic travelogue, who testified:

> A voice, to which that of Braham [John Braham, 1774–1858, born Abraham, son of a chazzan, Abraham Singer of Prossnitz, and a celebrated English tenor] in his best days was not superior, performs the solo parts of these extraordinary cantiques; while about a dozen voices or more, some of them being boys, fill up the glorious chorus. The volume of vocal sound exceeds anything

of the kind I have ever heard; and being unaccompanied by an instrument, it produces an effect equally singular and delightful.[15]

The first volume of *Schir Zion,* Sulzer's collection of synagogue music, appeared in 1840. The preface (written in 1838) contains some of Sulzer's objectives: "I see it as my duty . . . to consider as far as possible the traditional tunes bequeathed to us, to cleanse their ancient and decorous character from the later accretions or tasteless embellishments, to restore their original purity, and to reconstruct them in accordance with the text and the rules of harmony."[16] Sulzer also endeavored to attain

A restoration that had to rest upon historical foundations. . . . One had to resume the given tradition and restore it in a dignified and artistically correct manner. . . . The Jewish liturgy . . . must not renounce its Jewish character . . . the old national melodies and modes had to be rediscovered, collected and arranged according to the rules of art.[17]

Several of Sulzer's objectives require a commentary.

Until the end of the eighteenth century—and in some small eastern European communities as late as the Holocaust—the music of the synagogue was transmitted largely orally, as it passed down from one cantor to another. These cantors were unconcerned with such things as western musical notation and vocal technique.[18] But in the Enlightenment capitals of Germany and Austria, Sulzer epitomized a new type of cantor who was schooled not only in traditional Jewish learning but also in western music, music theory, and composition.[19] He thus appealed to Viennese community leaders who wanted a cantor with a voice that was trained according to western aesthetic standards and with competence in composition and choral technique, together with sound Hebrew grammar. In 1845, similar demands were made of Abraham J. Lichtenstein (1806–1880), who was appointed to succeed Ascher Lion in Berlin. Lion's musical ability was so slight that he had been unable to decipher handwritten scores of *Schir Zion* obtained from Vienna, and a young *meshorer,*[20] Louis Lewandowski (to whom we shall return),

had to come to his assistance. By contrast, Lichtenstein was
required to obtain one letter testifying to his musical knowledge,
and another attesting to his Hebraic literacy.[21]

By "later accretions or tasteless embellishments," Sulzer
meant those musical characteristics of a tradition in decline,
which had been so evident in the late eighteenth century, particularly among professional itinerant chazzanim who served
the larger communities. The traditional modal prayer chant had
been neglected while third-rate, late baroque instrumental or
operatic music was absorbed or parodied. Some composers even
attempted to imitate instrumental forms, especially the dance
forms of the rococo, without regard to the meaning of the text
(see examples 1–3).[22]

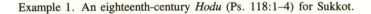

Example 1. An eighteenth-century *Hodu* (Ps. 118:1–4) for Sukkot.

Example 2. An eighteenth-century setting of *Lekha Dodi* (hymn welcoming the Sabbath).

Example 3. An eighteenth-century setting of *Melekh Elyon* (a holy day *piyyut*).

We even know of small rural Hungarian communities still largely unaffected by social and religious changes where Orthodox synagogues utilized the dance and vocal models of the minuet, *Ländler* (a slow Austrian dance), *csardas* (a fast Hungarian dance), march, and operatic aria.[23]

Harmony was not entirely unknown in the European synagogue, but it was a three-part harmony, a form of organum, and was performed by *meshorerim* such as Burney had heard in Amsterdam—although usually with a boy soprano, or *singerl,* and a bass. They accompanied the cantor, singing in octaves, thirds, and sixths, and also provided musical interludes, frequently in the form of vocalises (wordless songs) in imitation of musical instruments. The vocalise was used by the cantor as well (see example 4, a Kaddish by Joseph Goldstein, written c. 1791, in Bavaria).

Example 4. A Kaddish setting (c. 1791) by Joseph Goldstein.

Like other chazzanim of his generation, Sulzer had apprenticed as a *meshorer*. He even brought with him two of his own *meshorerim* to Vienna, but they were to supplement a four-part choir—instead of the traditional three-part variety—and they were no longer to sing in the improvised manner. Actually, the first four-part choir had been formed by Israel Lovy in Paris in 1822, and in 1832 a stylized trio style was established by Maier Kohn in Munich.[24] But of the various choirs, Sulzer's had the most impact. The old style survived in eastern Europe while increasingly, in the west, it was considered indecorous and detrimental to a devotional spirit.[25] Still, aspects of the *meshorer* idiom continued to pervade some arranged and composed nineteenth-century music, as in a setting of *Lekha Dodi* by Sulzer himself (see example 5)[26] where the three-part harmony provides a textural contrast between the solo section of the cantor and the tutti refrain of the choir.

Example 5. A *Lekha Dodi* setting by Salomon Sulzer.

True to his stated objectives, Sulzer reworked the sung portions of the liturgy, seeking clean-cut melodic lines without excessive coloratura. Giving the meaning of the texts the highest priority, he refrained from breaking up phrases and repeating words. Unfortunately, the free rubato, recitative style was often forced into a regular meter, which does not fit Hebrew prosody, and the modal flavor was sometimes compromised by concessions to western tonality (such as the use of leading tones and transformations of traditional modes to major and minor keys). Similarly, choral responses to a modal chazzanic chant were sometimes awkward (see examples 6a and 6b).

Example 6a. A *Semiroth Israel* setting (1845) by Hirsch Goldberg.

Example 6b. A *Semiroth Israel* setting (1864) by Samuel Naumbourg.

In Sulzer's *Schir Zion* we find some recitatives based on the traditional Jewish modes alone, and others in which the modes were augmented by a variety of choral responses. In some of the choral parts of *Schir Zion* 1 Sulzer was assisted by a number of leading Viennese composers, most of them non-Jewish; even Franz Schubert wrote one setting.[28] They composed primarily for liturgical sections that lacked a definitive *nusach* (customary prayer chant) or conventional musical emphasis. In *Schir Zion* 2 the traditional element clearly predominates. In his settings for the festivals and High Holy Days we see Sulzer's skill in restoring "old melodies . . . arranged according to the rules of art." The juxtaposition of tasteful choral sections and refined but expressive modal recitatives is shown in the following excerpt from the prayer for *Tal* (dew), recited on Passover (see example 7).[29]

Example 7. Excerpt from a *Tal* setting by Salomon Sulzer.

Innumerable cantors came to Vienna to study with Sulzer, some at the request and expense of their own communities. Most came from western and central Europe; others came from the east, from as far away as Odessa. Among these latter were Osias Abrass (1820–1884), Baruch Schorr (1823–1904), and Pinchas Minkowsky (1859–1924).

Hirsch Weintraub and Samuel Naumbourg

Another regenerator of synagogue music was Hirsch Weintraub (1811–1881). He had studied general music and violin in Vienna and Berlin. After first succeeding his father, a cantor in Poland, he was appointed chief cantor in Königsberg in 1838. His eclectic collection, *Schire Beth Adonai* (1859), provides a fascinating reflection of a community in transition from east and west. On the one hand, he included traditional chant settings, and often designated them as *Alte Melodie,* or even *Uralte Melodie,* and indicated their connection to the eight western medieval and Renaissance church modes. On the other hand, there are chorales, some utilizing traditional themes and others new in inspiration. Some have fugal endings and a few are to be sung in German, whether as translations of well-known prayers or for new occasions such as confirmation. The final section of the publication includes the highly elaborate recitatives of his father, to which he added his own simplified versions that were more in accord with the tastes of his congregants.

In 1845, on the recommendation of Jacques Halevy, Samuel Naumbourg (1815–1880), once a chorister with Maier Kohn in Munich, was appointed cantor in Paris, where he proved instrumental in the musical revival of the French synagogues. His three-volume *Semiroth Israel* (1847–1864), based on his own native south German chant, contains some of the most archaic elements of Ashkenazi song. Despite the imprint of *opera comique* here and there, most melodies are worshipful and exude a delicate quality. Several contributions were made by Halevy and Meyerbeer. Another Naumbourg work (copublished with Vincent d'Indy), a study of the newly discovered synagogue music of Salamone de Rossi (c. 1570–c. 1630), represents one of the first contributions to the historical study of Jewish music.

Louis Lewandowski

Only Louis Lewandowski (1823–1894) rivaled Sulzer as a composer of synagogue music.[30] The first Jew admitted to the Royal Academy of Arts in Berlin, Lewandowski studied with Adolf Bernhard Marx, the music theorist, and Eduard Grell, contrapuntalist and organist. Though born into a cantorial family, Lewandowski functioned not as cantor but as director of music, the first Jew to hold such an office in the history of the synagogue. Appointed to this position in Berlin's Alte (Old) Synagogue in 1844, he directed a choir considerably larger than Sulzer's in Vienna. From 1845 on Lewandowski worked with Abraham J. Lichtenstein, the chief cantor, whose recitatives he studied and rearranged. In 1866 Lewandowski transferred his activities to the cathedral-size Neue (New) Synagogue, which had been provided with an organ (although he personally opposed its use in the synagogue).

Lewandowski's first significant publication was the *Kol Rinnah U'T'fillah* (Berlin, 1871), for cantor and two-part choir for Sabbaths, festivals, and the High Holy Days. It supplied an immediate need of smaller and medium-sized congregations that had neither the means nor the ability to perform the complex compositions of Sulzer or Weintraub. Despite the rapid urbanization of German Jewry at this time, most Jews still lived in smaller towns and villages. *Kol Rinnah* offered these communities an opportunity to participate in simplified congregational singing. Sulzer himself had already compiled a collection of simple rearrangements of some of his pieces entitled *Dudaim* (Vienna, 1860), intended for school children and smaller congregations; and Naumbourg, too, later produced a collection of songs, *Agudat Shirim* (Leipzig, 1874), that was far superior to Sulzer's. The most interesting feature of Naumbourg's work was the inclusion of Sephardi melodies as part of a plan to fuse the Sephardi and Ashkenazi rites. After years of negotiations, the plan was narrowly rejected. Even so, some Sephardi tunes did enter Ashkenazi synagogues.[31]

Lewandowski can thus be credited with setting modern synagogue congregational song on a firm foundation. Critical of Sulzer for providing choral sections that required the choir to lead the congregation in its responses and thus, in effect, silenced the congregation, Lewandowski provided congregational tunes to be sung with or without the choir, in addition to the two-part choral compositions. He also criticized some of Sulzer's monotonal choral responses and attempted instead to write responses to fit the *nusach* of a particular section of the service (see example 8).[32]

Example 8. A choral response from Louis Lewandowski's *Kol Rinnah* (1871).

The *Kol Rinnah*'s chant settings served many a cantor of modest vocal abilities, giving rise to a generation of *Kol Rinnah* chazzanim. Lewandowski also simplified many of Lichtenstein's recitatives, which were decreasingly appreciated by the congregations[33] (see examples 9a and 9b).[34]

Example 9a. A *Barukh atah Adonai* setting by Lichtenstein.

Example 9b. Simplified version of Lichtenstein's setting of *Barukh atah Adonai* by Louis Lewandowski.

Lewandowski himself excelled in the cantabile style—that region between recitative and more metrical, tuneful melody. While Sulzer often reflected the style of Schubert, Lewandowski was deeply influenced by Mendelssohn.

Lewandowski's full potential was realized through his *Todah W'simrah* (Berlin, 1876 and 1882), for four-part choir, cantor, congregation, and organ. The organ accompaniment usually only doubled the choral parts, making most pieces suitable for use in synagogues that had no organ. Lewandowski's music thus cut across denominational lines,[35] and his influence extended far beyond Berlin.

Reform in Eastern Europe

Eastern Europe, home to the largest numbers of Jews who lived under medieval-like conditions, did not remain immune to western developments. Larger communities instituted a *Chorshul* (literally, choir synagogue) modeled on the Vienna rite but nominally Orthodox and never with an organ. The chazzanut of the *Chorshul* remained typically eastern European, that is, unashamedly oriental in conception; modal, with frequent modulations, often rising to tonal levels similar to the *maqamat* of Arabic and Turkish music; highly improvisational and melismatic; and unrestricted by regular meters. However, to this style was added a western-inspired choral element.

The leading center of the eastern European *Chorshul* was Odessa. This cosmopolitan port laying outside the Pale of Settlement—the area of dense Jewish settlement in eastern Europe—rapidly became home to the most important Jewish institutions in Russia.[36] It was also the first Russian city to possess an opera house frequented by Jews and non-Jews alike, where cantors could hear the potential of contemporary non-Jewish music.

Appalled by the conditions existing in the main synagogue, a group of German-speaking Jews from Brody, in Galicia, an important center of *Haskalah* (the name applied to the Jewish Enlightenment), initiated a rival house of worship in 1840 known as the Brody Synagogue. Here Nissan Blumenthal (1805–1903) established a four-part choir.[37] Within a few years the Great Synagogue followed suit.

A galaxy of virtuoso chazzanim officiated in Odessa, raising chazzanut to new levels of artistry and competition: cantors like Abrass and Minkowski (mentioned above) and Ephraim Zalman Razumni (1853–1918)[38] were imitated throughout the Pale of Settlement, where the synagogue became the only center of musical performance. The Odessa synagogues also employed composer/music directors such as A. Dunajewsky (1843–1911) and David Nowakowsky (1848–1921). The latter's *Schirei David: Kabbalat Shabbat* (Odessa, n.d.) and *Schirei David: Schlußgebet für Yom Kippur* (Moscow, 1895) represent but a fraction of his compositions.[39] The stature of this gifted composer with remarkable contrapuntal skills is only slowly being recognized.

Nevertheless, we should not exaggerate the role of the *Chorshul* in the evolution of eastern European synagogue music, for it was but one band of the spectrum. "What is important here," writes Mark Slobin, "is . . . that every community supported a variety of synagogues, ranging from the purposely plain *shtiblakh* of Hasidic sects, who scorned ornament, through a badly heated *shnaydershul* (tailor's synagogue) to the grand edifices of the middle class."[40]

The Choir and the Organ: Two Symbolic Issues

The choirs that were introduced in western and central Europe were, at least in the first decades, for the most part comprised men and boys. With few exceptions the traditional separation of men and women in the synagogue remained in full force, even in "liberal" synagogues (as more conservative-oriented non-Orthodox synagogues were called later in the nineteenth century). For the Orthodox, there remained the Jewish legal proscription against listening to a woman's voice (for the historical context of this rule, see the discussion in Schleifer's essay, above). As early as 1814, members of the Vienna community had approached one of the leading rabbinical authorities of the day, Rabbi Moses Sofer (1762–1839), for guidance concerning the permissibility of performing a cantata for mixed voices written by Ignaz Moscheles (1794–1870) for a special service to commemorate the Austrian victory over Napoleon. The Rabbi's responsum was most strict in its condemnation and added considerable weight to the (musical) exclusion of women from public religious life.[41]

Before 1850 fewer than ten German communities possessed mixed choirs.[42] Independent synagogues, that is, synagogues existing outside the general community structure, such as the West London Synagogue (established in 1842), which introduced a mixed choir in 1859, felt freer to allow women to participate. However, the overwhelming majority of central European synagogues remained within the *Gemeinde* (community) so that issues concerning worship were decided, not by the rabbi or even the individual synagogue, but by the overall *Gemeinde* board, which frequently restrained those seeking changes. For example, there was no mixed choir in any Berlin *Gemeinde* synagogue until 1891, and only in 1893 did women sing in the choir of the Neue Synagogue.[43] In Vienna, only men and boys sang until 1939. German Orthodoxy never allowed the participation of women, but starting in the late 1880s mixed choirs began to be used in several middle-class London Orthodox synagogues.[44] The only city in eastern Europe with a mixed choir was Odessa, and here in but one synagogue.[45]

After 1850, many central European communities adopted the organ,[46] partially for aesthetic reasons, but also as a symbol of cultural and social parity with the gentile environment. In 1845, a Reform-dominated rabbinical conference sanctioned its use, even by a Jew on the Sabbath.[47] The Leipzig Synod of 1869 reconfirmed the 1845 permission and even commended the organ's introduction.

Nevertheless, the use of an organ remained a divisive issue throughout the century. By 1886, organs had been introduced into approximately sixty-five German communities,[48] though not without incurring considerable community bitterness. For instance, with respect to installing an organ in Berlin's Neue Synagogue, the *Gemeinde* board elicited opinions on the subject from seven rabbinical authorities, one of whom, the celebrated preacher and scholar, Michael Sachs, even resigned, largely over this issue.[49] While Budapest introduced the organ in 1853, Vienna never did so, at least for Sabbaths and festivals, even though Sulzer, unlike Lewandowski, favored the organ and had even drafted a written recommendation for its use. An 1856 conference of French rabbis permitted the organ on Sabbaths and Holy Days, provided it was played by a gentile; and by the century's end, most acculturated Orthodox synagogues under the supervision of the consistoire used the organ.[50] In eastern Europe, as we might expect, Odessa alone used the organ. In 1877 it was first used for a weekday Chanukah service in the Great Synagogue, while from 1901 it was introduced for regular worship in the Brody Synagogue.[51]

In Retrospect

In the early twentieth century, the attempt by Sulzer, Lewandowski, and others to obtain a musical synthesis of two cultures came under criticism. The mood was for a greater intensity of

Jewish musical spirit, often drawing upon Jewish folk music, its freer rhythms and modal tunes. A new harmonic language was sought for a music that was considered oriental, not western, in origin.

Nevertheless, nineteenth-century European achievements in the field of synagogue music are remarkable. Time-honored chants were restored and creativity awakened. The standards set by cantors and composers and the expectations of congregants were raised. The time was opportune for the Jewish composer to reconsider the music of Judaism as a fruitful and worthy field of endeavor. But above all, Judaism's musical response to the nineteenth century reflected the hopes, opportunities, and uncertainties of a Jewry undergoing a profound social transformation and religious adaptation.

NOTES

1. Cf. Hanoch Avenary, "Music: Modern Times," *Encyclopedia Judaica,* vol. 12 (Jerusalem, 1972), cols. 636–55; Abraham Z. Idelsohn, *Jewish Music* (New York, 1929), chapters 12–14; Michael A. Meyer, *Response to Modernity* (Oxford, 1988), chapters 1–5; Eric Werner, *A Voice Still Heard* (University Park, Penn., 1976), chapters 10–13.

2. The pace of this modernization varied from place to place. See Steven M. Lowenstein, "The Pace of Modernization of German Jewry in the Nineteenth Century," *Leo Baeck Institute Year Book* 21 (1976), pp. 41–56.

3. The author, a Christian, assumes the leaders of worship to be priests, whereas, in fact, they would have been cantors.

4. Charles Burney, *The Present State of Music in Germany, the Netherlands, and the United Provinces* (London, 1775), vol. 2, pp. 229–30.

5. The first such ordinance (Westphalia, 1810) became the prototype for others throughout Germany, especially in the 1830s and 1840s. They regulated all matters relating to liturgy, ritual, music, and decorum in the synagogue.

6. *Hebraische und deutsche Gesänge zur Andacht und Erbauung* (Cassel, 1810).

7. Ascher Lion (1776–1863).

8. Modern services did, however, continue in the community school. The musical standards of the Beer Temple were not very high; they were described by one visitor as containing an "out of tune organ and the new, clumsy, shrieking choir." See Nahum N. Glatzer, "On an Unpublished Letter of Isaak Markus Jost," *Leo Baeck Institute Year Book* 22 (1977), p. 131.

9. From 1818 to 1833 the hymnal that was used was compiled by Eduard Kley, who was originally associated with the Beer Temple in Berlin. Later the Hamburg Temple produced its own *Allgemeines israelitisches Gesangbuch* (Hamburg, 1833).

10. Moritz Henle, "Bemerkungen zum Gesang im Hamburger Temple," *Liberales Judenthums* 10 (July–August 1918), pp. 76–79. According to Henle, a disproportionately large section of the services was allotted to the singing of these hymns.

11. Meyer, *Response to Modernity,* p. 57. The Hamburg Temple, which continued in existence until 1939, later reintroduced cantillation, reduced the number of hymns, and restored the Ashkenazi chant.

12. Until 1848 only "tolerated" Jews—those who could afford the property and poll taxes—were allowed to dwell in the city. The Jews of Vienna thus comprised a social elite, similar to the Jews of Munich and, to some extent, Berlin, where immigration from Prussian Posen was restricted.

13. Joseph Mainzer, *Esquisses Musicales* (Paris, 1838), pp. 165–66. At that time Mainzer worked for the *Gazette musicale* and the *Nationale* in Paris. He later settled in England to found the forerunner of the *Musical Times.* See A. L. Ringer, "Salomon Sulzer, Joseph Mainzer, and the Romantic a cappella Movement," *Studia Musicologica* 2 (1969): 254–370. During one of his visits, Mainzer did not miss a single Sabbath service during a seven-month period.

14. Ringer, "Sulzer," p. 360.

15. Frances Trollope, *Vienna and the Austrians* (London, 1838), p. 373. Quoted in Ringer, "Sulzer," p. 356.

16. Quoted in Werner, *Voice Still Heard,* p. 213. On the 1840 date, see Hanoch Avenary, ed., *Kantor Salomon Sulzer und seine Zeit: Eine Dokumentation* (Sigmaringen, 1985), p. 250.

17. Salomon Sulzer, *Denkschrift* (Vienna, 1876). Quoted in Werner, *Voice Still Heard,* p. 212.

18. Even with the completion of *Schir Zion* 2 in 1865, significant sections of the synagogue services were still not notated.

19. Occasionally we find a musically educated cantor in the pre-Enlightenment era, such as Solomon Lipschütz (1675–1758), who held that "singing without musical knowledge is like prayer without true devotion." See his *Te'udat Shelomo* (Offenbach, 1715–1718), fols. 21b–22a.

20. Plural, *meshorerim:* singers known for their oral mastery of a large repertory. Dependent on oral transmission, cantors sought out *meshorerim* who could teach them traditional melodies.

21. Cf. Aron Friedmann, "Abraham Jakob Lichtenstein," in Aron Friedmann, ed., *Lebensbilder berühmter Kantoren,* part 1 (Berlin, 1918), pp. 78–81; and Lewandowski's "Erinnerungen," *Der jüdische Kantor,* vol. 3 ([Bromberg], 1882), no. 11, p. 82.

22. Examples are taken from Abraham Z. Idelsohn, *Thesaurus of Oriental Hebrew Melodies,* vol. 6: *The Synagogue Song of the German Jews in the Eighteenth Century* (Leipzig, 1932), reprint ed. (New York, 1973), pp. 1–194. Example 1 (no. 443), a *Hodu* (Ps. 118:1–4) for Sukkot, opens with the traditional melody but becomes a baroque instrumental suite. Example 2 (no. 300) utilizes a traditional tune for *Lekha Dodi,* the hymn welcoming the Sabbath, which is varied, however, in early classic concertante style. Example 3 (no. 332) is a High Holy Day tune to *Melekh Elyon* but is augmented with elements of the tune that Franz Joseph Haydn reworked in 1797 into "Gott erhalte unsern Kaiser."

23. Leopold Löw, "Der Gesang in den orthodoxen ungarischen Synagogen," *Ben Chananja,* vol. 6 (1863), p. 460.

24. Maier Kohn, arr., *Vollständiger Jahrgang von Terzett- und Chorgesängen der Synagoge in München* (Munich, 1839).

25. In some communities the rabbis took steps to abolish the *meshorerim* entirely. This first occurred in the Kingdom of Westphalia in 1810. An attempt was made to abolish them in Württemberg in 1838. See the *Gottesdienst Ordnung für die Synagogen des Königreiches Württemberg* (Stuttgart, 1838), part 2, paragraph 4.

26. *Schir Zion* 1, no. 1.

27. Example 6a (Hirsch Goldberg, *Gesänge für Synagogen,* 2nd ed. [Braunschweig, 1845], p. 65) is the cantor's chant and response for the first benediction before the *Shema* on Sabbath eve. The flatted seventh of the *Adonai Malakh* mode is sometimes disregarded and the response is forced into the key of F major. Example 6b (Samuel Naumbourg's *Semiroth Israel,* vol. 2 [Paris, 1864], no. 16) is a more authentic notation of the traditional formula, but it avoids the flatted seventh.

28. Cf. Eduard Birnbaum, "Franz Schubert as a Composer of

Synagogue Music," in Eric Werner, ed., *Contributions to a Historical Study of Jewish Music* (New York, 1976), pp. 228–40; Elaine Brody, "Schubert and Sulzer Revisited: A Recapitulation of the Events Leading to Schubert's Setting in Hebrew of Psalm 92, D. 953," in Eva Badura-Skoda and P. Branscombe, eds., *Schubert Studies: Problems of Style and Chronology* (Cambridge, 1982), pp. 47–60.

29. *Schir Zion* 2, nos, 180 and 181.

30. There is a discrepancy concerning Lewandowski's date of birth. Some consider it to have been 1821, but I have followed Eduard Birnbaum, "L. Lewandowski," *Jeschurun* [Tilsit], vol. 3 (1894), no. 8, p. 102; and E. Ehrenreich, "Der erster Synagogenchor in Berlin," *Gemeindeblatt der jüdischen Gemeinde zu Berlin,* vol. 19 (1929), no. 3, p. 108.

31. See Morton M. Rosenthal, "History and Stylistic Development of Synagogue Music in France in the Nineteenth Century" (Rabbinic thesis, Hebrew Union College–Jewish Institute of Religion, 1960), p. 38.

32. *Kol Rinnah* (Berlin, 1871), p. 15, no. 18. The congregational chant for the *Shema* continues in the same *nusach* as that intoned by the cantor for the previous blessings. It resembles Naumbourg (example 6). Prior to the regeneration of synagogue music in the nineteenth century it would appear that most congregational responses had degenerated into heterophony.

33. When plans were made for constructing the Neue Synagogue in Berlin, members of the community petitioned the Community board for, among other things, a "simplification of the mode of performance"—an indirect criticism of Lichtenstein, whose chant was by then considered too elaborate. See *An die geerhten Mitglieder der hiesigen jüdischen Gemeinde* (Berlin, 1865), p. 3.

34. Example 9(a): Lichtenstein MSS, Birnbaum Collection of Jewish Music, Mus. 125, HUC-JIR, Cincinnati. Example 9(b): Lewandowski, *Kol Rinnah,* p. 101, no. 154.

35. For example, the *Liturgisches Liederbuch* (Berlin, 1912), a songbook compiled by the *Gemeinde* of Berlin, is comprised largely of Lewandowski's melodies and responses and is intended for use by both Orthodox and Liberal synagogues and schools.

36. Steven J. Zipperstein, *The Jews of Odessa: A Cultural History 1794–1881* (Stanford, 1985), p. 47.

37. Nissan Blumenthal was probably the first Russian cantor to utilize Sulzer's *Schir Zion*. See Avenary, ed., *Kantor Salomon Sulzer,* p. 116.

38. For notations of a number of his recitatives, see Samuel

Alman's *Shirei Razumni* (London, 1930).

39. Most of Nowakowski's compositions remain in manuscript form.

40. Mark Slobin, *Chosen Voices: The Story of the American Cantorate* (Urbana, Ill., 1989), p. 18.

41. Saul J. Berman, "Kol 'Isha [A Woman's Voice]," in Leo Landman, ed., *Rabbi Joseph H. Lookstein Memorial Volume* (New York, 1980), pp. 45–66. R. Sofer's ruling was the most stringent of all interpretations based on the talmudic statement that "a woman's voice is a sexual incitement" (B. Ber. 24a). Rabbi Moses Sofer's extreme Orthodoxy spurned participation in western culture. By contrast, neo-Orthodoxy, represented by R. Samson Raphael Hirsch, sought a rapprochement with modernity. In Hirsch's synagogue, decorum as strict as any Reform synagogue was enforced and choral singing—male only— was introduced.

42. Steven M. Lowenstein, "The 1840's and the Creation of the German-Jewish Religious Reform Movement," in Werner Moss, ed., *Revolution and Evolution: 1848 in German-Jewish History* (Tübingen, 1981), Lowenstein, "Modernization of German Jewry," p. 269.

43. Aron Friedmann, *50 Jahre in Berlin* (Berlin, 1929), p. 20.

44. Indicative of the right-wing trend in post–World War II Orthodoxy in western Europe is the curtailment of the use of the organ in French synagogues and the abolition of mixed choirs in English Orthodox synagogues.

45. "Odessa," *Jewish Encyclopedia* (New York, 1905), vol. 9, p. 384.

46. Lowenstein, "German-Jewish Religious Reform Movement," pp. 255–97.

47. The legal (halakhic) issues involved are the ban against imitating gentile practices and the definition of work forbidden on the Sabbath. Reformers argued that the synagogue replaced the Temple, where musical instruments had indeed been played, even on the Sabbath. The organ was likened to the Temple *magrefa,* which was said to be one such musical instrument. It is highly doubtful that this was actually the case. See Joseph Yasser, "The Magrepha of the Herodian Temple: A Five-Fold Hypothesis," *Journal of the American Musicological Society* 13 (1960): 24–42.

48. *Magyar Zsido Szemele* (Budapest, 1886), pp. 506–7.

49. The opinions are summarized in A. Berliner, "Literargeschichtliche Belege über die christliche Orgel im jüdischen Gottesdienste," in A. Berliner, ed., *Zur Lehr' und zur Wehr* (Berlin, 1904), pp. 40–63.

50. S. Debre, "The Jews in France," *JQR*, o.s., 3 (1891): 366–435, gives an excellent description of *fin de siècle* Judaism in France.

51. Cf. Zipperstein, "Modernization of German Jewry," p. 133; *Jewish Encyclopedia*, s.v. "Odessa."

Christian Liturgical Music
from the Bible
to the Renaissance

MARGOT FASSLER AND PETER JEFFERY

THE NEW TESTAMENT
AND THE EARLY CHURCH

The earliest Christian musical tradition developed from a variety of sources, but especially from the Jewish and pagan customs of singing at gatherings around a meal. Though New Testament writers testify that some early Christians continued to worship in the Temple and the synagogue, even while gradually coming to feel unwelcome there (Acts 2:46–3:3, 5:20–42, 13:13–51, 17:1–15), neither the Temple nor the synagogue is likely to have been the immediate source of early Christian music. The elaborate Temple ritual, with its animal sacrifices, professional priests, and levitical "orchestra," could not have been duplicated in early Christian gathering spaces. In synagogue services, it is unclear whether any psalmody was used before 70 C.E., when attempts were made to develop the synagogue liturgy into a partial substitute for the destroyed Temple cult through the use of psalmody, the shofar, and certain other practices commemorating the sacrifices. Thus the most distinctively Christian gatherings of the early church were not Christianized synagogue or Temple services but, rather, the common meals, related to the ritualized Jewish banquets celebrated by groups of disciples gathered around an authoritative Rabbi or teacher, or the family-centered-meals that still

84

survive today in Jewish homes: at the Friday night supper that opens the Sabbath, for instance, or (especially) the Passover seder.

Held in private homes during the first two centuries, such meals typically included Scripture reading, religious instruction, prayer, and singing, and they often had messianic or eschatological significance. We find examples in the literature of Qumran,[1] the *Letter of Aristeas*,[2] and especially Philo's *The Contemplative Life*.[3]

Among the pagans, too, common banquets had long provided important occasions for philosophical and religious discussion as well as for religious and secular song. This was the original meaning of the word *symposium* (literally, drinking together), as illustrated in the dialogues of that name written by Plato, Xenophon, and Plutarch. The banquets celebrated by the early church were seen as commemorating, and in a sense continuing, the meals Jesus himself had celebrated with his disciples, and from such meals the Christian eucharist and the lamplighting or vespers services developed. The similarity of the early Christian feasts to Jewish and pagan practices alike provides the context for interpreting our earliest evidence regarding Christian music. The repeated admonitions of early Christian writers to shun intoxicating pagan revelry in favor of spirit-filled rejoicing (Eph. 5:18–20) echo Philo and other Jewish writers.[4] The musical practices of Philo's Therapeutae so closely resemble early Christian music that Eusebius of Caesarea, the fourth-century "father of church history," insisted that Philo must have been describing a Christian group.[5]

The oldest sources describe early Christian music with words such as "psalms, hymns, and spiritual songs" (Eph. 5:18). Rather than the names of three musical genres, these words were probably loose synonyms used interchangeably with other terms as well. From a modern perspective, however, it is helpful (albeit anachronistic) to distinguish three types of texts that were sung during the early period: (1) psalms, namely, the 150 Psalms of the Bible; (2) canticles or odes, psalmlike poems found in other books of the Bible (e.g., Exodus 15, Habakkuk 3); (3)

hymns, which are nonscriptural compositions of any kind, whether anonymous or written by poets whose names we know. The earliest Christian hymns often resemble the Psalms and canticles in form and structure, but most include at least some specifically Christian content, usually dealing with the identity of Christ or with the meaning of his life and death. The pagan writer Pliny the Younger describes Christians of the early second century as singing "a hymn to Christ, as to a God."[6] The texts of many such christological hymns are quoted in the New Testament itself (e.g., John 1, Phil. 2:6–11, Col. 1:15–20), and an early collection of hymns of this kind may survive in the so-called Odes of Solomon.[7] Indeed, the apocryphal Acts of John describes Jesus singing a song about himself while leading a dance after the Last Supper (cf. Matthew 26:30).[8] Though Gnostic and other heretical hymnodists provoked sporadic attempts to restrict the use of nonscriptural hymns in favor of the biblical psalms and odes,[9] Christian poets and composers never ceased to create new hymns throughout the history of the church.

Some of the earliest hymnodists seem to have been bent on promoting heterodox Christologies. The first important orthodox hymnodists include Ephrem the Syrian (c. 306–373 C.E.), who composed sermonlike *memre* and strophic *madrashe,* and Ambrose of Milan (c. 339–397), whose strophic Latin hymns are still sung today in modern translations. The most significant Greek hymnodists were both Syrians by birth: Romanos the Melode (sixth century), who may have been of Jewish origin and who mastered the kontakion, or metrical sermon; and John of Damascus (seventh to eighth centuries) whose kanons presented a series of stanzas meant to be interpolated among the verses of the biblical odes. Monostrophic or single-stanza hymns, most generally called *troparia* (though they also have other names), were composed by many authors; for instance, the troparion "O Only-begotten Son" of the Byzantine liturgies' little entrance is attributed to Emperor Justinian (483–565). The Gloria patri ("Glory be to the Father") and the Trisagion ("Holy God, Holy Mighty One") are used in the liturgies of almost all Eastern and Western churches.

THE CONVERSION OF THE ROMAN EMPIRE

The conversion of the emperor Constantine at the beginning of the fourth century signaled an important shift in Christian musical history, though the gradual transition from a pagan to a Christian empire took several centuries. With the end of persecution, Christians were free to leave their house-churches and to worship openly, and as a result the liturgy began to develop in two new directions, cathedral liturgy and monastic liturgy.

"Cathedral" or "Stational" Liturgy

In each city of the empire, the entire Christian community gathered together for worship under the leadership of the bishop, assisted by presbyters (elders or priests), deacons, and lower-ranking clergy. These celebrations were held in the great basilicas, modeled on imperial courthouses, built to hold the large crowds of new Christian worshipers. On each major feast the entire clergy and populace of the city would assemble in a different church and then go in procession to the basilica where the eucharist would be celebrated (the *station*). Thus in the course of a year, celebrations would be held throughout the whole city. The most important station, reserved for the most solemn days, was at the cathedral, the bishop's "headquarters" church where his *cathedra* (chair) was located.

With its large crowds of worshipers and numerous clergy, its impressive buildings and lengthy processions, stational liturgy soon became more elaborate and formalized than worship had been in the days of the house-churches. Because the bishop was now an imperial as well as an ecclesiastical official, the Christian liturgy absorbed some of the elements of secular ceremonial that his civil office entitled him to use. This privilege included the right to be met by a choir when he entered the basilica at the beginning of the liturgy, a practice that may have developed into what we know as the introit.

Congregational singing was also important. It is frequently mentioned in the sermons of the great Church Fathers of the late fourth and early fifth centuries. Most often, congregational singing took the form of responsorial psalmody, in which a soloist (an ordained reader or cantor) sang the verses of a psalm, and the congregation joined in at the end of each verse with an unvarying refrain, usually derived from a verse of the same psalm. This type of psalmody is first mentioned in connection with vigils, services that lasted much of the night and ended in the morning. But responsorial psalms were also included among the scriptural readings at mass, which is why they were mentioned in so many sermons of the period. They were also sung during communion and at other points during the mass and office.

Along with responsorial psalmody two other types of psalmody were also important in the cathedral office. St. Basil described one of them in a letter dated 375:[10] In antiphonal psalmody two choirs, or two halves of the congregation, took turns singing the verses in alternation (i.e., one choir sang the odd-numbered verses, the other the even-numbered ones). Later, there was also a refrain or antiphon sung after each verse, though Basil did not mention this. In its classic Western form, antiphonal psalmody ended each psalm or group of psalms with the trinitarian hymn Gloria patri. In direct psalmody the entire psalm was sung straight through by all with no alternation or refrain.

Monastic Liturgy

Many lay Christians of both sexes wanted a more rigorous and heroic spirituality than the emerging civic Christianity seemed to offer. They found it in the wilderness outside the cities, particularly in the deserts of Egypt, where they grouped together in the first monastic communities. The worship of the monks aimed at the ideal of unceasing prayer (1 Thess. 5:17) by means of a regular cycle of daily and nightly communal services that featured recitation of the psalms and meditation on the Scriptures as well as group prayer. Most psalms were chanted by a soloist while the other monks listened, though the last psalm of each office was performed responsorially with the word *Alleluia* serving as the refrain. Monastic liturgy tended to be more austere than the cathedral type, partly because of the simpler and more ascetic way of life followed by the monks in the wilderness, and also because the monastic communities were originally made up of laymen or laywomen with few or no clergy. Originally, the monks were reluctant to use the nonscriptural hymns of the cathedral liturgy, with their beautiful poetry and melodies. This reluctance gradually weakened, however, as the cathedral and monastic types of worship began to merge.

THE EARLY MEDIEVAL SYNTHESIS

The Blending of the Two Types of Liturgy

Even as they were first emerging during the fourth century, the cathedral and monastic types of worship were already influencing each other. Some monastic communities that were established in or near cities participated in the services of the stational liturgy in addition to their own monastic services; this was so in Jerusalem when Egeria described its liturgy during the early 380s. In addition, as monks who had originally been laymen became increasingly clericalized, even to the point where it was normal for a monk to be a priest, they took part in both cathedral and monastic liturgies. Thus the fully formed liturgies of the Middle Ages were actually hybrid traditions, built up from varying syntheses of cathedral and monastic elements that were combined differently in each major center. Liturgical historians still disagree often about the cathedral and monastic elements and the processes by which they were mingled to form the rites we find in the earliest surviving liturgical books, most of which date from the seventh to the tenth centuries.

The monasticizing of the urban clergy along with other factors promoted a clericalizing of the liturgy, an increasing tendency to regard the liturgy as an activity carried out within the clerical community on behalf of the whole church, rather than as an act of the whole assembly. At the same time, membership in the Christian laity seemed less distinctive now that it included almost everyone in the empire. As liturgical traditions began to be written down and organized into liturgical books, and as literacy and education also became a largely clerical preserve, it was inevitable that the role of the laity in public worship would diminish considerably. More of the responsibility for singing fell to the choir, made up of low-ranking clergy. Thus most of the liturgical music that we have from the Middle Ages is the music of the monasteries, cathedral chapters, and other clerical and religious communities that were so numerous during the medieval period.

But two common misconceptions should be avoided. First, congregational singing and other forms of participation did not completely die out during the Middle Ages. Second, the pressures that tended to clericalize the liturgy did not spring from a desire for musical expertise and virtuosity, as some modern writers, seeking to discourage the use of Gregorian chant by modern congregations, have claimed. Such a desire would in fact have been completely contrary to the early monastic spirit.

The Medieval Repertories

Initially, every city or region seems to have developed its own local rite and chant repertory, with particular chant texts, prayers, readings, and other materials fixed into standardized orders of service according to the local liturgical calendar. This may have happened first at Jerusalem, where a complete annual cycle of responsorial psalms for the mass already existed in the early fifth century; it now survives only in the old Armenian lectionary, translated from the lost Greek original.[11] The first real chant book, containing the texts of all the scriptural and nonscriptural chants, arranged by the date and time each text was sung during the year, was also compiled at Jerusalem, probably by the seventh century; it survives only in a Georgian translation from the original Greek, and thus bears the Georgian title *Iadgari*. In the Latin West, such a book was called an *antiphonale;* the earliest surviving copies, dating from the eighth century, represent the uses of Milan and Rome. The earliest antiphonalia that are fully supplied with musical notation for the melodies date from the early tenth century. Notated Greek manuscripts survive from the mid–tenth century onward.

At first, the musical signs, or neumes, indicated only the general direction of melodic movement up or down; they served mainly to assist the memories of singers who were well-trained in the chant tradition. Between the eleventh and the thirteenth centuries, both Western and Eastern notational systems were refined so as to show exact pitch, but this was done in different ways. In the West it meant the invention of the staff, which is still the basis of Western pitch notation today. The Byzantine East opted for a "digital" system, in which each sign indicated a specific diatonic interval, higher or lower than the pitch indicated by the preceding sign. This notation was simplified and modernized in the early nineteenth century, when a few of the signs were retained to represent invariable degrees of the diatonic scale.

Eventually the traditions of the most important centers began to overwhelm, replace, or merge with those of the smaller and less powerful ones. Among the most significant were Orthodox Christians—divided by a variety of languages—and Roman Catholic Christians.

Among Greek-speaking Orthodox Christians, the two strongest traditions—the Divine Liturgy of Constantinople's cathedral (Hagia Sophia) and the monastic office of Palestine—gradually merged to form what we know as the Byzantine rite. It absorbed or supplanted the smaller, more local traditions of Antioch, Jerusalem, Alexandria, southern Italy, and even the cathedral office of Constantinople itself. This hybrid Byzantine tradition was introduced by Greek Orthodox missionaries into the Slavic world, where it survives today (after many adaptations) in the Bulgarian, Russian, LTU Rusin, Serbian, Ukrainian, and Rumanian chant traditions.

Eastern Christians who spoke languages other than Greek, and who subscribed to theological views unaccepted by Rome and Byzantium, managed to hold onto more of their own traditions. The Armenian church, for instance, derived its liturgies from the pre-Byzantine Greek worship of Jerusalem, experienced periods of Byzantinization and Romanization, but in general retained its independence. The neighboring Georgian Orthodox church, on the other hand, originally followed a later form of Jerusalem ritual, but about the twelfth century was completely Byzantinized. Many Armenian and a few Georgian medieval manuscripts contain musical neumes that cannot now be deciphered. The Armenian notation, like the Greek, was modernized and simplified in the early nineteenth century.

Syriac-speaking Christians divided into three main traditions: First, the Jacobite, west Syrian or Syrian Orthodox (Monophysite) church preserved translations of much Greek material from Jerusalem and Antioch that was lost from Greek-speaking Christianity after these early centers were Byzantinized. (In more recent times a branch has also been established in India; part of it has entered communion with Rome and is known as the Malankar rite). Second, the east Syrian or Assyrian Orthodox (Nestorian) church of the East, in the Persian Empire in Mesopotamia, possessed the only ancient liturgical tradition that developed outside the Hellenistic world; a group that united with Rome in the sixteenth century is known as the Chaldean church. During the Middle Ages the Assyrian tradition was brought all the way to China and India by Nestorian missionaries; the Catholic branch that survives in India is known as the Malabar rite. Third, the Maronites of Lebanon, united with Rome since the Crusades, preserve an independent synthesis that seems originally to have been more closely related to the east Syrian tradition but now shares a great deal with the west Syrian tradition also. None of these three traditions ever adopted written musical notation, and their melodies are transmitted orally to this day. However, the Syrian Melkites, or "Royalists," who sided with the Byzantine emperor during theological controversies, gradually adopted the Byzantine liturgy in Syriac translation, producing a fourth Syriac liturgical tradition. This adoption included unsuccessful attempts to introduce Greek neumes, and a few neumated Melkite manuscripts still survive.

The chant of the Coptic Orthodox (Monophysite) church of Egypt includes some material of Greek origin, but it never developed a notational system, despite some limited medieval attempts to do so. As a result, much of the ancient melodic repertory has been lost. Only the music for the Divine Liturgy and the most common other services has been passed down by oral tradition.

Though the Ethiopian Orthodox church was theoretically a branch of the Coptic church, much of its liturgy, particularly its chant repertory, developed in relative isolation from Egyptian traditions. A fully developed notational system emerged in the sixteenth century, and is still in use today.

Hardly any evidence survives regarding the chant of the Nubian church, which once existed in what is now the Sudan, but which by the fourteenth century had been completely overwhelmed by Islam.

Gregorian Chant

In the Latin-speaking West, the Gregorian chant tradition ultimately prevailed. Gregorian chant may have been a synthesis of Roman and northern (Gallican or Frankish) traditions, for the earliest surviving manuscripts (from the eighth to the tenth centuries) do not come from Rome but from farther north, mostly from within the Frankish Kingdom or Carolingian Empire. Thus they date from the period when a standardized liturgy of Roman origin (but one that included non-Roman elements) was being assembled and imposed on all the churches in the domain ruled by Charlemagne (c. 742–814) and his successors. But scholars still fiercely debate the origins of the chant along with its problematic relationship to its namesake, Pope Gregory the Great (reigned 590–604). Though tradition credited Gregory with the compilation of the antiphonale, there seems to have been no music notation in use during his time. More troubling still, the earliest manuscripts from Rome (from the eleventh century) preserve a different tradition (usually called *Old Roman* chant), with most of the same texts as Gregorian chant but with melodies that are somehow related yet quite different. Nevertheless, the medieval belief that the "Gregorian" repertory was Roman assured its eventual hegemony over most of the other Western local traditions. These included the Gallican chant of France (eighth–ninth centuries); the Beneventan and other traditions of southern Italy (early ninth century); the northern Italian traditions of Ravenna and Aquilea (not much later than the early ninth century); and the Mozarabic chant of Spain following the withdrawal of the Muslims during the eleventh-century Reconquista (though the Mozarabic rite has been permitted to survive in one chapel of the Toledo cathedral). By the thirteenth century, Gregorian chant was being used even in the papal court, and in this form, as part of the liturgy of the Roman curia, it supplanted even the Old Roman chant that had survived up until then in the Roman basilicas. Only the local tradition of Milan, called Ambrosian chant because it was alleged to have been created by St. Ambrose, managed to survive into the twentieth century, despite some Romanization during the sixteenth century.

Genres of Chant

In all of these medieval traditions, the older practices of responsorial, antiphonal, direct, and solo psalmody survived, though they were sometimes abbreviated or altered in various ways: verses were omitted, refrains were sung less often. In the West, some psalms that had traditionally been direct or solo came to be performed by alternating choirs as if they were antiphonal; in the East the opposite sometimes happened. Antiphonal psalms, responsories, and strophic "Ambrosian" hymns were the main genres of chant in the medieval Western office, which retained a distinction between cathedral and monastic forms. Though they used most of the same material, each was differently arranged, the monastic arrangement being based on the early sixth-century Rule of St. Benedict. Kanons and troparia dominated the Byzantine monastic office, which eventually completely replaced the Constantinopolitan cathedral office.

In the medieval Roman mass, the antiphonal introit psalm was shortened to include only the antiphon, the first verse of the psalm, and the Gloria patri, while the responsorial offertory and antiphonal communion chants eventually lost their verses altogether. The responsorial psalm following the first reading was shortened to a refrain and one verse; in time it came to be called the *gradual* because it was sung from the steps (*gradus*) of the ambo. (The replacement of the shorter medieval graduals by longer responsorial psalms has been one of the more striking and popular of the reforms following Vatican II.) The alleluia before the gospel had also been a complete responsorial psalm at Jerusalem but seems always to have had only one verse in the West. On the other hand the tract, solo psalmody that replaced the alleluia during Lent, retained many verses, but by the late Middle Ages it was being sung antiphonally in some places. All of these chants varied both in text and melody for each day of the liturgical year. The series of chants proper to each liturgical day therefore became known as the *proper* of the Mass for that day (see table 1). The annual cycle of proper

Table 1

Sung Portions of the Medieval Mass, Roman Rite

Ordinary Chants	Proper	Priest's Prayers	Readings
	Readings		
	Introit		
		Collect	
Kyrie			
Gloria			
			Epistle
			(subdeacon)
	Gradual		
	Alleluia		
	(or Tract)		
			Gospel
			(deacon)
Credo			
	Offertory		
		Preface	
Sanctus			
		Pater	
		noster	
		Peace	
Agnus Dei			
	Communion		
		Postcommunion	
Ite missa est			

Mass chants was the first part of the Gregorian chant repertory to be collected and written down in a book, called the *Antiphonale Missarum* or the *Graduale* (perhaps a hint that the graduals were collected first?). The responsorial graduals and Alleluias and the solo tracts were collected separately in a book for the soloist called the *Cantatorium*.

The Roman mass had other chants with relatively fixed texts that did not vary much from day to day; these came to be called the *Ordinary* of the Mass, in contrast to the proper. Of the six chants typically included, four were short: The Kyrie eleison probably marked what had originally been the point where the participants in the stational procession, upon arriving at the church for Mass, sang a litany while entering and approaching the altar. The Sanctus, or canticle of the heavenly seraphim (Isaiah 6:3), was sung within the anaphora, separating what came to be called the Preface from the Canon Missae. The litanic Agnus Dei, introduced by Pope Sergius I (687–701), was sung during the fraction of the bread like the proper *confractorium* of the Gallican Mass. The Ite Missa est, changed to Benedicamus Domino on lesser days when the Gloria in excelsis was omitted, signaled the dismissal. The older of the long ordinary chants, the Gloria in excelsis, or canticle of the angels (Luke 2:34 plus additional material), was sung in the morning office in most other rites. In the Roman mass it was at first sung only on Christmas, perhaps following the gospel story in which it occurs (Luke 2:13–14). Pope Symmachus (498–514) is said to have authorized that it be sung on other major feasts when the mass was celebrated by a bishop, and it may then have migrated forward to its modern position following the introit and Kyrie. In this position it corresponds to the morning chants that began the mass in certain other rites: Daniel 3 (in the Septuagint, the Song of the Three Children) and Luke 1:68–79 in the Gallican mass, Psalm 95 in the Byzantine Divine Liturgy. During the eighth century, the Credo, or Nicene Creed, was inserted into the Western mass after the gospel, though it was not sung at Rome until 1014. In other traditions, the Creed received other positions, such as just before the anaphora (in the Byzantine Divine Liturgy) or before the Lord's Prayer as a preparation for communion (in the Mozarabic mass).

In the East, variability was more typical of the office, much less so in the Divine Liturgy, where, for instance, even the types of chants that could vary did not vary every day (see table 2). For the prokeimenon (the responsorial psalm that precedes the reading from the Apostle), the alleluia, and the koinonikon

Table 2

Sung Portions of the Medieval
Byzantine Divine Liturgy (simplified)

Choir	People	Deacon	Priest	Reader
Readings				
		Litany		
3 antiphonal psalms and troparia				
Trisagion				
Responsorial psalm				
				Epistle
		Gospel		
		Litanies		
Cheroubikon				
		Litanies		
	Creed			
			Preface dialogue	
Holy, holy, holy				
			Words of Institution and Epiclesis	
Theotokion				
		Litany		
	Our Father			
			Peace	
Koinonikon				
		Litany		
			Dismissal	

(the chant accompanying the communion of the clergy) small collections of a few dozen texts were used on multiple occasions during the year. For the eisodikon (the entrance chant) and the cheroubikon (the hymn sung at the Great Entrance when the bread and wine are brought to the altar), the same text was used almost always; alternative texts were substituted on only a few occasions during the year.

NEW MEDIEVAL DEVELOPMENTS

Notation and Music Theory

Once the basic repertories were formed, musicians began to seek ways to standardize and improve the teaching and performance of chant. This led to the widespread adoption of the system of the eight church modes, which probably originated in seventh- or eighth-century Palestine, and which spread to Syria, Armenia, Byzantium, and the West during the two centuries following. It also led to the development of music notation in both the Latin (by about 900) and Greek churches (by about 950). These developments were further refined by the creation of a new literature of music theory, one that adapted some of the concepts and terminology of classical Greek music to describe such musical phenomena as the range and tuning of the available pitches and the characteristics of the modes. This development went further in the West, where theoretical literature began to emerge in the ninth century with the writings of such figures as Aurelian of Réôme (fl. c. 840–850) and especially Hucbald of St.-Amand (d. 950), who relied for their information about classical Greek music upon such late antique Latin writers as Boethius (c. 480–524), Cassiodorus (c. 485–580), and Isidore of Seville (c. 560–636). These additions culminated in the invention of the staff, more or less as we know it today, by the most important medieval Western theorist, Guido of Arezzo (d. after 1033). He is also credited with organizing the solmization system that developed into our "Do, Re, Mi. . . ." Over many centuries, the synthesis of ancient Greek terminology, the modal system, and the Gregorian chant repertory grew into the basis of the highly refined music theory so characteristic of Western classical music today.

New Western Forms:
Ninth through Eleventh Centuries

In the East, ninth-century Constantinople began to eclipse Palestine as the chief center of Byzantine hymnography, with the activity of monks like Theodore the Studite (759–826), Joseph the Hymnographer (d. 816), and the nun Kassia. In the West, the standardized repertory of Gregorian chant was now in use almost everywhere, and in many regions new types of music and texts were being created to decorate and expand the repertory, particularly in the Carolingian Empire, England, northern Italy, and Benevento. Both the textual and musical styles of the new material differed somewhat from region to region, and everywhere they differed from the classic Gregorian corpus. Where the texts of Gregorian chant were frequently excerpted and paraphrased from the Bible, the new texts were more often poetic or literary, full of biblical allusions but not extracted from any single biblical passage. Much of the new music was monophonic, like the chant itself, a single vocal line of great sophistication and beauty but often different in style from the older Gregorian melodies. Some of the new music was polyphonic, however, consisting of one or more additional harmonizing melodies to be sung simultaneously with the chant.

Although scholars have not yet established a fully consistent terminology for the new monophonic chants (the medieval terminology was inconsistent also), we can divide them into four broad categories: (1) pneumata or neumae, (2) tropes, (3) prosulae, and (4) sequences. From the testimony of ninth- and tenth-century writers such as Amalarius of Metz (c. 780–850/1), and the parallel witness of the earliest chant manuscripts, it is clear that there was a tradition of singing decorative, untexted melodies, the neumae, at various points in the mass and office.[12] Neumae were often sung, for example, following the gospel antiphons (i.e., the antiphons of the canticles Luke 1:46–55 and

1:68–79) at lauds and vespers, and at the close of the alleluia at Mass, where they were often called *jubili* or *sequentiae*. In a famous passage, Notker Balbulus (d. 912), the poet of St. Gall, spoke of his difficulty in remembering these very long melodies that were sung at the alleluia.[13] Unfortunately, the

Example 1. Beginning of the Gloria in Excelsis Deo with interpolated tropes. From the manuscript Vatican City, Bibliotheca Apostolica Vaticana, MS Vaticanus Urb. lat. 602, ff. 34r–36v, as published in John Boe, ed., *Beneventanum Troporum Corpus*, vol. 2: *Ordinary Chants and Tropes for the Mass from Southern Italy, A.D. 1000–1250*, part 2: *Gloria in excelsis*, Recent Researches in the Music of the Middle Ages and Early Renaissance, vols. 23–24 (Madison, Wisc., A–R Editions, 1990), pp. 149–50.

Translation: GLORY TO GOD IN THE HIGHEST
[Trope 1:] Whom the citizens of heaven proclaim with lofty
voice to be the Holy One.
AND PEACE TO PEOPLE OF [GOD'S] GOOD WILL.
[Trope 2:] As the [angelic] ministers of the Lord promised
to people on earth through the incarnate word.
WE PRAISE YOU.
[Trope 3:] In your praises the morning stars persevere.

evidence for reconstructing this early practice, which existed, after all, in an oral tradition, is slim, and it had apparently diminished greatly by the close of the tenth century, the period from which we first have substantial numbers of chant manuscripts.

The manuscript tradition is far stronger for the three other categories. Tropes, additions of both text and music to Gregorian chants, were created in the greatest numbers to accompany introits;[14] but certain other chants of the proper (offertories and communions) and of the ordinary of the Mass[15] could also have tropes (see example 1).

Prosulae, purely textual additions to the melismatic sections of Gregorian chant (i.e., places where many notes had originally been sung to a single syllable) were written especially for alleluias and Kyries, as well as for certain melismas in offertories, Glorias, and the great responsories of matins (see example 2).[16]

Example 2. Beginning of a Kyrie in two versions: (top) melismatic version without prosula; (bottom) syllabic version with prosula *Fons bonitatis*. From the manuscript Naples, Biblioteca Nazionale, MS VI.G.34, 25v and 29v, as published in John Boe, ed., *Beneventanum Troporum Corpus*, vol. 2: *Ordinary Chants and Tropes for the Mass from Southern Italy, A.D. 1000–1250*, part 1: *Kyrie eleison*, Recent Researches in the Music of the Middle Ages and Early Renaissance, vols. 20–21 (Madison, Wisc.: A–R Editions, 1989), pp. 116–17.

Translation: [Top:] LORD, HAVE MERCY
[Bottom:] LORD, fount of goodness from whom all good things
  proceed, HAVE MERCY.

The most important single addition to the Gregorian repertory, the sequences, constitute a liturgical genre in their own right, with a history extending for several centuries. Although they may well have begun as a kind of prosula for the long neuma sung after the alleluia at mass, by the end of the ninth century, sequences, or *proses* (as they are also often called), were composed as independent pieces both east and west of the Rhine, as well as in Italy and England. Early medieval sequences, the type written from the ninth to the eleventh centuries, commonly are made up of prose couplets of varying lengths, with different music for each successive couplet of text.[17] It was a common practice to quote from a particular alleluia melody at the opening of the sequence melody, thereby referring to the historical connection between alleluia and sequence. Many sequence melodies became popular and were set numerous times, the oldest ones being found in several traditions.

The liturgical texts and music created to expand upon the Gregorian repertory constitute the most important music composed in northern Europe during the centuries immediately following the Carolingian Renaissance. Although there is great variety in the texts and music of these repertories from region to region, most fall into specific genres whose liturgical function determines both the melodic style and the nature of the exegesis found in the texts. Introit tropes, for example, are expository, and serve to establish the theme of the feast; texts written for alleluia prosulae, on the other hand, offer praise along with the angelic hosts. Thus tropes, sequences, prosulae, etc., were designed to provide the scriptural texts of the Gregorian canon with medieval exegetical interpretations. It was also within these repertories that specific regions (and even individual religious institutions) customized their liturgical practices and preserved vestiges of the traditions displaced by the Gregorian repertory. Yet in spite of the widespread acceptance of tropes and sequences throughout Europe and in Italy, some institutions never used them to any great degree; for example, the Benedictine abbey at Cluny in France, famous for its elaborate offices and votive services, apparently never incorporated great numbers of tropes and sequences into its liturgy.

During this same period (ninth–eleventh centuries), new

monophonic melodies continued to be generated in the older musical genres of Gregorian chant. Many new melodies for the chants of the ordinary of the mass were created throughout northern Europe, and for the first time they began to be written down in a kind of book known as the *Kyriale*. [18] This was also a time of great expansion of the office, with new texts and music being composed in abundance for the hundreds of new saints added to the calendars of various regions and centers. Like the trope and sequence repertories described above, these office texts and music were, to a great degree, particular to specific regions in both the choice and ordering of pieces. They are significant resources for studying unique regional characteristics of medieval liturgies. [19] Some new offices were modally ordered, their chants composed to pass through all the modes in numerical order. Rhymed offices or *historiae* had rhyming poetic texts that contrast markedly with the prose texts of the older repertory.

Organum, the practice of performing Gregorian chant polyphonically, usually with improvised harmonizing parts, is described in treatises of music theory as early as the tenth century. Octaves, fifths, and fourths were the preferred intervals, and the newly composed part (*vox organalis*) usually had only one note for each note of the original chant (now called *vox principalis*). Written examples of polyphony (differing melodic lines performed simultaneously) are scarce from this period, but the ones that survive suggest that a variety of techniques were being used to decorate the chant melodies. The most important polyphony to survive from before the early twelfth century comes in manuscripts from Winchester (c. 1000, polyphonic alleluias) and Chartres (late eleventh century, polyphonic alleluias and graduals). [20]

Western Liturgical Chant:
Twelfth and Thirteenth Centuries

The Gregorian reform movement (named for Pope Gregory VII, 1073–1085) began in the second half of the eleventh cen tury, and within one hundred years it had inspired a variety of changes in western European musical and liturgical practices. These changes can be observed not only in the liturgies of newly formed religious orders—the Cistercians and the Augustinian canons regular, for example—but also in the liturgies of cathedrals, especially in dioceses with reform-minded bishops. Augustinian canons, the group most closely associated with the specific agenda of the Gregorian reform movement, usually followed the liturgical use of the diocese in which their particular house was located. But no matter where they were located, Augustinians were particularly fond of sequences and led the way in the development of the new style of sequence that emerged in the late eleventh century and came to triumph throughout northern Europe in the century following. Late sequences, like their predecessors, were organized in double versicles, but their texts were written in accentual rhythmic poetry; this change in poetic style affected musical style as well: many late sequences were designed so that each textual unit, be it phrase, line, or strophe, had its own sharply marked group of notes, and thus the structure of the music perfectly reflects the text. Certain carefully constructed melodies were set repeatedly, such as the famous melody "Laudes crucis," providing a plan for great numbers of new texts.[21] The Augustinian interest in sequences did not extend to tropes for the propers. In fact, whenever possible, these were omitted from the liturgies they inherited.

The best known of all liturgical and musical reforms of the twelfth to the thirteenth centuries are those of the Cistercians, an order of reformed Benedictine monks. The Cistercians attempted to return to a strict interpretation of the Benedictine rule and thus sought a liturgy and music that reflected their understanding of what liturgical practice had been in Benedict's time, the sixth century. According to the writings of Chrysogonus Waddell, the leading modern authority on the subject, the first Cistercian liturgy was an adaptation of the liturgy and chant of Marmoutier. In subsequent decades, the Cistercians attempted to get back to the time of St. Benedict by studying the chant of Metz (believed to be the purest dialect of Gregorian chant) and the hymns of St. Ambrose as preserved in the Milanese tradition. Standardized in the late twelfth century, the Cistercian liturgy and chant is essentially Gregorian, but has certain striking modifications. Many chants of both the mass and office were reworked to fit the Cistercian understanding of the modes and were stripped of very long melismatic passages as well. The hymns of the office were reordered and only a small group of these pieces were retained.

Because the reform movement focused great energy on the secular clergy, it fostered interest in cathedral liturgies and the music written for them. Just as the twelfth and thirteenth centuries witnessed the building of many new Gothic cathedrals in western Europe, they also saw a refurbishing of the liturgies designed to fill these buildings. Although very few liturgical books survive from cathedrals of the twelfth century and earlier, many books remain from the thirteenth century, including a representative selection of ordinals, liturgical books that provide detailed ceremonial directions as well as incipits for the mass and office chants throughout the entire year. Thus, complete outlines of the thirteenth-century liturgies from several cathedrals in France, including Chartres, Amiens, Bayeux, and Laon, for example, as well as from cathedrals in England, Italy, and centers west of the Rhine, including a magnificent fourteenth-century ordinal from Trier[22] are available for study.

Medieval cathedral liturgies are characterized by a matins service with nine readings (as distinct from the Benedictine twelve). This characteristic is a reliable first step in distinguishing cathedral chantbooks and calendars from monastic ones. Northern European cathedral liturgies were still stational during the thirteenth century, with the bishop and his entourage visiting specially designated churches on appointed major feasts. In several French cathedrals, an elaborate vespers service was sung during Easter week, a practice that may have derived from the descriptions of ninth-century Roman liturgies found in the commentaries of Amalarius of Metz.[23] Considerable evidence suggests strongly that proper tropes were never as important in cathedral liturgies as they were among some Benedictines. The commentator Johannes Beleth, writing in Paris in the mid–twelfth century, stated that introit tropes were especially favored by monks,[24] and the vast number of surviving manuscripts of tropes are indeed found in monastic rather than cathedral books.

Other monophonic repertories created in the twelfth–thirteenth centuries are less directly related to religious reform movements. The versus or conductus[25] were composed in France to provide incidental music during the mass and office, and to ornament the Benedicamus Domino, the chant that closed each of the office hours.[26] Elaborate musical plays written in the twelfth century and designed to be performed at the close of matins or vespers came to be associated with the special services put on by cathedral canons and choral vicars during the weeks immediately following Christmas.[27]

The new music written for the mass and office in these two centuries also reflected the increasing devotion to the Virgin Mary being felt throughout Europe in the period. By the end of the twelfth century, both monastic and cathedral liturgies commonly had special offices for Mary as well as an increasing number of feasts in her honor. Furthermore, previously existing marian feasts were elevated to higher ranks. They required an even greater number of special texts and music and thus provided a great number of marian sequences and hymns from this period.

Polyphony of the Twelfth and Thirteenth Centuries

The first extensive repertories of written polyphonic music survive in four manuscripts from southern France. This Aquianian repertory consists primarily of versus, verse tropes for the Benedicamus Domino, and sequences. The manuscripts, which were prepared throughout the entire twelfth century and into the thirteenth, demonstrate changes in notational practice as well as in musical and poetic taste.[28] Much of the music of the southern repertory differed from earlier polyphonic repertories like the alleluias of Winchester. Instead of the added voice being closely tied to the original chant, with one or a few notes for each note of the chant melody, the added voice in the Aquitanian florid style was freer and consisted of an elaborate countermelody. The added polyphonic voice was often the more active voice, providing a group of notes for each individual pitch of the original chant. As a result the chant melody came to be sung more slowly, in notes that were held a relatively long time. For this reason, this part came to be called the *tenor* (from the Latin for "holding fast").

Although there are few correspondences between the polyphonic repertories of southern and northern France in the twelfth century, the few manuscripts that preserve the northern repertories testify to the importance of the florid or melismatic style there as well.[29] The most important northern liturgical polyphony from the late twelfth–thirteenth centuries was apparently composed for the cathedral of Notre Dame in Paris. Notre Dame polyphony (as it is often called) was written first for the parts of the service that traditionally belonged to soloists—that is, the intonations and verses of the responsorial graduals and alleluias of the mass and great responsories of the office. The choir responded to the soloists in monophonic chant. The music, as preserved in manuscripts dating from the mid–thirteenth century, represents the practices of at least three generations of Parisian composers. The earliest layer of music consists primarily of organum purum, very long pieces with the original chant held in long notes while the added voice(s) are in florid or melismatic style. In sections where the original chant was melismatic, on the other hand, the added voices were composed in discant style, moving at approximately the same speed as the chant, with a small number of notes for each note of the tenor. Short sections consisting of a chant melisma in the tenor with added voice in discant style are known as *discant clausulae.*

At the end of the twelfth century and in the early thirteenth century, Parisian composers (and subsequently the theorists and notators who preserved their music) began to organize the polyphony into rhythmic patterns, slowly replacing a practice that had hitherto been rhythmically unpatterned. By the mid–thirteenth century, a liturgical polyphony existed that was expressed in rhythmic notation, so that, for the first time in the history of Western music, duration was indicated precisely. In this system long and short notes were organized into ternary patterns called *rhythmic modes*. Music notation that relies on these patterns is called *modal notation*. Later in the century, the notation became even more sophisticated as precise note shapes came to have specific rhythmic meanings. The classic form of this notation is called *Franconian,* after Franco of Cologne, a Parisian theorist who flourished in the third quarter of the thirteenth century.

Several genres of compositions grew out of the first layers of Parisian polyphony. Some popular melismas had numerous discant settings written for them. Because modern scholars think these settings were interchangeable in some instances, they are known today as *substitute clausulae*. By the early thirteenth century, it became common to set texts to the upper voices of substitute clausulae, and thereby the first motets were formed. The conductus, too, came to be set polyphonically in the first half of the thirteenth century.

Although the organa pura, the clausulae, and some early motets and conductus were meant to be sung within the liturgy, the great number of motets composed in the second half of the thirteenth century were increasingly secular in nature and many, clearly, were not designed for liturgical use. Yet the motet was the most important polyphonic genre of the century, and by writing such pieces composers learned to control three voices with different levels of rhythmic activity, thereby gaining the skills necessary to develop the more rhythmically complicated polyphonic liturgical music of the fourteenth century. It is well to remember, however, that although the polyphonic repertories dominate modern histories of the thirteenth- and fourteenth-century liturgical music, and even though they were the most innovative repertories of music created during the time, they would not have been performed in the monasteries and, indeed, even in most northern European cathedrals during this period. Throughout the Middle Ages and the Renaissance, Gregorian chant and the sequences prevailed throughout Europe as the common repertory of liturgical music.

THE LATE MIDDLE AGES AND RENAISSANCE

In the East

During the final flowering of the Byzantine Empire, the "Palaeologan Renaissance" (1261–1453), the synthesis of Palestinian monastic and Constantinopolitan cathedral elements was finally achieved. A new style of music, the kalophonic, or "beautiful-sounding," style emerged under the leadership of John Koukouzeles, who had been a monk on Mount Athos.[30] Though still monophonic, the new style was much more florid and ornamental than the old and required a wider vocal range. Original compositions in this style by named composers are preserved in manuscripts called *akolouthiai* (orders of service) from the fourteenth century onward.

In the West

The Patronage System. In the West, beginning in the four-teenth century, the social context for music making began to change dramatically with the rise of the patronage system. While cathedrals and monasteries never ceased to celebrate musical liturgies, leadership in musical creativity passed to a new kind of institution: the private court chapel. Such a privately owned church formed part of the court household of a wealthy lay nobleman or of a high-ranking ecclesiastic, such as a cardinal or the pope. To enhance his reputation as a patron of the arts, the nobleman or ecclesiastic would hire musically trained clerics, the most expert he could find, to staff his private chapel and perform music at his court. Each musician would be paid by means of one or more benefices—that is, he would be appointed to a well-paying ecclesiastical post (bishop and abbot were especially desirable) and thus have the right to collect the income accruing to it, though in practice he would be exempt from actually having to reside or perform any duties at the church that was paying him. Though an obvious abuse, this practice did make possible the rise of the highly trained, specialized musical professional and the vast repertories of exquisite music that such musicians composed and performed. The extensive use of absentee benefices to support musicians may have been begun by the Avignon popes of the fourteenth century, and it only started to be curtailed by the Counterreformation popes of the sixteenth. As this source of income became scarce, musical patrons found other ways to pay musicians, who by the seventeenth century were more likely to be laymen than clerics. In this form, noble patronage continued into the nineteenth century. The last major composer whose entire career was supported by it was Franz Joseph Haydn (1732–1809). The gradual decline of the aristocracy and of noble patronage during the nineteenth century paralleled a shift toward music as a commodity, bought and sold widely in the form of concert tickets, sheet music, and, more recently, in the many forms of recorded and electronic media.

The Ars Nova. The music of the fourteenth century was described by its practitioners as a "new art" (*Ars Nova*), and earlier polyphonic compositions from the thirteenth century were relegated to the category of "old art" (*Ars Antiqua*).

Characteristics of the New Art included (1) isorhythm, or the practice of assigning a fixed sequence of rhythmic durations to the pitches of the tenor; (2) hocket ("hiccup"), in which two or more singers alternate notes and rests; and (3) notational advances that permitted each beat to be subdivided into two equal smaller notes as well as the traditional three, paving the way for the development of duple meters (e.g., our 2/4 and 6/8 meters) alongside the triple meters of modal and Franconian notation (our 3/4 and 9/8 meters). Although Pope John XXII, in a famous bull of 1322, forbade the use of most of these techniques in church music, his wishes were completely ignored. The fourteenth century saw the first written polyphonic settings of the ordinary of the mass and of the strophic hymns of the office, though these genres may have been performed earlier in improvised polyphony. Each portion of the ordinary is set in one of three styles: (1) resembling the contemporary isorhythmic motet, that is with an isorhythmic, often Gregorian tenor and faster-moving upper parts; (2) resembling the polyphonic secular French chanson, with the greatest musical interest in the highest-pitched melodic part; (3) in a simultaneous style, with all parts moving in the same rhythm. Simultaneous style may owe something to the older practice of improvising polyphony, about which we know so little. While some large collections of polyphonic mass movements survive from the period, we can also observe a tendency to assemble one movement of each type (i.e., one Kyrie, Gloria, Credo, Sanctus, Agnus, Ite) to form an entire polyphonic mass, even though the movements were created independently and even by different composers. Masses of this sort are preserved in manuscripts from Tournai,[31] Toulouse, Barcelona, and the Sorbonne, the last of which, more progressive than the others, contains works that exhibit some musical relationships between the movements, for the Agnus incorporates material from the Kyrie and the Sanctus. What appears to be the first polyphonic setting of the complete mass by a single person is *La Messe de Nostre Dame* by the most important composer of fourteenth-century France, Guillaume de Machaut (d. 1377), a canon of Reims cathedral who held posts at several royal courts. Johannes Ciconia (d. 1411) wrote several pairs of Gloria and Credo movements, each pair being musically unified by stylistic similarities.

In the early fifteenth century musical leadership shifted to English composers, led by Leonel Power (d. 1445) and especially John Dunstaple (d. 1453). The new English style was admired on the continent for its avoidance of dissonances and its frequent use of the intervals of the third and the sixth. These English composers also developed the *cantus firmus* mass, the first fully unified settings of the entire mass ordinary, achieved by the technique of basing all of the movements on the same tenor melody, or cantus firmus, often a Gregorian chant or a secular song. From this time on, the five-movement ordinary (Kyrie, Gloria, Credo, Sanctus, Agnus Dei) became the most important sacred musical form in the West. Several writers of the period regarded the new English style as a new beginning in music history, and for music historians today the period still marks the end of the Middle Ages and the beginning of the Renaissance.

The English innovations were soon adopted by the next generation of continental composers, led by the Burgundian Guillaume Dufay (d. 1474), who spent some years as a singer in the pope's own private chapel before retiring as a canon at Cambrai. The leading composer of the next generation, Johannes Ockeghem (d. 1497), spent his career in the French royal chapel. His mass compositions include the earliest extant polyphonic Requiem, consisting of introit, Kyrie, gradual, tract, and offertory, and using the chant melodies as cantus firmi. A number of masses that lack cantus firmi display his outstanding technical expertise, being held together by elaborate contrapuntal techniques. The greatest composer of the Renaissance, Josquin Des Prez (d. 1521), belonged to a generation that included many talented and distinguished composers. Their use of imitative counterpoint and other techniques enabled them to treat all the polyphonic voices equally and gave them unprecedented control over their material. As Martin Luther remarked in his *Table Talk,* Josquin was a "master of the notes. They must do as he wills, whereas other masters are forced to do as the notes will." Josquin inaugurated some important developments of the sixteenth century. His *Missa Mater patris* is a major early example of *imitatio* (later called "parody") technique, in which the music is based on multiple voices of a polyphonic model rather than on a monophonic cantus firmus.[32] In his motets he revealed a special interest in the expressive possibilities of an unusually broad range of affective texts, exploring an area that would increasingly occupy composers for the rest of the century. Josquin's contemporary Heinrich Isaac (d. 1517) attempted to set to music the complete cycle of mass propers for the entire liturgical year. It was published after his death with the title *Choralis Constantinus* (1550–1555) after the city of Constance, Switzerland, though much of it was originally composed for the Hapsburg court chapel.

This new emphasis on the texts had a number of interrelated historical sources: humanistic interest in literature and poetry, the greater availability of books due to the invention and rise of printing, and the religious controversies over the Bible and other texts during the Reformation. The musical directives issued during and after the Council of Trent emphasized the intelligibility of texts and the elimination of secular elements as the two most important characteristics of sacred music. These directives led to a number of experiments by composers who sought to present the Latin text more understandably, by respecting the proper accentuation of the words and by minimizing highly florid passages and the simultaneous singing of different syllables in different parts. The most famous experiment of this kind, the *Missa Papae Marcelli* of the Roman composer Giovanni Pierluigi da Palestrina (1525–1594), became the object of a romantic legend that Palestrina had it performed at the Council of Trent itself, averting at the eleventh hour a determined attempt by the assembled bishops to ban all polyphony from the Catholic liturgy. Palestrina's subsequent reputation during the seventeenth to early twentieth centuries wrenched him from his historical context and exaggerated his importance and influence by presenting him as the greatest of Renaissance composers (a distinction many today would confer on Josquin) and the model Counterreformation musician. But in fact his personal life was not especially exemplary, and his commitment to musical reform less palpable than that of lesser composers like Vincenzo Ruffo (c. 1508–1587) and Jacobus de Kerle (1531–1591), whose *Preces speciales* (1561–1562) actually were written for and performed at the council. It is best to see Palestrina as the culmination of one stream within Renaissance music, equal, but not superior, to such very different contemporaries as the prolific and cosmopolitan Orlando di Lasso (1532–1594) of the ducal court in Munich, and the multifaceted William Byrd (1543–1623), organist of the English Chapel Royal, who managed to remain a Catholic even though it was then illegal, and who composed music for both Catholic and Anglican services.

We still know less than we should about the late medieval and Renaissance liturgical practices that created the context for which so much polyphony was composed. We cannot merely assume that a mass or motet with a Gregorian chant tenor was composed to be sung at the date and time to which the chant was traditionally assigned. It is clear that it often was not, and the popularity of cantus firmi taken from secular songs seems to show that the selection of a cantus firmus was mainly a musical rather than a liturgical question, left to the composer's choice rather than determined in advance by liturgical regulations. The so-called a capella ideal often attributed to Renaissance music is a nineteenth-century exaggeration. Except in the pope's private chapel and perhaps a few other places, instruments were often used to accompany vocal polyphony in church.

THE LEGACY OF MEDIEVAL
AND RENAISSANCE MUSIC TODAY

The concern for textual declamation and emotional expression ultimately brought Renaissance polyphony to an end, leading to the development of opera and the new Baroque style. For a long time, however, Renaissance music continued to be studied and performed in churches, for which it was thought more suitable. Baroque church music composed in Renaissance or pseudo-Renaissance style came to be known as *stile antico* (antique style), and counterpoint textbooks claiming to teach the style of Palestrina had an important place in music pedagogy down to our own century, the most important being the *Gradus ad Parnassum* of Johann Joseph Fux (1725).

The Eastern churches continued to cling to their monophonic chant, as most still do to this day. The first to make extensive use of polyphonic music was the Russian Orthodox church, influenced first by German Lutheran chorales and then by Italian operatic music. Some Russian composers of the eighteenth century actually studied in Italy or with visiting Italians such as Baldassare Galuppi (1706–1785), who directed the private chapel of Catherine the Great in St. Petersburg in 1765–1768. The monophonic Slavonic chant also continued to be sung, particularly among the Old Believers, with the old neumatic notation signs or *znamenny,* whence it has come to be called Znamenny chant.[33] However, a modified staff notation (called *Kievan notation*) was also introduced under Western influence and is commonly used in the Russian Orthodox church. Polyphony has been sung in the Armenian Orthodox church since at least the nineteenth century. In the early nineteenth century, both the Armenian and the Greek Orthodox churches experienced a modernization of their medieval neumatic notation, with the result that the notation of the medieval sources ceased to be understood. Though modern scholars have made much progress in deciphering the Greek neumes, some problems of interpretation remain unsolved, and Armenian neumes are still not decipherable.

In the West, the nineteenth century saw the beginning of a great revival of both medieval chant (particularly by the Benedictines of the abbey of Solesmes) and Renaissance polyphony (the Cecilian movement). This "Early Music" revival continued into the twentieth century where it was greatly helped by the new availability of recordings. The ideals of the nineteenth century were enshrined in Pope Pius X's *motu proprio* entitled *Tra le sollecitudini* of 1903, often described as the charter of the liturgical movement. In this document the pope taught that Gregorian chant was the supreme model of liturgical music, and that of other musics, Renaissance polyphony came the closest to it in spirit. As a result, for the first half of the twentieth century, the promotion of congregational singing of Gregorian chant was a major goal of the liturgical movement. After Vatican II, however, the disappearance of Latin and the new openness to the worldwide spectrum of folk and popular music led to a general abandonment of Gregorian chant and to a polarization between those church musicians who wished to preserve chant, polyphony, and classical music and those who thought it more important to promote popular music in the renewed liturgy. After a quarter-century standoff, however, it is time to move to a new synthesis. Chant and polyphony will not go away, indeed they are more popular among some of the general public than they have been for centuries. Just as the church, while it must be open to new theological insights from every quarter, can never abandon its biblical and historical Greek and Latin heritage, so the church, while it must penetrate and redeem every culture in the modern world, can never forget its historic musical heritage. The chant and the liturgy developed together as a single organic growth; the music, like the liturgical texts, is imbued with the spirit of the biblical and patristic traditions, an extraordinary treasury of profound musical wisdom. The tropes and polyphony that developed out of the chant partake of this spirit just as medieval commentaries and theological writings grew out of the biblical and patristic heritage. And just as theology today cannot ignore the historical development of doctrine from the early church to the present, so our musical life will not be healthy if it is expected to operate in a historical vacuum cut off from its past. The continued study and performance of this treasury of sacred music are therefore not optional but essential, and would have the beneficial side-effect of dramatically improving the standards of quality expected of all the other kinds of music performed in modern worship. The more serious one is about fully incarnating the gospel in the culture of the modern world, the more respect one will have for the liturgical song that is at the root of our own musical culture, the ancient and venerable ancestor of the many kinds of music we perform and enjoy today.

NOTES

1. G. Vermes, *The Dead Sea Scrolls in English* (New York, 1975), pp. 32, 81–82.

2. "Aristeas to Philocrates (Letter of Aristeas)," in Moses Hadas, ed. and trans., *Jewish Apocryphal Literature,* vol. 2 (New York, 1951), pp. 175–215.

3. Philo of Alexandria, *The Contemplative Life, The Giants, and Selections,* trans. David Winston, Classics of Western Spirituality (Mahwah, N.J., 1981).

4. James McKinnon, *Music in Early Christian Literature* (Cambridge, 1987), pp. 1–5.

5. Ibid., p. 98.

6. Ibid., pp. 27, 98–99.

7. Ibid., pp. 23–24.

8. Ibid., p. 25.

9. Ibid., p. 119.

10. Ibid., pp. 68–69.

11. John Wilkinson, *Egeria's Travels to the Holy Land,* rev. ed. (Jerusalem, 1981), pp. 253–77.

12. For the history of one famous neuma, see Thomas F. Kelly, "Neuma Triplex," *Acta Musicologica* 60 (1988): 1–30.

13. See Richard Crocker, *The Early Medieval Sequence* (Berkeley, 1977), p. 1.

14. See Ellen Reier, "The Introit Trope Repertory at Nevers: Mss Paris, BN lat. 9449 and Paris, BN lat. 1235" (Ph.D. dissertation, University of California at Berkeley, 1981).

15. See Alejandro Planchart, *The Repertory of Tropes at Winchester,* 2 vols. (Princeton, 1977). Trope texts are now being published systematically in the volumes of the *Corpus Troporum.*

16. See Ruth Steiner, "The Prosulae of the MS Paris, Bibliothèque Nationale, f. lat. 118," *Journal of the American Musicological Society* 22 (1969): 367–93.

17. See Crocker, *Early Medieval Sequence.*

18. For bibliography, see David Hilley, "Ordinary of Mass Chants in English, North French, and Sicilian Manuscripts," *Journal of the Plainsong and Medieval Music Society* 9 (1986–1987): 1–128.

19. For bibliography, see Ritva Jonsson, *Historia: Etudes sur les genèse des offices versifiés* (Stockholm, 1968); Andrew Hughes, "Modal Order and Disorder in the Rhymed Office," *Musica Disciplina* 37 (1983): 29–51; and Andrew Hughes, "Research Report: Late Medieval Rhymed Offices," *Journal of the Plainsong and Medieval Music Society* 8 (1985): 33–49.

20. See Andreas Holschneider, *Die Organa von Winchester: Studien zum ältesten Repertoire polyphonischer Musik* (Hildesheim, 1968); and Marion Gushee, "Romanesque Polyphony: A Study of the Fragmentary Sources" (Ph.D. dissertation, Yale University, 1964).

21. Margot Fassler, "Accent, Meter, and Rhythm in Medieval Treatises *De rithmis,*" *Journal of Musicology* 5 (1987): 164–90.

22. Adalbert Kurzeja, *Der älteste Liber Ordinarius der Trierer Domkirche: London Brit. Mus., Harley 2958, Anfang 14. Jh.* (Münster, 1970).

23. See Guy Oury, "La structure des Vêpres Solennelles dans quelques anciennes liturgies françaises," *Etudes grégoriennes* 13 (1972): 225–36.

24. Johannes Beleth, *Summa de ecclesiasticis officiis,* ed. H. Douteil, Corpus Christianorum Continuatio Medievalis 41 (Turnhout, 1976), ch. 59, pp. 107–8.

25. Religious Latin Lyric poems in rhythmic style set to music; see Leo Treitler, "The Aquitainian Repertories of Sacred Monody in the Eleventh and Twelfth Centuries" (Ph.D. dissertation, Princeton University, 1967); and Thomas B. Payne, "*Associa tecum in patria:* A Newly Identified Organum Trope by Philip the Chancellor," *Journal of the American Musicological Society* 39 (1986): 233–54.

26. See Anne Walters Robertson, "*Benedicamus Domino:* The Unwritten Tradition," *Journal of the American Musicological Society* 41 (1988): 1–62.

27. See Wulf Arlt, *Ein Festoffizium des Mittelalters aus Beauvais in seiner liturgischen und musikalischen Bedeutung,* 2 vols. (Cologne, 1970); and Margot Fassler, "The Feast of Fools and the *Danielis Ludus:* Popular Traditions in a Medieval Cathedral Play," in Thomas Forrest Kelley, ed., *Chant in Context* (Cambridge, forthcoming).

28. See Sarah Fuller, "The Myth of 'St. Martial' Polyphony," *Musica Disciplina* 33 (1979): 5–26.

29. Michel Huglo, "Les débuts de la polyphonie à Paris: Les premiers *organa* parisiens," *Forum Musicologicum* 3 (1982): 93–117.

30. First half of the fourteenth century; see Edward Williams, "John Koukouzeles' Reform of Byzantine Chanting" (Ph.D. dissertation, Yale University, 1968).

31. Jean Dumoulin et al., *La Messe de Tournai* (Louvain, 1988).

32. Howard Mayer Brown, "Emulation, Competition, and Homage: Imitation and Theories of Imitation in the Renaissance," *Journal of the American Musicological Society* 35 (1982): 1–48.

33. See Joan Roccasalvo, "The Znamenny Chant," *Musical Quarterly* 74 (1990): 217–41.

SUGGESTIONS FOR FURTHER READING

General

Duckles, Vincent, and Michael Keller, *Music Reference and Research Materials: An Annotated Bibliography,* 4th ed. (New York, 1988).

Fellerer, Karl Gustav, *Geschichte der katholischen Kirchenmusik,* 2 vols. (Kassel, 1972–1976).

Grout, Donald, and Claude Palisca, *A History of Western Music* (New York, 1988).

Hoppin, Richard H., *Medieval Music* and *Anthology of Medieval Music* (New York, 1978).

Hughes, Andrew, *Medieval Music: The Sixth Liberal Art,* rev. ed., Toronto Medieval Bibliographies 4 (Toronto, 1980).

The New Grove Dictionary of Music and Musicians, ed. Stanley Sadie, 20 vols. (London, 1980).

New Oxford History of Music 2: *The Early Middle Ages to 1300,* rev. ed., ed. Richard Crocker and David Hiley (Oxford University Press, 1990).

Wilson, David Fenwick, *Music of the Middle Ages: Style and Structure* and *Music of the Middle Ages: An Anthology for Performance and Study* (New York, 1990).

Yudkin, Jeremy, *Music in Medieval Europe* (Englewood Cliffs, 1989).

The New Testament and Early Church

Bartlett, John, *Jews in the Hellenistic World: Josephus, Aristeas, the Sibylline Oracles, Eupolemus* (New York, 1985).

Ferguson, Everett, "Hymns," "Music," "Psalms," *Encyclopedia of Early Christianity,* ed. E. Ferguson et al. (New York, 1990), pp. 441–43, 629–32, 763–65.

Jeffery, Peter, "Werner's *The Sacred Bridge,* Volume 2: A Review Essay," *Jewish Quarterly Review* (1987): 283–98.

McKinnon, James, *Music in Early Christian Literature* (Cambridge, 1987).

Philo of Alexandria, *The Contemplative Life, The Giants, and Selections,* trans. David Winston, Classics of Western Spirituality (New York, 1981).

Quasten, Johannes, *Music and Worship in Pagan and Christian Antiquity,* trans. Boniface Ramsey, OP (Washington, DC, 1983).

Smith, William, *Musical Aspects of the New Testament* (Amsterdam, 1962).

Vermes, G., *The Dead Sea Scrolls in English,* 2nd ed. (New York, 1975).

The Conversion of the Empire

Brock, Sebastian P., *The Luminous Eye: The Spiritual World Vision of St. Ephrem* (Rome, 1985).

Carpenter, Marjorie, trans., *Kontakia of Romanos, Byzantine Melodist,* 2 vols. (Columbia, MO, 1970–1973).

Jeffery, Peter, "The Introduction of Psalmody into the Roman Mass by Pope Celestine I (422–432): Reinterpreting a Passage in the *Liber Pontificalis,*" *Archiv für Liturgiewissenschaft* 26 (1984): 147–65. *Re-Envisioning Past Musical Cultures: Ethnomusicology in the Study of Gregorian Chant* (Chicago, 1992).

The Early Medieval Synthesis

Apel, Willi, *Gregorian Chant* (Bloomington, IN, 1958).

Cody, Aelred, "The Early History of the Octoechos in Syria," *East of*

Byzantium: Syria and Armenia in the Formative Period, ed. Nina Garsoïan et al., Dumbarton Oaks Symposium 1980 (Washington, DC, 1982): 89–113.

Conomos, Dmitri E., "Change in Early Christian and Byzantine Liturgical Chant," *Studies in Music from the University of Western Ontario* 5 (1980): 49–63.

Dyer, Joseph, "Monastic Psalmody of the Middle Ages," *Revue Bénédictine* 99 (1989): 41–74. "The Singing of Psalms in the Early Medieval Office," *Speculum* 64 (1989): 535–78.

Fassler, Margot E., "The Office of the Cantor in Early Western Monastic Rules and Customaries: A Preliminary Investigation," *Early Music History* 5 (1985): 29–51.

Gillespie, John, "Coptic Chant: A Survey of Past Research and a Projection for the Future," *The Future of Coptic Studies,* ed. R. McL. Wilson, Coptic Studies 1 (Leiden, 1978): 227–45.

Hage, Louis, *Le Chant de l'église maronite* 1: *Le chant syro-maronite,* Bibliothèque de l'Université Saint Esprit 4. (Beirut, Lebanon, 1972).

Harrison, Frank Ll., *Music in Medieval Britain,* 4th ed. (Buran, Netherlands, 1980).

Hiley, David, "Recent Research on the Origins of Western Chant," *Early Music* 16 (1988): 203–13.

Mother Mary and Kallistos Ware, *The Festal Menaion* (London, 1969), *The Lenten Triodion* (London, 1978).

Nersessian, Vrej, ed. *Essays on Armenian Music* (London, 1978).

Shelemay, Kay Kaufman, and Peter Jeffery, *Ethiopian Christian Chant: An Anthology,* 2 vols., Recent Researches in Oral Traditions of Music 1. (Madison, WI, 1991).

Strunk, Oliver, *Essays on Music in the Byzantine World* (New York, 1977).

Szövérvy, Josef, *Die Annalen der lateinischen Hymnendichtung: Ein Handbuch,* 2 vols. (Berlin, 1965). *A Guide to Byzantine Hymnography,* 2 vols. (Brookline, MA and Leyden, 1978–1979).

Wellesz, Egon, *A History of Byzantine Music and Hymnography,* 2nd ed. (Oxford, 1961; reprinted 1971).

Wilkinson, John, *Egeria's Travels to the Holy Land,* rev. ed. (Jerusalem, 1981).

New Medieval Developments

Arlt, Wulf, *Ein Festoffizium des Mittelalters aus Beauvais in seiner liturgischen und musikalischen Bedeutung,* 2 vols. (Cologne, 1970).

Corpus Troporum 1– , ed. Ritva Jonsson [now Jacobsson], et al., Studia Latina Stockholmiensia 21– . (Stockholm, 1975–).

Beleth, Johannes, *Summa de ecclesiasticis officiis,* ed. H. Douteil, Corpus Christianorum Continuatio Medievalis 41–41A (Turnhout, Belgium, 1976).

Crocker, Richard, *The Early Medieval Sequence* (Berkeley, 1977). "Matins Antiphons at St. Denis," *Journal of the American Musicological Society* 39 (1986): 441–90.

Fassler, Margot, "Musical Exegesis in the Sequences of Adam and the Canons of St. Victor" (Ph.D. diss., Cornell University, 1983). "Who Was Adam of St. Victor? The Evidence of the Sequence Manuscripts," *Journal of the American Musicological Society* 37 (1984): 233–69. "Accent, Meter, and Rhythm in Medieval Treatises 'De rithmis,'" *Journal of Musicology* 5 (1987): 164–90. "The Feast of Fools and the *Danielis Ludus:* Popular Tradition in a Medieval Cathedral Play," *Plainsong in the Age of Polyphony,* ed. Thomas Forrest Kelly (Cambridge, 1992), pp. 65–99. *Gothic Song: Augustinian Ideals of Reform in the Twelfth Century and the Victorine Sequences* (Cambridge, forthcoming).

Fuller, Sarah, "The Myth of 'Saint Martial' Polyphony." *Musica Disciplina* 33 (1979): 5–26.

Gushee, Marion, "Romanesque Polyphony: A Study of the Fragmentary Sources" (Ph.D. diss., Yale University, 1964).

Hiley, David, "Ordinary of Mass Chants in English, North French and Sicilian Manuscripts," *Journal of the Plainsong and Medieval Music Society* 9 (1986–1987): 1–128.

Holschneider, Andreas, *Die Organa von Winchester: Studien zum ältesten Repertoire polyphonischer Musik* (Hildesheim, 1968).

Hughes, Andrew, "Modal Order and Disorder in the Rhymed Office," *Musica Disciplina* 37 (1983): 29–51. "Research Report: Late Medieval Rhymed Offices," *Journal of the Plainsong and Medieval Music Society* 8 (1985): 33–49.

Huglo, Michel, "Les débuts de la polyphonie à Paris: Les premiers *organa* parisiens," *Forum Musicologicum* 3 (1982): 93–117.

Kurzeja, Adalbert, *Der älteste Liber Ordinarius der Trierer Domkirche: London Brit. Mus., Harley 2958, Anfang 14. Jh.* (Münster, 1970).

Jonsson, Ritva, *Historia: Etudes sur la genèse des offices versifiés* (Stockholm, 1968).

Kelly, Thomas F., "Neuma Triplex," *Acta Musicologica* 60 (1988): 1–30.

Marcusson, O., "Comment a-t-on chanté les prosules? Observations sur la technique des tropes de l'alleluia," *Revue de Musicologie* 65 (1979): 119–59.

Oury, Guy, "Les Matines Solennelles aux grandes fêtes dans les anciennes églises françaises," *Etudes grégoriennes* 12 (1971): 155–62. "La structure des Vêpres Solennelles dans quelques anciennes liturgies françaises," *Etudes grégoriennes* 13 (1972): 225–36.

Payne, Thomas B., "*Associa tecum in patria:* A Newly Identified Organum Trope by Philip the Chancellor," *Journal of the American Musicological Society* 39 (1986): 233–54.

Powers, Harold S., "Mode," *The New Grove Dictionary of Music and Musicians,* ed. S. Sadie (London, 1980), 12: 376–450.

Planchart, Alejandro, *The Repertory of Tropes at Winchester,* 2 vols. (Princeton, 1977).

Reier, Ellen, "The Introit Trope Repertory at Nevers: Mss Paris, BN lat. 9449 and Paris BN lt. 1235," (Ph.D. diss., University of California at Berkeley, 1981).

Robertson, Anne Walters, "*Benedicamus Domino:* The Unwritten Tradition," *Journal of the American Musicological Society* 41 (1988): 1–62.

Stäblein, Bruno, *Schriftbild der einstimmigen Musik,* Musikgeschichte in Bildern 3: Musik des Mittelalters und der Renaissance 4 (Leipzig, 1975).

Steiner, Ruth, "The Prosulae of the MS Paris, Bibliothèque Nationale, f. lat. 1118," *Journal of the American Musicological Society* 22 (1969): 367–93. "The Music of a Cluny Office of Saint Benedict," *Monasticism and the Arts,* ed. Timothy Verdon (Syracuse, 1984), pp. 81–113.

Treitler, Leo, *The Aquitainian Repertories of Sacred Monody in the Eleventh and Twelfth Centuries* (Ph.D. diss., Princeton University, 1967).

Waddell, Chrysogonus, OCSO, ed. *The Twelfth-Century Cistercian Hymnal,* 2 vols., Cistercian Liturgy Series 1–2 (Trappist, Kentucky, 1984).

Wright, Craig, *Music and Ceremony at Notre Dame of Paris, 500–1550* (Cambridge, 1989).

The Late Middle Ages and Renaissance

Apel, Willi, *The Notation of Polyphonic Music, 900–1600,*5th ed. (Cambridge, MA, 1961).

Brown, Howard Mayer, *Music in the Renaissance* (Englewood Cliffs, 1976). "Emulation, Competition, and Homage: Imitation and Theories of Imitation in the Renaissance," *Journal of the American Musicological Society* 35 (1982): 1–48.

Conomos, Dmitri E., *Byzantine Trisagia and Cheroubika of the Fourteenth and Fifteenth Centuries: A Study of Late Byzantine Liturgical Chant* (Thessaloniki, 1974). *The Late Byzantine and Slavonic Communion Cycle: Liturgy and Music* (Washington, DC, 1985).

Cummings, Anthony M., "Toward an Interpretation of the Sixteenth-Century Motet," *Journal of American Musicological Society* 34 (1981): 43–59.

Dumoulin, Jean, et al., *La Messe de Tournai* (Louvain, 1988).

Leech-Wilkinson, Daniel, *Machaut's Mass: An Introduction* (Oxford, 1990).

Lockwood, Lewis, *The Counter-Reformation and the Masses of Vincenzo Ruffo* (Venice, 1970). *Giovanni Pierluigi da Palestrina: Pope Marcellus Mass* (New York, 1975).

Lowinsky, Edward E., with Bonnie J. Blackburn, eds., *Josquin des Prez: Proceedings of the International Josquin Festival–Conference Held at the Juilliard School at Lincoln Center in New York City, 21–25 June 1971* (London, 1976).

Reynolds, Christopher, ''Musical Careers, Ecclesiastical Benefices, and the Example of Johannes Brunet,'' *Journal of the American Musicological Society* 37 (1984): 49–97.

Joan Roccasalvo, ''The Znamenny Chant,'' *Musical Quarterly* 74 (1990): 217–41.

Tischler, Hans, *The Earliest Motets (to circa 1270): A Complete Comparative Edition,* 4 vols. (New Haven, 1982).

Williams, Edward, *John Koukouzeles' Reform of Byzantine Chanting* (Ph.D. diss., Yale University, 1968).

The Legacy of Medieval and Renaissance Music Today

Brown, Howard Mayer, and Stanley Sadie, eds., *Performance Practice: Music Before 1600,* The Norton/Grove Handbooks on Music (New York, 1990).

Combe, P., *Histoire de la restauration du chant grégorien d'après* des documents inédits (Solesmes, 1969).

Haskell, Harry, *The Early Music Revival: A History* (London, 1988).

Jeffery, Peter, ''Chant East and West: Toward a Renewal of the Tradition,'' *Concilium: International Review of Theology,* No. 222 (March 1989): *Liturgy 1989: Music and the Experience of God* (Edinburgh, 1989): 20–29.

McGee, Timothy, *Medieval and Renaissance Music: A Performer's Guide* (Toronto, 1985).

Christian Liturgical Music
in the Wake of
the Protestant Reformation

Robin A. Leaver

From its beginnings in the early sixteenth century the Reformation was essentially a theological phenomenon. It began as a search for an answer to the typically medieval question: How can I be saved?[1] The search revealed this question in the New Testament. But the working-out of the Reformation was more than just the posing of a theological question within a medieval framework, and more than a rediscovery of biblical thinking. More than the intellectual probing of a theological possibility unrelated to the world of time and space, the question was an existential imperative: How can I be saved, today, within the realities of the society in which I have to live and work.

Thus, while fundamentally a theological and religious phenomenon, the Reformation nevertheless had implications for every aspect of human activity. Not only affecting the structure of the Christian church, together with its liturgical forms and worship patterns, the movement also brought about changes in society at large. The Protestant understanding of the doctrine of the priesthood of all believers, the commonality of all church members,[2] contributed to the transformation of medieval thinking and action. The Reformation era left in its wake new policies for education; for the governance and political life of important European cities, princely territories, and nations; for commerce in banking, printing, and publishing; the rise of both the tenant-farmer and the independent artisan; new directions in the visual, plastic, and musical arts. In all these areas of life and work the far-reaching influence of the Reformation can be clearly seen.

Admittedly, these changes had already begun to take place before the Reformation had become an identifiable movement. For example, the Renaissance in general and humanism in particular embraced a "new learning" that involved a rediscovery of classical literature in its original languages, including the Hebrew and Greek literatures of Hebrew Scripture and the New Testament. Such new learning influenced the worlds of education, politics, commerce, art, and music. Thus it can be argued, with equal validity, that the Reformation was as much conditioned *by* social change as it was an instrument *of* social change.[3] Nevertheless, it remains essentially a theological phenomenon that manifested itself in sixteenth-century European society, rather than being a socioeconomic phenomenon *per se*.[4]

The liturgico-musical aspects of the Reformation were materially affected by two simultaneous and interrelated developments within society at large: changes in the social standing of musicians, and the expanding importance and influence of printing.

Sacred music in the late medieval period was largely in the hands of the clergy: choir members were either ordained priests or held minor orders. But at the beginning of the sixteenth century sacred music was beginning to move in a nonclerical direction, reflecting the changes within society at large, where the profession of musician was gaining in independent status.[5] Within the Lutheran church in Germany a new musical profession developed, that of cantor, personified by Johann Walter, who had moved on to Torgau from Wittenberg in the mid-1520s and is commonly regarded as the first Lutheran cantor.[6] Thereafter, the music of the Lutheran church rested securely in the hands of gifted professional musicians and composers who functioned primarily within the church. Similarly, in Elizabethan England the organists of cathedrals and collegiate chapels exercised professional leadership for the liturgical music of the English church. The climate in England, however, differed somewhat from Germany, and music as a profession became increasingly extraliturgical.[7]

The technological revolution that materially advanced the spread of the Reformation was the refinement of the printing press, which made possible the relatively cheap production of a vast supply of broadsheets, pamphlets, and booklets. During the first half of the sixteenth century more than ten thousand individual titles were produced in German-speaking lands alone.[8] When Luther drew up his *Ninety-five Theses* on indulgences in 1517, they were first issued in broadsheet form in Wittenberg. Even though only three extant reprints—published in Nuremberg, Leipzig, and Basel—have survived,[9] many other pirated versions must have been printed and circulated, since the *Theses* were being discussed in detail at major European universities, including those in England, within a matter of weeks after having been posted in Wittenberg at the end of October. A vast popular literature included the pamphlets of reformed, vernacular liturgies, as well as the broadsheets and small collections of vernacular hymns and other congregational songs.[10] Thus the changes that occurred in sacred music as part of the Reformation movement, although driven by theological principles, were nevertheless inextricably bound up with other changes within European society in general.

The liturgico-musical responses to the social changes of the Reformation era in both Germany and England blended continuity and discontinuity, familiar tradition with unfamiliar innovation. Tradition provided a sense of security in a changing world; innovation, a sense of progress beyond the confines of the unchangeable past.

LUTHERAN MUSICAL RESPONSES

For some reformers, the new awareness of biblical doctrine, together with the perception of the shortcomings of the contemporary church in the light of this doctrine, led them to conclude that the Reformation must mean a complete break with everything that the church of Rome stood for, especially with its liturgy and music. Thus Zwingli had banished all music from the sanctuaries of churches in Zurich by 1525, and a generation later Calvin had reduced the music of the worship at Genevan churches to metrical psalmody sung by the congregation in unaccompanied unison. At an early stage of the reforming movement in Wittenberg, one of Luther's colleagues, Andreas Carlstadt, was also influenced by Zwingli's views.[11] Luther dismissed this position in his preface to Johann Walter's so-called *Chorgesangbuch,* printed in Wittenberg in 1524. The reformer states that he was not "of the opinion that the gospel should destroy and blight all the arts, as some of the pseudo-religious [*abergeistlichen*] claim"—clearly a reference to Carlstadt and others like him—"but I would like to see all the arts, especially music, used in the service of him who gave and made them."[12] Music, Luther never tired of saying, is the handmaid of theology. Indeed, since music and prophecy were inextricably intertwined in the Hebrew Bible, he claimed that music is the bearer of the Word of God, the *viva voce evangelii,* the living voice of the gospel.[13]

When Luther addressed the question of liturgy and music, two elements of continuity and discontinuity operated side by side; he was at the same time a conservative and a radical liturgical reformer. His first liturgical order was issued in 1523: *Formula Missae et Communionis pro Ecclesia Vuittembergensi (An Order of Mass and Communion for the Church in Wittenberg).*[14] His conservatism compelled him to retain most of the Latin mass, complete with its plainchant monody and polyphonic settings of the ordinary. He allowed some changes, however, such as the use of a complete psalm for the introit, the omission of long graduals, and the drastic reduction of sequences—an anticipation of the reforms of the Council of Trent later in the century. On the other hand, his radicalism led to the elimination of all references to the sacrifice of the mass, which meant that the canon was severely truncated. He left only the *verba testamenti,* the words Jesus used to institute the eucharist. This same radicalism influenced Luther's choice of music for his Latin liturgy. In the traditional Roman mass of his day were two basic silences, the silence of the priest as he inaudibly recited the canon, the prayer of consecration, and the silence of the people as they attended the mystery. For Luther both silences were to be replaced by the sound of music. In place of the traditional silence of the priest, Luther directs the celebrant to chant the *verba testamenti,* since he understands these words not as priestly prayer spoken to God but as prophetic announcement spoken to the people, who need to hear the proclamation of forgiveness. In place of reducing the role of the people at mass to silent spectators, Luther introduced congregational song in order to demonstrate the doctrine of the priesthood of all believers and to articulate a corporate response to God's Word.[15]

Luther and his Wittenberg colleagues specifically provided congregational hymns. In them, one can detect the twin themes of continuity and discontinuity. Some translated and adapted traditional Latin hymns, familiar to the people even though they would not actually have sung them in their original Latin form. Other hymns reworked old German folk hymns, the fifteenth-century *Leisen* (medieval vernacular hymns) sung after mass at the major festivals of the church year (see example 1).

Example 1. Comparison of the Easter sequence "Victimae paschali laudes"; the *Leise,* or German folk hymn, "Christ ist erstanden," based on the sequence; and Luther's "Christ lag in Todesbanden" (1524), which originally appeared with the heading "Der lobgesang 'Christ ist erstanden' gebessert" ("The hymn 'Christ ist erstanden' improved").

However, by the beginning of the sixteenth century, some congregations sang them at festivals within the mass, in connection with the sequence of the day. In addition to these traditional elements, Luther and his friends also created new strophic texts and melodies for congregational singing, using the style of art songs of the day—the *Hofweise,* songs in the courtly manner—as the model. Thus the continuity of the older hymnody blended with the discontinuity of the newly created hymns.

The old and the new mingled in the same way in which hymns were performed in Wittenberg liturgy. The first Wittenberg hymnal, Walther's *Chorgesangbuch,* was issued, not as a congregational collection, but as a set of part books for choral use. It contains polyphonic settings of five Latin motets and thirty-eight hymn or chorale melodies. The style simplifies choral polyphony as exemplified in the works of Josquin des Prez and others. But whereas these Catholic compositions were more extensive, employing plainchant *cantus firmi* (preexisting melodies used as the basis for later compositions), which are not always audible, Walter's more concise settings are based on the Wittenberg hymn melodies, which are almost always clearly heard (see example 2).

Example 2. The opening of Johann Walter's setting of "Aus tiefer Not."

The technique of using settings composed on preexisting melodies offered continuity; setting briefer compositions based, not on melodies of clerical monody, but on congregational hymnody provided discontinuity. These settings of Walter were sung by Wittenberg's choir, which alternated with the congregation singing its stanzas in unison. At first, 1523–1524, the members of the congregation used broadsheet copies of the hymns, but after 1525 they had a more permanent hymnal. Thus the old practice in the medieval church of the choir answering monodic chant with polyphonic settings was replaced in Witten-

berg by the congregation answering choral polyphony with
unison hymnody.

This corporate expression of unanimity obviously provided
a source of encouragement to the people in these times of
dramatic change. In the old church, the individual Christian often
felt very much on his or her own, despite the stress on the
communion of the saints. Each person went to confession,
received individual absolution, performed an individual penance,
and individually attended mass. But the new church, which by
no means underestimated the individual's responsibility before
God, found a new expression of the people's solidarity. Together
they faced the world, the flesh, the devil, and all opposition—
including the Catholic church if need be!—and sang with Luther,
"nun freut euch, lieben Christen g'mein":

> Dear Christians, one and all, rejoice
> with exultation ringing,
> and with united heart and voice
> and holy rapture springing.
>> Proclaim the wonders God has done,
>> how his right arm the victory won.
>> What price our ransom cost him!

Or the fourth stanza of his *Ein feste Burg:*

> The Word they still shall let remain
> nor any thanks have for it.
> He's by our side upon the plain
> with his good gifts and Spirit.
>> And take they our life,
>> goods, fame, child, and wife,
>> though these all be gone,
>> our victory has been won.
>> The kingdom ours remaineth.[16]

In 1526 Luther's German liturgy was issued: *Deudsche Messe
und ordnung Gottis dienstes (German Mass and Order of Worship).*[17] Luther did not intend this German liturgy to replace

his earlier Latin liturgy. Indeed, he expressly states that where Latin is understood—that is, in the Latin schools of towns and in the universities of cities—the basic Latin service, which could have some German elements in it, should continue. In principle Luther favored worship in the two biblical languages as well as Latin and German: "And if I could bring it to pass, and Greek and Hebrew were as familiar to us as Latin and had as many fine melodies and songs,[18] we would hold mass, sing, and read on successive Sundays in all four languages, German, Latin, Greek, and Hebrew."[19]

The *Deutsche Messe* was designed primarily for small towns and villages where Latin was not understood. However, in practice, the many Lutheran church orders that were published later conflated Luther's two liturgies and mixed Latin and German. In the *Deutsche Messe* congregational hymnody was increased by vernacular hymnodic versions of the ordinary of the mass, such as the Kyrie, Gloria, Credo, and so forth, sung congregationally either in place of the Latin texts or after the choir had sung the Latin versions, either in plainchant or polyphony. (The latter became the usual practice.)

Example 3. The *verba testamenti* from Luther's *Deutsche Messe* (1526).

Another feature of this German liturgical order actually was the melodic formulas that the celebrant used when singing the *verba testamenti*. Luther had given three specific groups of lectionary tones for the chanting of the gospel, one for the words of the Evangelist, another for the words of other people within the narrative (generally within the tenor range), and a third for the words of Jesus alone (pitched lower, in the bass range). As a result, the congregation knew that the music for the words of Jesus differed from all the rest. When his words, the *verba testamenti*, were heard again later in the eucharist they too were to be sung to the same melodic patterns as Jesus' part during the earlier chanting of the gospel for the day (see example 3). Thus the same basic melodic form unified the proclamation of God's good news of forgiveness and grace, in both the chanting of the gospel and in the *verba testamenti*. Here is a mark of Luther's genius: he gave practical expression to his theoretical assumption that theology and music intertwined in the proclamation of the Word, certainly a brilliant innovation connected to the past. The chant that Luther employed grew out of the long Judeo-Christian tradition of liturgical chant.[20]

ANGLICAN MUSICAL RESPONSES

The Reformation in England began very much in Luther's shadow, even though Erasmus had complained as early as 1519 that English polyphonic music for the liturgy was "so constructed that the congregation cannot hear one distinct word."[21] Avoiding this lack of comprehension was to become an important principle for English Reformers, but it was Luther's theology that grabbed their attention in the first place.

Already by 1520 a group of Cambridge theologians were meeting in the White Horse Inn in order to discover Luther's writings. One of them, Miles Coverdale, issued around 1535 an English translation of a good many of the Wittenberg hymns, together with their melodies.[22] About six years later Coverdale published a tract that called for English liturgical reform along the lines of Lutheran churches in Denmark and Germany.[23] Unlike areas influenced by Saxon Germany, the theological situation in Anglo-Saxon England was more complex. Loyal Catholics maintained an allegiance to the pope in Rome; English Catholics retained traditional theology but ecclesiologically supported Henry VIII's break with the papacy; moderate reformers, such as Thomas Cranmer, archbishop of Canterbury, were generally Lutheran in theological perspective, at least at an early stage of the reforming movement; and then there were the more radical reformers, such as John Hooper, who had studied in Zurich under Heinrich Bullinger, Zwingli's successor. Henry VIII himself remained with the old theology, and while he was alive the reforming movement was largely kept in check. After Henry's death and the accession of his youthful son, Edward VI, in 1547, however, reform was openly pursued— and the four-cornered factions vied with each other for ascendancy. The old Catholics wanted the tradition to remain unchanged, but the new Catholics wanted some innovation, at least in terms of a vernacular liturgy. On the other hand, the moderate Protestants wanted to retain at least some traditional practices, but radical Protestants wanted to change everything. By and large the reformers were more influential than the Catholics in Edwardian England, and the moderate reformers outweighed the more radical, but just barely. Therefore, the first English prayer book, issued in 1549, was a compromise for everyone: it was thus simultaneously too traditional and too novel— depending on a person's point of view.

The Anglican prayer book was, like Luther's liturgical provisions, a blend of the two elements of continuity and discontinuity. In drawing on traditional elements, Cranmer did not confine himself to the Latin mass but developed the English vernacular liturgy against the background of Greek and, possibly even, Hebrew forms. He drew from the Liturgy of St. John Chrysostom, producing ''A Prayer of St. Chrysostom'' at the end of the English litany. Cranmer also may have been aware of Hebrew forms through Paul Fagius, the Strassburg reformer whom, with others, Cranmer invited to England. Although

Fagius died shortly after having arrived in England in 1549 and therefore could not have had any personal involvement in the subsequent revision of the Edwardian prayer book, he might have provided Cranmer with some Hebrew perspectives through a pioneering book published some years before, *Precationes Hebraicae* (*Hebrew Prayers;* Isny, 1542). In the preface to these Latin translations of Hebrew prayers Fagius, the earliest Protestant to do so, drew attention to the similarities between the Jewish *Kiddush* and the Christian eucharist. He suggested that a knowledge of Jewish rites contributes greatly to an understanding of Christian usage.[24] This fruitful comparison of the two related traditions undergirded his own view of the eucharist as a social celebration, an emphasis that is clearly marked in Cranmer's revised prayer book of 1552. In this new form of the eucharist the isolation of priest and altar is replaced by a free-standing table in the body of the church, around which the congregation gathers as a family for this social celebration of the meal of faith.

While drawing on older liturgical traditions, Cranmer was aware also of the new developments in vernacular Protestant liturgies. He was particularly conscious of Lutheran orders, having traveled throughout Germany in around 1530. Indeed, he stayed with Lucas Osiander in Nuremberg while Osiander was working on the Brandenburg-Nuremberg church order, eventually published in 1533. In Edwardian England, Cranmer had access to a broad group of contemporary liturgical scholars: Martin Bucer, the architect of the Strassburg German liturgy, who so influenced Calvin; Valerandus Pollanus, also from Strassburg, who developed a liturgy for exile for French weavers in Glastonbury; the Polish reformer Joannes á Lasco, who compiled independent forms for the "stranger" churches in London; and Martin Micron from Ghent, who produced a Dutch version of Lasco's liturgy for the "strangers" from the Low Countries living and working in the capital city.

Though the liturgical music of Anglicanism, like that of Lutheranism, was also made up of traditional and novel aspects, the English solution was less integrated than the German.

Lutheran church music was unified in a basic tradition: monody and polyphony, organ and other instrumental accompaniment, choral and congregational music were all held together by the common thread of the chorale. By contrast, Anglicanism never expressed an unequivocal and common doctrinal position, as did Lutheranism. One of the consequences of this broader base was that English church music developed in two directions simultaneously: the choral tradition of the cathedrals and collegiate chapels, based on the multivoiced settings of the prayer book services, on the one hand; and the congregational tradition of the parish churches, devoted almost exclusively to metrical psalmody, on the other.[25] Cathedrals stressed artistic celebration and parish churches emphasized the social celebration, but the same prayer book liturgy united both Anglican music traditions.

During the mid–sixteenth century, English choral, liturgical music underwent a dramatic change. Though the polyphonic settings of the Latin ordinary of the mass were magnificent, with architectonic compositions of layers of rolling sound, little attention was given to the words. But for the new vernacular prayer book service, the composers—often the same ones who had written for the Latin mass, such as Tallis and Tye—adopted an almost uniformly homophonic style with virtually no text overlap and with each syllable sounding simultaneously in each voice part (see example 4).[26]

Example 4. The opening of Thomas Tallis's setting of the prayer book "Benedictus" for four men's voices.

There was continuity in the choral settings of the liturgy, but discontinuity in the declamatory style, created by the reformers' desire for the sung word to be heard and understood. Indeed, Cranmer and others commended the principle of "one note per syllable" in liturgical music.[27]

These new, homophonic, predominantly four-part, choral settings nevertheless continued the tradition of *cantus firmus* composition, as exemplified in the older polyphonic masses. They were frequently based on plainchant.[28] The traditional plainchant was often modified and simplified, but usually in a creative way, reflecting the different inflections and stresses of the English language when compared with the Latin.

In the liturgical monody for the new prayer book liturgies a similar process can be detected in as early as *The booke of Common praier noted,* issued semiofficially in 1550.[29] The composer John Marbeck, organist at St. George's Chapel, Windsor Castle, developed a brilliant, rhythmically measured adaptation of traditional plainchant to match the sounds and rhythms of the English liturgical language. He often greatly simplified the traditional chant but was always sensitive to the basic integrity of the ancient monody (see example 5).

Example 5. Comparison of the Sarum Kyrie from *Missa pro defunctis* and John Marbeck's Kyrie "At the Communion" from *The booke of Common praier noted* (1550).

As well as adapting traditional plainchant, Marbeck also created new monodic chants, much wider in range than the traditional melodies, the two notable examples being his settings of the Gloria and Creed in the communion service, although even these are redolent of traditional melodies. Thus, for the polyphony and monody that was used with the prayer book services in cathedrals and collegiate chapels, the new was created out of the old, and the old continued in a modified form.

In the parish churches of English towns and villages virtually the only music for worship was the congregational metrical psalm, although some parishes in larger towns and cities maintained a choral tradition throughout the remainder of the sixteenth century (these latter, however, were exceptional). The English metrical psalm was developed by Sternhold and Hopkins during the reign of Edward VI. This early English psalmody was apparently, like the choral tradition in the cathedrals, a four-part tradition, with the principal melody sounding in the tenor voice (see example 6).[30]

Example 6. The opening of the anonymous metrical version of Psalm 100 in the Lumley part books (London, British Library, Royal App. MS. 74–76), c. 1549.

Only later, after contact with continental custom during the Marian years, did English psalmody become an essentially unison practice. There is, however, an oral tradition, which may or may not be accurate, that suggests that the early metrical psalms were sung to popular melodies. It is known that tunes were specifically composed for them, and the evidence found in two Edwardian collections of metrical psalms[31] suggests that tunes were also crafted out of the basic plainchant psalm tones.[32] The two Anglican traditions of church music resemble one another: both employed four-part singing, both utilized the older traditional plainchant, and both depended on elements of continuity and discontinuity.

CONTEMPORARY IMPLICATIONS

Amid the great social changes of the sixteenth century and though different in detail, the musical responses of Lutheranism and Anglicanism blended creatively the continuity of the past with the discontinuity of the present. The music of the reforming movement, itself concerned with change within the sometimes violent mutations of the sixteenth century, was therefore neither reactionary nor rootless. Through the music from the past, contemporary Christians were given insight and encouragement to live in the present: through the music of the present, worshiping congregations saw that God was not only the God of yesterday but also the God of today. Continuity overstressed creates the danger of fossilization, an escapism that lives only in the past, willfully blind to the present. When discontinuity predominates, there is danger of disintegration, a different kind of escapism that lives only in the present, an existentialism that denies all traditional values. If either continuity or discontinuity displaces the other then disastrous social consequences follow, as later history demonstrates. In England the metrical psalm-singing puritans under Oliver Cromwell pursued discontinuity so tenaciously that they created a civil war. In Germany, earlier in our own century, Lutherans were so concerned with the authentic continuity of their fine tradition of church music from the past that they could not see where Hitler was leading them in the present.

In the reformation era in both Germany and England, continuity and discontinuity balanced in a creative tension. In late twentieth-century North America, we have been passing through a period of significant societal change that, in the process, has brought about a "restructuring of American religion," as the research of sociologist Richard Wuthnow has perceptively demonstrated.[33] As in the sixteenth century, there has been a concern to explore biblical theology and relate that exploration to contemporary society; to reach people outside ecclesiastical circles in order to share with them the insights of religious faith; and to find new, expressive, and inclusive ways of worshiping. Like the people of the sixteenth century, we too have been influenced by interrelated changes in the status of church musicians and in the emergence of a new technology.

Collaboration between minister and musician and the acknowledged dependence on each other's expertise is changing dramatically. The theologian Luther knew it was necessary, when drawing up patterns of worship for Wittenberg, to call on the expertise of the gifted musician Johann Walter. Even Calvin, who was much more suspicious and restrictive than Luther about music in the liturgy, nevertheless knew the wisdom of working with such notable composers as Louis Bourgeois and Claude Goudimel in the provision of music for the Genevan psalter. Indeed, when the significantly expanded Genevan psalter of 1551 was being prepared for publication, Bourgeois also produced a small tract—presumably with Calvin's encouragement—dealing with the basic rudiments of music that individuals in the congregation required for singing the metrical psalms.[34] Today, congregations are led to believe that only music in a simplistic style is appropriate for worship and that professionally competent musicians are unnecessary. This extreme position deprives congregations of the breadth and depth that professional musicians can offer as partners with the clergy and the people.

Like the receivers of the new technology of printing in the sixteenth century, we, at the end of the twentieth century, also have new technologies of communication. Television is more pervasive than the sixteenth-century pulpit; and computer communication, more immediate than the sixteenth-century broadsheet. The growth of these electronic technologies in our society also brings with it the desire to control the flow of information. Various forms of censorship, or "rights of access," now operate in ways that endanger our freedom by undermining the First Amendment.[35] A similar censorship also operates with regard to the sacred music transmitted through the electronic media. The facile medium of television has produced its "lowest-common-denominator" approach in the worst excesses of televangelism,[36] in which only one type of music is heard, one that reflects the materialistic desires of our society rather than the deeper spiritual concerns of our faith. Similarly, the advent

of electronic publishing in connection with sacred music is likely
to promote only a narrow range of anodyne and "popular"
music, unless other publishers rise to the challenge of the
medium.[37]

We appear to be in a period of transition, unsure where the
future may take us. Despite positive possibilities,[38] the signs
favor discontinuity at the expense of continuity. As Eric Werner
has pointed out,[39] the synagogue of the Diaspora has been completely thrown off balance by the Holocaust, being dominated
by survivalist policies; and the Catholic church, since Vatican
II, has in large measure given up much of its musico-liturgical
tradition.[40] Many Protestant churches are little different in their
preference for the "instant" music of contemporary commer-
cialism and for the dismissal of the church music of continuity
as either "churchy" or "elitist." But we need the music of
the past as well as the music of the present, as the German and
English reformers discovered in the sixteenth century. They
developed a sacred bridge linking continuity at one end with
discontinuity at the other, a sacred bridge that must be kept
accessible and serviceable for present as well as future generations of worshipers.

NOTES

1. See, for example, Robin A. Leaver, *Luther and Justification*
(St. Louis, 1975), especially p. 13 and following.

2. See especially Gert Haendler, *Luther on Ministerial Office and
Congregational Function,* trans. Ruth C. Gritsch, ed. Eric W. Gritsch
(Philadelphia, 1981).

3. For older literature, see, for example, Ernst Tröltsch, "Ren-
aissance and Reformation," *Gesammelte Schriften* 4 (Tübingen,
1925), pp. 261–96; Patrick C. Gordon Walker, "Capitalism and the
Reformation," *Economic Review* 8 (1937): 1–19; Hajo Holborn, "The
Social Basis of the Reformation," *Church History* 5 (1936): 330–39.
All three articles can be found, with some abbreviation, in L. W.
Spitz, ed., *The Reformation: Material Or Spiritual?* (Boston, 1962).
For more recent discussions, see the Harold J. Grimm Festschrift,

Lawrence P. Buck and Jonathan W. Zophy, eds., *The Social History of the Reformation* (Columbus, 1972); the bibliographic essay by Thomas A. Brady, Jr., "Social History," in Steven Ozment, ed., *Reformation Europe: A Guide to Research* (St. Louis, 1982), pp. 161–81; and Kyle C. Sessions and Phillip N. Bebb, eds., *Pietas et Societas: New Trends in Reformation Social History. Essays in Memory of Harold J. Grimm,* Sixteenth-Century Essays and Studies 4 (Kirksville, Mo., 1985).

4. For such an interpretation, see Eva Priester, *Kurze Geschichte Österreichs* (Vienna, 1946), pp. 111–19, trans. in W. Stanford Ried, ed., *The Reformation: Revival or Revolution?* (New York, 1968), pp. 98–105.

5. See Walter Salmen, *The Social Status of the Professional Musician from the Middle Ages to the Nineteenth Century* (New York, 1983); Frank L. Harrison, "The Social Position of Church Musicians in England, 1450–1550," *Report of the Eighth Congress of the International Musicological Society,* vol. 1 (Kassel, 1961), pp. 346–56; John W. Barker, "Sociological Influences upon the Emergence of Lutheran Music," *Miscellanea Musicologica: Adelaide Studies in Musicology* 4 (1969): 157–98.

6. See, for example, Walter E. Buszin, "Johann Walther: Composer, Pioneer, and Luther's Musical Consultant," *The Musical Heritage of the Church* 3 (1947): 78–110.

7. Sometime around 1576, the composer Thomas Whythorne, who had published a set of madrigals in 1571 and a few years later became the master of music to Matthew Parker, archbishop of Canterbury, wrote in his manuscript autobiography: "Now I will speak of the use of music in this time present. First, for the Church, ye do and shall see it so slenderly maintained in the cathedral churches and colleges and parish churches, that when the old store of musicians be worn out, the which were bred when the music of the church was maintained (which is like to be in short time), ye shall have few or none remaining, except it be a few singingmen and players on musical instruments" (*The Autobiography of Thomas Whythorne: Modern Spelling Edition,* ed. James M. Osborn [London, 1962], p. 204).

8. For an excellent survey and bibliography, see Steven Ozment, "Pamphlet Literature of the German Reformation," in Ozment, ed., *Reformation Europe,* pp. 85–105.

9. See *Luther's Works,* ed. Jaroslav J. Pelikan and Helmut T. Lehmann (St. Louis and Philadelphia, 1955–   ), vol. 31, pp. 22–23.

10. See Kyle C. Sessions, "Song Pamphlets: Media Changeover in Sixteenth-Century Publicization," in *Print and Culture in the Renaissance: Essays on the Advent of Printing in Europe* (Newark, 1986), pp. 110–19.

11. See Charles Garside, *Zwingli and the Arts* (New Haven, 1966), pp. 54–56.

12. *Luther's Works*, vol. 53, p. 316.

13. See further, Carl Schalk, *Luther on Music: Paradigms of Praise* (St. Louis, 1988).

14. For a translation of the *Formula Missae*, see *Luther's Works*, vol. 53, pp. 19–40.

15. See further, Robin A. Leaver, "*Verba Testamenti* versus Canon: The Radical Nature of Luther's Liturgical Reform," *Churchman* 97 (1983): 123–31; Robin A. Leaver, "The Whole Congregation Sings: The Sung Word in Reformation Liturgy," in *Drew Gateway* 60 (1990–1991): 53–73.

16. Composite translations.

17. For a translation of the *Deutsche Messe*, see *Luther's Works*, vol. 53, pp. 61–90.

18. Luther was clearly unaware of the interrelationships between Hebrew, Greek, and Latin chant.

19. *Luther's Works*, vol. 53, p. 63.

20. For a summary of the Lutheran tradition that proceeded from Luther, see Robin A. Leaver, *The Liturgy and Music: A Study of the Use of the Hymn in Two Liturgical Traditions*, Grove Liturgical Study 6 (Bramcote, 1976), pp. 14–24.

21. Quoted in Peter le Huray, *Music and the Reformation in England 1549–1660* (Cambridge, 1978), p. 11; see also C. A. Miller, "Erasmus on Music," *The Musical Quarterly* 52 (1966): 332–49.

22. [Miles Coverdale], *Goostly Psalmes and Spiritual Songes* (London, c. 1535).

23. Miles Coverdale, *The order that the churche and congregation of Chryst in Denmark, and in many places, countries and cities of Germany doth use* (c. 1543), reprint ed. in G. Pearson, ed., *Writings and Translation of Myles Coverdale* (Cambridge, 1844).

24. See further Jerome Friedman, *The Most Ancient Testimony: Sixteenth-Century Christian-Hebraica in the Age of Renaissance Nostalgia* (Athens, 1983), pp. 102–6.

25. Historical surveys of the two traditions can be found in Edmund H. Fellowes, *English Cathedral Music*, Jack A. Westrup, ed.

(London, 1969); and Nicholas Temperley, *The Music of the English Parish Church*, 2 vols. (Cambridge, 1979). A recent study, Stanford E. Lehmberg, *The Reformation of Cathedrals: Cathedrals in English Society, 1485–1603* (Princeton, 1988), investigates the role of cathedral establishments during the far-reaching political and theological changes of the English Reformation era; a social history, the work stresses particularly the liturgical and musical consequences of those changes (see especially chapters 4, 6, and 8).

26. See Huray, *Music and the Reformation*, pp. 172–226; Denis Stevens, *Tudor Church Music* (New York, 1973), pp. 86–112.

27. See Fellowes, *English Cathedral Music*, p. 24.

28. See the articles by John Aplin: "A Group of English Magnificats 'Upon the Faburden'," *Soundings* 7 (1978): 85–100; "The Survival of Plainsong in Anglican Music: Some Early *Te Deum* Settings," *Journal of the American Musicological Society* 32 (1979): 247–75; "'The Fourth Kind of Faburden': The Identity of an English Four-Part Style," *Music and Letters* 61 (1980): 245–65.

29. See *The booke of Common praier noted* 1550, Robin A. Leaver, ed., Courtenay Facsimile 3 (Appleford, 1980), especially the introduction; and Robin A. Leaver, *The Work of John Marbeck*, Courtenay Library of Reformation Classics 9 (Appleford, 1978).

30. See Robin A. Leaver, *'Goostly Psalmes and Spiritual Songes': English and Dutch Metrical Psalms from Coverdale to Utenhove 1535–1566* (Oxford, 1991).

31. Robert Crowley, *The psalter of Dauid newely translated into Englysh metre* (London, 1549); F. Seagar, *Certayne psalmes select out of the Psalter of Dauid, and drawen into Englyshe Metre, wyth Notes to euery Psalme in iiij parts to Synge* (London, 1553).

32. A number of the French Genevan psalm tunes were also crafted out of traditional plainsong; see Pierre Pidoux, *Vom Ursprung der Genfer Psalmweisen* (Zurich, 1986), pp. 14–17.

33. See especially, Robert Wuthnow, *The Restructuring of American Religion: Society and Faith since World War II* (Princeton, 1988); and Robert Wuthnow, *The Struggle for America's Soul: Evangelicals, Liberals, and Secularism* (Grand Rapids, 1989).

34. Louis Bourgeois, *Droict Chemin de Musique* (Geneva, 1550); see facsimile and English trans. by Bernard Rainbow, *The Direct Road to Music* (Kilkelly, Ireland, 1982).

35. See Ithiel de Sola Pool, *Technologies of Freedom* (Cambridge, Mass., 1983).

36. The issues are more complex and far-reaching than can be dealt with here; see, for example, the discussions of Wuthnow cited in note 33, above.

37. For example, with traditional methods of music publishing, the costs of producing some compositions are currently prohibitive, but the prospect of producing copies "on demand" from electronic databanks opens up new possibilities.

38. See, for example, Robin A. Leaver, ed., *Church Music: The Future. Creative Leadership for the Year 2000 and Beyond. October 15-17, 1989, Westminster Choir College, Conference Papers* (Princeton, 1990).

39. See the preface to Eric Werner, *The Sacred Bridge: The Interdependence of Liturgy and Music in Synagogue and Church during the First Millenium,* vol. 2 (New York, 1984), p. xi.

40. See, for example, Thomas Day, *Why Catholics Can't Sing: The Culture of Catholicism and the Triumph of Bad Taste* (New York, 1990), a perceptive diagnosis that lacks a coherent prescription.

PART 2

Exploring the Present:
Sacred Sound in
North America Today

Introduction

Part 2 of this volume moves directly from the past to the present, our own era of reformation in church and synagogue. Whether recognized officially or not, diversity of membership has always characterized religious denominations and movements. Certainly that is the case today, with the obvious result that we are unable in any one volume to provide a full gamut of opinion within any one of the two liturgical traditions in question. Nor could we hope to cover every change, every challenge, and every musical debate in every church and every synagogue body. Nonetheless, the three authors whose essays constitute part 2 represent a particular segment of Catholic, Protestant, and Jewish traditions in the throes of current change. Each has chosen specific currents in his or her contemporary church or synagogue music, with the belief that these are central matters that will continue to demand our attention in the future. The authors focus on the trends that they consider pivotal in the direction our sacred music will take.

Miriam Therese Winter is professor of liturgy, worship, and spirituality at Hartford Seminary in Connecticut. Her compositions include *Mass of A Pilgrim People,* which was premiered at Carnegie Hall. Since 1968, however, she has also been named annually to the Popular Awards List of ASCAP. Her appreciation of both the classical musical heritage of the Catholic church and of the popular sounds that emanate authentically from a people's lived situation form the basis of her challenge to the church to take advantage of the revolutionary new possibilities of the postconciliar era, by acting prophetically to sing a new world into being. Whereas other authors in this book decry

secularity (see the remarks by Samuel Adler, for instance),
Winter celebrates its possibilities, in that it represents the
workplace, the marketplace, and the real life-space of the people
whom the church is called to liberate—hence her emphatic
attention to the prophetic task of religion in general and religious
music in particular.

The broad gamut of churches we call *Protestant* are represented here by a particular case study: the music of the Reformed
churches in North America and, particularly, their historical
penchant for psalmody. What has happened to the Calvinist ardor
for meshing liturgy with a social order? asks Horace T. Allen.
Allen is in a good position to ask that question. He surveys the
movement in America away from social responsibility and
toward individual salvation, and he calls on the Reformed
churches to reengage themselves with their Hebrew scriptural
musical bases, to the end that proper praying will support "doing
justly" in this "paganized, consumerized, and competitive
culture."

Finally, Benjie-Ellen Schiller gives us the case of North
American Reform Judaism. A cantor herself, Schiller teaches
the Jewish musical heritage at the Hebrew Union College's
School of Sacred Music. She is as well a prominent composer
for the synagogue, and as such, she struggles with the issues
that she describes in historical overview here. Her survey of
the official hymnals that have guided Reform synagogues since
1897 turns up several trends in American Jewish identity, most
recently a recapturing of tradition that past generations threw
away (like the psalmody for which Allen yearns?) and yet, on
the other hand, a recognition of the validity of musical diversity to match a worshiping constituency that is far from homogeneous (recalling Winter's observations on Catholic polity,
certainly).

There are patent differences in each of these articles—to note
that we share a "second reformation" is not to imagine that
we all do so to the same extent or in the same way. Surely our
diverse histories and traditions channel contemporary challenges
in denominationally unique ways, just as our social situations
demand different responses. But points are shared in common

here, above all, perhaps, an accent on sacred song as the people's prayer, and a recognition of the pluriformity of the worshiping community, with a resulting eclecticism in musical taste.

Catholic Prophetic Sound
after Vatican II

MIRIAM THERESE WINTER

Twenty-five years after the conclusion of Vatican II, a whole new sound resonates from the Catholic church in America: the sound of people singing—in choirs, in the pews, in ad hoc or more permanent groups dedicated to a less formal style or repertory; the sound of hymn, psalm, chant, song, antiphon, and acclamation in the language of the people, spontaneously composed or classically constructed, both complex and rudimentary, in unison or in harmonies either articulated or implied; the sound of full-bodied organ and steel-string guitar, of keyboard, woodwind, percussion, and brass; the sound of rhythmic clapping, of a community of believers come to life and open to making music. Not all the time. Not in every parish. But enough times in enough cathedrals, local churches, seminaries, schools, religious houses, and small Christian communities to confirm a paradigmatic shift in the character of music-making from what existed before the council. This century has seen in the Catholic church significant change—ecclesiological, liturgical, and social—and that change has occurred in association with music.

Sometimes music precipitated change, causing the church to reorder its practices in ways far beyond anything anyone could have anticipated. For example, the popularity of vernacular hymn and psalm singing in the dialogue or low mass of the fifties[1] helped influence the council to define liturgy in terms of the active participation of the people and to be open to the use of the vernacular. Before long, the categories of *high* and

150

low mass were eliminated as the vernacular language became the liturgical norm. The full participation of women in choirs for many years prior to the council led the church to recognize officially all church choirs and to accept the equal status of women within them, overturning an ecclesiastical law that had excluded women from membership in official liturgical choirs.[2] A singing congregation and a full choir were catalysts for the architectural redesign of parish churches from the long, narrow, spectator style with choir and organ in a loft in the rear to a circular, more inclusive orientation with the choir visible in front and with a less strong demarcation between narthex, body, and sanctuary, between laity and clergy. The free and informal folk style of the sixties, aided both by quick and easy access to new songs through parish duplicating machines and by inexpensive missalettes, became so widespread and so prolific that any attempt to enforce an officially approved repertory was useless and the practice was quietly discontinued. The use of guitar and even percussion precipitated a reclassification of musical instruments that had formerly been banned from liturgical use on both aesthetic and theological grounds. Today all instruments are potentially liturgical.

In a variety of ways the impact of music forced the Catholic church of this century to change, yet at other times music reflected changes that had already arisen in some other arena and then found their expression in musical form. For example, the liturgical emphasis on participatory acclamations has led to the proliferation of musical fragments in the eucharistic liturgy. Some celebrations now consist solely of musically disconnected amens, alleluias, antiphons, hosannas, and an anaphora acclamation. The emergence of the responsorial psalm as the primary people's response during the liturgy of the word has given rise to various collections of sung psalms and refrains, establishing a responsorial relationship between cantor and community that remains to this day. The liturgical decision to promote active participation through musical means opened the door to all manner of composers who brought to the ritual all kinds of music. The length of time it took to complete the revision of all liturgical books meant that the music of the immediate postconciliar period was guided by no firm criteria, and the result was a musical pluriformity historically uncharacteristic of the institutional church.

Without a doubt the struggle for musical literacy in the American Catholic church has coincided with a ritual and social reformation. An initial stage of liturgical and musical reform precipitated a period of genuine renewal. The people were claiming their church. From the perspective of the hierarchy and the average American parish, some sense of stability exists at present. The genius of past experimentation has been absorbed into the mainstream of the tradition. It is possible once again to describe and define what is essential to Catholic liturgical music.

From a liturgical point of view three guidelines have emerged: (1) it is essential that the people sing whenever it is possible and appropriate for them to do so, for through song and the act of singing people experience a sense of community and express the presence of God among them; (2) it is essential that the singing be ritually integrated within the given liturgical moment and that the musical expression be appropriate to the ethos of the liturgical action taking place; and finally, (3) it is essential that the music be pastorally sensitive to the celebrating assembly, reflecting a style and level of difficulty appropriate to those participating. These guidelines leave room for considerable differences on aesthetic matters, with critics taking contrary positions, for instance, on what is musically essential. Some have made a concerted effort to return to a set of uniform aesthetic values, if not a uniform musical praxis, that reflects the ethos of a ''lost'' tradition. Yet parishes continue to have differing standards of performance, interpretation, and style. Although parishes differ significantly according to region, religious majority/minority status, urban/rural location, ethnicity, size, structural complexity, and the dynamism of programs and loyalties,[3] the Sunday morning liturgies of many American Catholic churches reflect an emerging ''American way'' of doing the liturgy, even as diversity persists. Parishes have begun to model preconciliar hopes and decretal definitions. The institutional church in our day seems finally to have found its voice.

Such an overall impression, while true, is also somewhat

misleading. Radical fringe elements in music and in ritual have not really disappeared. They have simply changed location. While designated liturgical rites remain relatively normative for the average American parish, rituals rehearsed in indigenous base communities scattered around the globe and existing here and there in America have begun to presage a new social order within and beyond the church. There are rumblings beneath the surface of structured religious practice that bear a striking similarity to preconciliar disenchantment. Then and now, prophetic individuals and communities have intuitively sensed an integral relationship between the elements of authentic ritual and the way people order their lives. Then and now, music appears to function as the sign and symbol of a transformative vision experienced or proclaimed. Who we are is how we pray, and how we pray is who we are becoming.

This is essentially why we sing: to express who we are and are becoming. When Vatican II took its decisive step in the direction of a search for meaning, it boldly—albeit, no doubt, unwittingly—invited local churches to discern their culturally conditioned identity and to discover how to pray authentically and contextually. Any journey into meaning, culture, context, and self-understanding is necessarily open ended. The church in America is still in the process of becoming. Its roots are cross-culturally so complex that no one has yet been able to say exactly what it means to be an American Catholic. If we do not yet know who we are, how can we be so absolutely certain about what we ought to sing and how we ought to pray? A second-generation postconciliar church is experimenting with alternative ways of being in community and is searching for opportunities to transform the social order into a foretaste of the new creation. Its ritual and social behavior, rooted in the spirit of justice and equality, is modeling on the margins of institutional life what may one day be a legitimate expression of the Catholic church in America. Nonterritorial parishes, house churches, and alternative communities of faith and inspiration determined by gender, ethnicity, sexual orientation, broad ecumenical perspective, religious vows, or comprising other types of Catholics who feel excluded from full participation in the church, meet to discern the Word of God and make eucharist together

as they experiment with styles of leadership and participation
and with images, language, and forms. The songs that arise from
such liturgical celebrations may well be paving the way for yet
another institutional upheaval.

Although the Catholic church has moved beyond an emphasis
on reform into a condition of renewal, it has not gone far enough.
The institutional church has made significant changes but has
stopped short of a radical systemic change that would ensure
the inclusion of all of its people—women, people of color, gays
and lesbians, those who have divorced and remarried—as full
participants in the fullness of its life and meaning. Nevertheless,
once the church stepped out of its archaic past into a dynamic
present, seeds were sown for a future time of radical transformation. Those seeds are beginning to germinate; signs of
spontaneous growth are popping up all around. This may be
neither what the council fathers intended nor what seasoned
liturgists and professional musicians would even recommend,
but the worldview of the Holy Spirit often clashes with institutions and their plans.

EXPERIENCING A MUSICAL REFORMATION

Immediately after Vatican II, Catholics were inundated with
change. A rigid, inflexible, impersonal tradition suddenly
adopted a pastoral orientation, with the result that people were
caught up in the pragmatics of how-to, what-to, and when-to
do what had never been done before. Music bore the brunt of
the changes. Latin gave way to the vernacular language,
liturgical chant and classical polyphony were replaced by congregational song, musical leadership shifted in many instances from
the professional to the inexperienced, and good will replaced
credentials when it came to the dynamics of implementing the
spirit of Vatican II. Some communities of faith flourished.
Others were devastated by a sense of loss and a feeling of having
been betrayed. Hundreds of years of musical tradition were
replaced by unfamiliar pieces and by a new set of musical values.

Participation, not aesthetics, was the criterion by which one measured failure or success. Relevance, not longevity, was a primary principle informing musical selection. Local adaptation, not universality, guided the development of repertory. Individuals charged with helping the congregation find its voice asked a different set of questions, such as, Will it work?—not, Will it last?

Rites were revised to recover ancient forms that predated centuries of accretion. Ritual books were rewritten; rubrics, simplified; rules, changed. New ministries were identified and established, among these, the ministry of music. Choirs moved from the edge to the center. Women not only participated in the liturgical choir but in some cases directed it. Cantors led musically illiterate assemblies into some semblance of congregational response. Slowly repertories began to grow and, even more slowly, to become familiar.

Toward the end of this period of intense reform, further experimentation of a systemic nature was officially discouraged. Innovations were more carefully channeled to enhance, and not restructure, existing liturgical forms, and music was once again at the service of the designated rites.

For professional musicians the period of reform was a time of personal crisis, as all that they held precious seemed to be threatened with extinction. Talent, training, and years of experience were suddenly insufficient for the job. Instead, amateur musicians with folk-style songs, guitars, and enthusiastic support groups enabled an immediate realization of the council's key liturgical principle: active participation. Their less formal style and repertory encouraged people to get involved, and the sound they brought with them left a permanent mark. Eventually, however, the professionally trained again took charge of the musical agenda, and as they did so, they made friends with the participatory people's song and pushed it to new possibilities, adding genres of their own. Vocal and instrumental arrangements gave the vernacular sound a well-deserved legitimacy. Compositions proliferated, reflecting a variety of styles and forms for the congregation and the choir. Songbooks featuring individual composers, anthologies of contemporary songs, psalm settings with seasonal antiphons, and revised hymnals for congregational use are among the scores of publications that have been produced in the postconciliar years.

Yet not all are satisfied. Liturgist Mark Searle says: "The reason that Catholic congregations do not sing at Mass is not that they do not *want* to sing; it's because what they are given to sing *they do not like*."[4] Elsewhere, Searle reports:

> The church's ideal of a sung liturgy with full and active congregational participation appears most often to be realized in those parishes which provide hymnals rather than missalettes, which make careful selection of the music to be sung and which judiciously deploy the music between choir or folk group, cantor and congregation.[5]

Searle is correct in concluding that people ordinarily sing when they like the music and refuse to sing when they do not. What people like to sing, however, is not necessarily found in hymnals or in missalettes. The issues are not hymnals or missalettes but control, mainstream values, the continuity of a particular tradition over against freedom and spontaneity, an openness to the Spirit making all things new. Ironically, contemporary congregational song was born from liturgical need because traditional music was so rigid and so removed from the realities of everyday life. Yet some liturgists, particularly those with a monastic bent, long for a return to the sounds and symbols of a more reasoned rite, and they support musicians who share that view.

Decisions about what and how much people sing are based not only on liturgical criteria but also on sociological realities. The pace of reform, the depth of renewal, and the level of satisfaction among American Catholics are related to the sociological profile of the parish and conflicting models of parish identity. Today's "upwardly mobile but very heterogeneous U.S. Catholic population . . . has reached a level of educational, social, and economic development where it has all the capabilities to be a participating people" and consequently has a lot in common with the mainline confessional and sacramental Protestant population.[6] Yet these middle-class American parishes are not the only parish model.

Alongside the post–World War II generations and the post–Vatican II parishes are the working-class peoples . . . the "immigrant church" . . . educated Catholics in their 40s and 50s who . . . have a yearning for the order, the legal clarity or the devotional comfort of the church as it was—"growing up Catholic." Enough with experimentation, enough with pluralism! Back to the one way. . . . There is a sense of community in the knowledge that all around us share the same spiritual folkways and rules.[7]

The Notre Dame Study of Catholic Parish Life points out that "pluralism and heterogeneity are found not only between parishes" but also "within the same parish."[8] Some parishes are more prophetic than others, and even within a single parish there are a variety of visions. Music inevitably reflects these differences.

Sociological diversity often means pluriform perspectives on music expressed, not only in terms of genre and style, but often as a preferential bias toward either the traditional heritage or contemporary innovations. Both emphases are supported by the institutional church. While concililar documents give theological priority to a cathedral liturgy, with its attendant formality, tradition, and emphasis on transcendence, the council's pastoral challenge to cultivate and communicate a sense of community lies with the liturgy of the local parish. These two types of liturgy imply two radically different styles and conflicting expectations with regard to liturgical song.

Two streams of music, rooted in diverse theological orientations and validated by the legislation, now coexist in the Catholic Church. Both are affirmed by *Sacrosanctum concilium* and are clearly represented there. The first is promoted by chapter one in all those liturgical principles and norms that call for active participation and imply the value of pastoral song. The second is supported by chapter six and calls for a continuation of the Church's rich musical tradition, both in the preservation of its precious heritage and by transmitting its values through future compositions. Nobility and solemnity, celebrational modes more appropriate to a cathedral liturgy, and the kind of religious singing where the voices assembled ring out, are qualitative criteria that meet and clash in the average parish liturgy. Later legislation shows that these tensions

surface in regard to music quality and style. The music given
priority in chapter six has vestiges of "only the best for God." . . .
The music promoted by chapter one is music of and for the people.
It can be any style or genre and respects a culture's songs.[9]

Some musicians have helped to diffuse this conciliar dualism
by incorporating both past and present forms into their parish
music programs. Others have made peace with types of music
they once opposed and now concentrate on selecting what is
liturgically appropriate for the season and the ritual moment
and what is pastorally appropriate for those who are assembled
to sing. But even as mainline Catholicism allows itself to be
shaped by the first fruits of its internal reformation, seeds of
transformation sown by that same council, but not predicted
by it, are quietly taking root both inside and outside the parish
structure. Once again, those seeds are deeply embedded in
contemporary liturgical song. They await a nurturing environment in order to spring fully into life.

SEEDS OF TRANSFORMATION

The church in America awaits an *American Manifesto* around which
good, faithful musicians can rally and throw off the trappings of
unthinkingly monarchical and moribund liturgical music. This will
be the beginning of a new age of the Western church, because
American music, nurtured in pluralism and crafted by an ancient
faith nuanced by twentieth-century theological insight, will form
the next generations of Christians.[10]

From the fourth century onward, the church tried to control
its song through its leadership and its legislation. That control
ended officially after Vatican II, and in the view of those who
cherish tradition, everything fell apart. Professional church
people—bishops, clergy, musicians, liturgists—are by institutional definition the guardians of tradition. They control the
ritual's song and, consequently, the continuity of the tradition
in the life of the institutional church. But another revolution
is in the making.

What are the seeds of transformation that are already becoming a viable force for further systemic change in the institutional Catholic church? They are sociological and ecclesiological perspectives that are taking root in the experience of faith-filled people and are slowly but surely maturing. Central to these are (1) a change in ritual language, (2) a change in the church's foundational image and in its overall perception, and (3) a whole new experience of church. The development of all of these is related to the evolution of contemporary song.

Ritual Language

In the decades prior to Vatican II, advocates of the liturgical movement promoted the singing of Gregorian chant. Sociologically, it was an impossible task. Most members of the average American Catholic parish did not know Latin, so they refused to sing. As the problem seemed to be a matter of comprehension, liturgists lobbied for the use of the vernacular, and a change in the language of the liturgy was one of the outcomes of the council. At the same time, a new repertory developed to replace the music of the past, and most Catholics settled into the change. Some, however, did not. The use of the vernacular precipitated a new set of problems at each end of the liturgical spectrum. Supporters of the Tridentine tradition mourned the loss of the sense of mystery associated with a hieratic language that they did know and comprehend. Proponents of the vernacular were surprised to discover that the sense of the sacred that had been transmitted by traditional texts was lost to them in translation. An overwhelming experience of irrelevance and the discovery of ecclesiastical error triggered a deeper dissatisfaction among those who had advocated change. The issue was no longer textual comprehension but the content of the rite. Some pursued textual revision while others began a lengthy search for a new symbolic language and text that would speak to the pluriform, broadly inclusive reality of today.

Image of the Church

The shift in language, however, traumatic as it was for some, was not the most major innovation. A change in the foundational image or metaphor of church from *Body of Christ* to *people of God* was the paramount breakthrough, in that it heralded a paradigmatic shift from the static to the dynamic, from uniformity to unity-in-diversity, from centralization to decentralization, from rigid universal application to local and particularized adaptations. This ecclesiological change has become a seed of transformation.

Just as seeds grow in the right environment, the climate was right for the concept *people of God* and for the people themselves to grow and develop far beyond anyone's expectation. The new image affirmed individuality. Already in the early days after the council, the image undergirded the right of individuals to sing their own songs. The people felt no need for credentials or permissions. Had not the council demonstrated that the Spirit was vitally alive in our midst, surprising us all with radical new insights, speaking through unexpected channels? In this spirit of freedom that was the spirit of the sixties, the early folk singers absolutely believed that they were singing the Spirit's songs, and many others who shared that conviction sang along with them. Although institutional leaders of the church have continued to resist individuality and freedom, these seeds already have given rise to irrepressible new growth.

New Experience of Church

Thus has arisen the third of the radically new perspectives listed above: a novel experience of church itself. Ecclesiologically, the image *people of God* validated the laity as primary to the definition of *church*. Eventually, designated groups within the laity began to assert themselves, namely, the young, cultural and ethnic minorities, and those disenchanted with the system, particularly women. Bringing with them the concerns and the agendas of their world, laypeople integrated these with a newly emerging consciousness that they were the church. This shift from "going to church" to "being church" has also been a seed of transformation, as is the understanding of church as *sacramentum mundi,* a sacrament in the midst of the world and for the world, God's Word made flesh and visible now. Catholic laypeople have changed much since Vatican II, and they are still in the process of changing. They are changing not only within themselves, and consequently altering the reality of church experienced through them, but they are also affecting the institutional church, which is still uneasy with its newly inherited images and their implications. As such, the people are bound to precipitate further change.

Lay leadership and lay presence remain an unpredictable source of energy and power within American parishes. In many instances laity surpass the clergy in their understanding of issues that significantly influence the development of faith and commitment, such as human love and sexuality, gender and racial equality, family life and professional life, the economics of survival, and the politics of war and peace. The people are growing in their ability to interpret and articulate a position, and in their openness to hear divergent views, and they are claiming their place in the parish. By 1984, 83 percent of the leadership within Catholic parishes were laypersons. Shared responsibility for ministries was then and still is a fact of parish life.[11] Today, scores of priestless parishes are being administered by a layperson, while other parishes have lay associates as part of their pastoral team. Today's Catholic laity is less estranged from other Christian traditions. Through education, intermarriage, and participation in ecumenical programs, classical divisions between Catholics and Protestants have blurred. One result has been a substantial sharing of one another's music. The rich heritage of vernacular Protestant hymns is now available to American Catholics. The laypeople are also establishing among themselves communities of support and inspiration in the form of the house church or small Christian communities within or beyond the territorial parish. There they can more freely sing songs of their own choosing and test their creative and theological limits. These deeply committed and faith-based communities are significant seeds of transformation. Theologian Leonardo Boff calls them a new experience of church:

We have witnessed the creation of communities in which persons actually know and recognize one another, where they can be themselves in their individuality, where they can "have their say," where they can be welcomed by name. . . . This phenomenon exists in the church as well: grassroots Christian communities, as they are known, or basic Christian communities. . . . The laity carry forward the cause of the Gospel here, and are the vessels, the vehicles of ecclesial reality even on the level of direction and decision-making. This shift of the ecclesial axis contains, in seed, a new principle for "birthing the church," for "starting the church again" . . . a genuine "ecclesiogenesis."[12]

CULTURAL DIVERSITY

When first raised by Vatican II in its pastoral constitution on The Church in the Modern World (*Gaudium et spes*), the question of culture did not seem particularly pertinent to the church in America. Culture and the need to indigenize were considered third-world issues. But we have come to an acute awareness that American culture consists of a variety of subcultures and ethnic particularities and that the Catholic church in America is in dire need of enculturation. Prior to the council, subcultural diversity flourished in America in so-called national churches but was factored out of the ritual experience of mainline American Catholicism. The revised Roman ritual reflected a universal sameness that fit no particular culture but was intended instead to be supracultural. Ritual music was the universal church's song, not the people's song. Now authentic ritual, even in America, is understood to be rooted in culture, and it has been recognized that a variety of cultures related to age and ethnicity are what make up America. The church continues to search for ways to incorporate into its liturgical expression some of the characteristics of its cultural diversity. The most persistent examples stem from the demands of various age groups, as well as from ethnic and racial minorities.

Children, particularly the very young and teenagers, have their own culture. The church has been liturgically sensitive to its young ones. As early as 1973 the United States' bishops issued a *Directory for Masses with Children,* suspending a number of its regulations in order to accommodate children. However, it has been far less sensitive to the particular needs of teenagers. Parents often complain that their teen-aged children stay away from the liturgy because it has little meaning for them. The world of today's teenager is very different from the world of the past, and many teenagers have little patience with what they feel are archaic sounds or old-fashioned forms. What was radical music to our generation is past history to young people today, yet the principle of incorporating appropriate secular music still remains relevant. Secular songs of the sixties and seventies found their way into experimental liturgies and were sacred to those who espoused them. The generation that canonized Bob Dylan, Peter, Paul, and Mary, and a host of other secular composers should not deny the youth of today their own secular/sacred songs. Today's sound is the sound not exclusively, but certainly, of a chaotic world—loud, intense, rhythmic, with a hard, driving beat. And some of the texts are acceptable. Our youth are questioning our supposedly more enlightened understanding of *musica sacra* and challenging our definitions of sacred and secular song. Not to include their expressions in the collective voice of tradition is to suggest once again that culturally specific and time-conditioned forms have no liturgical or pastoral possibility. Even more tragic is the silencing yet another time of the voice and the creativity of some of the people of God. Today's youth can certainly learn to share and even love repertories different from their own, but not if the church categorically denies the validity of their own experience in its sacramental rites, especially in its music.

The concerns of ethnic and racial groups are critical to any consideration of culture. African-Americans, Hispanics, Asians, and Native Americans are just a few of the groups seeking a liturgical identity. Here again the people of God bring with them the agendas of the world in which they live. The scars of second-class status, poverty, lack of opportunity, and discrimination drive African-American Catholics to remain attuned to their collective struggle for liberation, first of all as African-Americans with a shared social and political agenda, secondarily as Catholic Christians. "Were you there when they crucified my Lord?" they sing. Where? In Selma. Harlem. Soweto. "We shall overcome," they sang back in the turbulent sixties, and they continue to sing today. We shall overcome all forms of racial discrimination, in the world and in the church. African-Americans bring an authentically American musical tradition of spirituals sung into life by the slaves of society and religion, as well as a repertory of Gospel music that has given rise to some of America's best secular genres, notably jazz and the blues. People of this rich heritage are looking for these culturally conditioned sounds in their liturgical life as well.

Hispanic Catholics, a minority moving quickly toward the majority, have an invisible status as far as the liturgy is concerned. They, too, are beginning to find their voice and are starting to demand their own distinctive sound—not simply songs translated into Spanish, but truly Hispanic music arising out of their creative midst. While there have been some efforts to meet their cultural needs, no obvious, organized plan integrates their influence into the mainstream.

Likewise, the art and experience of Asian and Native American cultures must be taken into account. The music of all people who make up North America, once validated, must enrich and energize our shared liturgical life. Emphasis on culture plants a seed of transformation. Popular culture is surely "a theological place—the locale in which one may encounter God."[13]

> If one believes . . . that people are sacraments of God, that God discloses Himself/Herself to us through the objects, events, and persons of life, then one must concede the possibility that in the sacramentality of ordinary folk, their hopes, their fears, their aspirations represent a legitimate experience of God, legitimate symbols of God, and legitimate stories of God.[14]

Opening up our rites to receive the gifts of other cultures means making our church big enough to embrace all of God's people. It means taking seriously our belief that the church is the people's church. It means opening ourselves to the Spirit, welcoming one another's aesthetic, and not dismissing what we do not understand.

INSIDERS AND OUTSIDERS: THE COMING RADICALIZATION OF THE NORM

Among the disenchanted who are part of parish liturgy are persons sensitive to forces of oppression and deeply concerned about social justice. They are one in spirit with the people of other nations who are struggling for liberation, and they are aware that third-world Christians, particularly those in base communities, have done a better job of integrating their agendas for justice with their liturgical life. For example, the Nicaraguan Mass, *La Misa campesina nicaraguense* by Carlos Mejia Godoy sings to "a God who sweats in the street . . . the worker God, the worker Christ." The entrance song says of God: "You stand in line in the camp so that they may pay you your wage. And you even protest for justice when they don't give you enough to eat." The Kyrie cries out: "Identify yourself with us, *Christo Jesus,* not with the oppressive class that squeezes and devours the community, but with the oppressed."[15] South African freedom songs offer similar illustrations of the integration of spirituality, justice, and liturgy. American liturgical music often lacks the honesty and the intensity of third-world songs of justice because American liturgy has denied victims of injustice their voice. Music that derives from middle-class values sings at best *about* the poor or on behalf of the poor but does not begin from the poor person's perspective. It rarely sings of justice with any specificity.

Secular songwriters and performers have stirred the consciences of many in the world and even within the church, supporting human rights issues and giving impetus to agendas for social justice within the Catholic church.[16] In 1984–1985, when it became known that famine threatened to decimate Ethiopia, rock stars sang the world to concerted action while the churches continued to sing in their separate assemblies, unable or unwilling to coalesce their own global constituencies in a similar way.[17] In 1986 alone, rock stars rallied on behalf of the hungry in Africa; the homeless, farmers, and AIDS victims in America; the anti-apartheid movement in South Africa; and the imprisoned around the globe. Contemporary musicians sang of the sanctuary movement, while some worshipers gathered in their sanctuaries and sang comfortable songs.

Clearly, it is not easy to change liturgical structures or influence the texts of ritual song. Some determined Catholics, dedicated to the vision of the gospel, continue to sing their liberation songs and to proclaim equity and equality on the margins of the church's designated rites. Women, for example, meet as women-church and sing Carolyn McDade's "Coming Out of Exile," Holly Near's "We Are a Gentle, Angry People," M. T. Winter's "A New Day Dawns." Women and men together struggle to overcome the homelessness, hunger, and poverty that stalk the streets of our nation's cities as they sing South African freedom songs: "We shall not give up the fight, we have only started"; "Freedom is coming, oh yes, I know. . . . O God give us power and make us fearless, O God give us power, because we need it."[18]

Together with a number of rock, folk, country, Gospel, and other secular music superstars, church people committed to social justice are convinced that the arbitrary line between the sacred and the secular needs to be erased. Two points are becoming clear: first, if the institutional church is to be an effective presence in the world, it must become more actively involved in the pain and suffering of the world; second, that kind of radical realignment of priorities and programs will happen only if we sing and pray about it together. Such a shift is critical for the well-being of the church as well as for the well-being of God's disadvantaged people. Noted sociologist Robert Bellah, coauthor of *Habits of the Heart,* said in his 1990 address to the American bishops:

> If the church is to be the church, it must not only practice its beliefs within the community, it must show forth what they imply for the larger society, not to coerce acceptance and not to be swept up into activism at the expense of spirituality, but to hold up an alter-

native vision of reality, to give witness to what, as best we can discern it, God is saying to the world today.[19]

The church must learn to integrate its experience of the world into the core of its sung prayer and praise. Justice-oriented individuals are pushing the church to rethink its militaristic images in light of its pursuit of peace and its symbols of abundance in a world of abject poverty and overwhelming need. A propensity to focus on other-worldly emphases; an avoidance of current issues and idioms, notably in liturgical texts, exclusive language, images, and practices: these are no longer acceptable in an institution that defines itself in terms of its people. Some ecclesiastics see these concerns as just so much political turbulence, signifying nothing, at least in religious terms. Those committed to justice see things differently and many feel that music is an agent of social change.

Jacques Attali associates music with power and speaks of "three strategic usages of music by power":

> Music is used and produced in the ritual in an attempt to make people *forget* the general violence. . . . It is employed to make people *believe* in the harmony of the world. . . . It serves to *silence,* by mass-producing a deafening, syncretic kind of music, and censoring all other human noises. Make people Forget, make them Believe, Silence them. In all three cases, music is a tool of power.[20]

Catholics are well aware of music used as a bureaucratic power to silence the opposition. For fifteen centuries liturgical legislation tried to keep music under tight ecclesiastical control. Why control the music? Because music has always been perceived as power—power to liberate or to enslave, power to shape the minds and hearts of the participating community. To lose control of the music is to lose control of the people. "We will become what you sing of us Tortuga!" So writes Rudolfo Anaya in his liberation novel, *Tortuga.* "Isn't that great! To become what you will make us in your songs!" The official church has finally relinquished its determination to legislate its music. Those committed to justice know that we can now sing the new world into being. It has been done before, and it can be done again. What we sing is what we will become.

The unrelenting persistence of women to speak and be heard signifies change. For women, music is indeed an agent of revolution. Women sang "I Am Suffragette" (1867) as they marched for the right to vote; "Bread and Roses" (now considered traditional) as they struggled to survive the injustices surrounding female labor at the beginning of this century; and more recently Judy Small's "Mothers, Daughters, Wives" (1984) as a protest against our propensity for war. Today a growing number of women are translating all songs into inclusive language and addressing God in female imagery, as *Bakerwoman, Mother, Shechinah*. More and more women are beginning to believe that what is sung will one day come to pass.

In her introduction to the field of women, music, and culture, Ellen Kossoff insists that "we must also begin to address the valuative role music plays in defining and reflecting established social and sexual orders and in acting as an agent in maintaining or changing such orders."[21] Bruno Nettl notes that the world of music is heavily weighted toward male musical practices and suggests that "this may result from the dominant role of men in determining approaches and methods."[22] Not only music is male-oriented. The exclusive patriarchal structures, rites, images, language, and general practices of the Catholic church are pushing many women toward more congenial communities, such as women-church and similar feminist collectives where they can find and express themselves without fear of intimidation or discrimination. Carol Robertson speaks of "social and ritual repertoires appropriate to the needs of women in transition" that are part of emerging cultures within complex societies: "As women's groups move from their culture of birth to their culture of choice they must recast notions of *value* that undergird musical interpretation, organizational styles, and habits of interaction."[23]

Women remain an oppressed group within institutional Catholicism, and liturgical ritual perpetuates that oppression. Women know from experience that "the *kinds* of power that exist within a social setting and the ways in which they are assigned to each gender establish order,''[24] and that ritual prayer and song confirm the established social order within the church. If, as Robertson states and many others would agree, ''women perform to create a catharsis of the spirit, both for themselves and their communities,''[25] then the Catholic reformation of this century has not been nearly receptive enough to women's intrinsic song. Many women who remain part of the institutional church are courageously defecting in place, forming the nucleus of the Spirit church which struggles to bring about an ecclesiological transformation, so that ageism, racism, sexism, classism, cultural discrimination and all other forms of patriarchal oppression will no longer be perpetuated by the forms and the content of the liturgy and its music. Such ecclesiological dissatisfaction is a multifaceted seed of transformation.

MUSIC: A CONTEMPORARY SACRAMENT

The Second Vatican Council enabled the Catholic church to open its windows to the Spirit and its doors to the world. Together the Spirit and the world broke down some of the walls separating Catholics from other people. Today the Spirit-church in the midst of the world and the institutional church on the margins of the world are trying to build a new structure together, a sacramental structure deeply rooted in both the sacred and the secular and therefore capable of bridging both realities. In biblical song the sacred and the secular have always been integral to one another, and in incarnational terms, they are one. Now contemporary song is testing the possibilities of recovering such a systemic integration.

Prior to the council, the liturgical focus was on the song itself, as legislation tried to protect the sacral quality of a designated repertory. Shortly after the council, when attention focused primarily on the act of singing, much energy went into facilitating the active participation of assemblies and, to some extent, cantors and choirs. More recently, the focus has shifted to the singers and the quality of their response. Music can be, and often is, a vehicle of personal and social transformation when the singer, the song, and the singing are inseparable, just as the proclamation of the Word, the proclaimer of that Word, and the very act of proclaiming were one Spirit-filled reality in the church of the New Testament. What was true of the *kerygma* can also be true of song, and such an integration is clearly sacramental.

To achieve this integration, we must be more concerned about the spirit and the meaning of what we are singing, more sensitive to its impact on the celebrating community, and less literal about preserving and transmitting the tradition (e.g., biblical and liturgical texts). We must also be as concerned about the quality of integration within the individual and the assembly as we are about the quality of the composition and its rendition. Grace truly abounds when the singer, the song, and the singing are one. Such integral harmony is a genuinely kerygmatic and, without doubt, a sacramental experience.

The conciliar effort to link liturgical ritual to its biblical tradition was, and still is, a turning point for liturgical music. The biblical psalm is the key to this transformation. We have not felt its transformative power because we have misunderstood the nature of the psalms and their primary message to us from their situation in the canon. The biblical psalms were songs of life before they were sacred songs, songs of the people in all their rugged humanity and in all their human secularity. Too often we have denied their secularity, editing them to fit our assumptions of what sacred songs should be. We will not allow secular songs to penetrate our praise. We have arbitrarily redefined these ancient songs of praise and then, on the basis of our redefinition, we have denied the entry of similar secular praise songs—chants, hymns, spirituals, Gospel, folk and folk-style songs—into our liturgical rites, thereby limiting our own access to ourselves and to God. In the cultic laments, curses, songs of trust, hymns of praise and thanksgiving that comprise the biblical psalter, the sacred and the secular, the word of God and the people of God merged through the medium of music. The astounding truth is that the inclusion of these songs of the people in the canon says to us that such songs can be sacred. We must learn to worry less about preserving the cult and our cultic traditions and more about affirming channels for God's word to permeate our culture.

For fifteen centuries the Catholic church told its people what to sing or not to sing as it legislated them into silence. The council's most radical action was to liberate its people and, perhaps inadvertently, give credence to their song. Once the people began to sing, the church could no longer designate the song, for the sound of people singing in the churches meant that some of the people some of the time would be singing their own songs.

Musically, socially, and liturgically, the Catholic church in America has moved from uniformity through diversity toward pluriformity; from adaptation toward indigenization; from reformation toward transformation. One day it may recognize that two streams of music emerging from Vatican II are really one, single, Spirit-inspired response arising from the people of God. Both the professional song and the popular song, the traditional repertory and contemporary compositions, are part of the church's precious heritage. Both modes of expression are, or can be, artistic. All song is the people's song. Some of the people are professional musicians, some of the professionals and nonprofessionals are artists who from time to time push human creativity to its limits and reveal to us a piece of ourselves we had never known before. The capacity to create truly sacramental music that liberates, integrates, and transforms individuals and society is a God-given gift. It can come from anyone, anywhere. It belongs to no single culture, nor does it require a particular style. When the song is the individual's best effort, when the singing is the community's best effort, then the best is still given to God. In fewer than twenty-five years, Catholic church music in America has undergone a paradigm shift in aesthetics, rendition, and theological understanding. What remains the same are its capacities to be a vehicle of prayer and praise and to call out in a prophetic voice within the tradition. The essentials have not changed.

NOTES

Copyright Medical Mission Sisters, 1992.
1. *The People's Hymnal* (World Library, 1955); *Our Parish Prays*

and Sings (1958); and the Psalms and Canticles set by Joseph Gelineau (1955–1956) were popular resources.

2. Pius X, *Tra le sollecitudini, motu proprio* on the restoration of church music, 22 November 1903, article 13.

3. "U.S. Parishes Today," the first report of the Notre Dame Study of Catholic Parish Life, *Origins* 14 (27 December 1984): 461.

4. Mark Searle, past-president of the North American Academy of Liturgy, is cited by Linda Clark of Boston University School of Theology in report 1 of her *Music in Churches Project* (27 June 1990), p. 1.

5. "Report on Parish Liturgical Celebrations," Notre Dame Study of Catholic Parish Life, *Origins* 15 (31 October 1985): 340.

6. "Who Participates in Local Communities?" Notre Dame Study of Catholic Parish Life, *Origins* 15 (13 June 1985): 51.

7. Ibid.

8. Ibid.

9. Miriam Therese Winter, *Why Sing? Toward a Theology of Catholic Church Music* (Washington, D.C., 1984), pp. 240–41.

10. Rory Cooney, "American Liturgical Music: Toward a Manifesto," *Modern Liturgy* 17 (October 1990): 23.

11. "U.S. Parishes Today," Notre Dame Study (1984), p. 465.

12. Leonardo Boff, *Ecclesiogenesis* (Maryknoll, N.Y., 1986), pp. 1–2.

13. Andrew Greeley, *God in Popular Culture* (Chicago, 1988), p. 9.

14. Ibid., p. 17.

15. Published by the Ministry of Culture, Managua, Nicaragua.

16. A partial list of the many whose music does more than entertain and may be potentially sacred because of its meaning and message would include the following performers and composers: Peter, Paul, and Mary; Joan Baez; Bob Dylan; Pete Seeger; Paul Simon; Harry Chapin; John Denver; Bruce Springsteen; John Cougar Mellencamp; U2; Tracy Chapman; Rosa Marta Zárata Macias; Mercedes Sosa; Sylvio Rodriquez; Pablo Milanes; Sara González; Victor Jarra; Sweet Honey in the Rock; Joan Armatrading; Aretha Franklin; Richie Havens; Ladysmith Black Mambazo; Holly Near; Pat Benatar; Cris Williamson; Meg Christian.

17. Cf. British rock star Bob Geldof's Band Aid and his consciousness-raising Christmas carol (1984); USA for Africa and "We Are the World," written by Lionel Richie and Michael Jackson and recorded by a cast of superstars (1985); fund-raising concerts such

as Live Aid, Farm Aid, Amnesty International's "Conspiracy of Hope" (1986); Human Rights Now! (1988).

18. From "Freedom Is Coming: Songs of Protest and Praise from South Africa," traditional songs collected and edited by Anders Nyberg (Uppsala, 1984; distributed in the United States by Walton Music Corporation).

19. "Leadership Viewed From the Vantage Point of American Culture," *Origins* 20 (13 September 1990): p. 223.

20. Jacques Attali, *Noise: The Political Economy of Music* (Minneapolis, 1985), p. 19.

21. Ellen Koskoff, ed., *Women and Music in Cross-Cultural Perspective* (New York, 1987), p. 15.

22. Bruno Nettl, *The Study of Ethnomusicology* (Urbana, 1983), pp. 334–35.

23. Carol Robertson, "Power and Gender in the Musical Experiences of Women," in Ellen Koskoff, ed., *Women and Music* (New York, 1987), p. 241.

24. Ibid., p. 244.

25. Ibid.

Present Stress
and Current Problems:
Music and the Reformed Churches

HORACE T. ALLEN, JR.

The ecclesial scope or "space" with which this essay intends to speak in both a historical and an analytical way is often described as "mainline Protestantism." More specifically, however, because of its subject matter, the definition may be narrowed to refer to the psalm- and hymn-singing traditions as they developed out of the Calvinist churches of northern Europe and Great Britain. This could be taken to embrace the Lutheran and Anglican traditions as well, if only because psalmody and hymnody have always functioned in an ecumenical way. The significant difference lies in the fact that these latter two traditions have always used psalms and hymns in the context of a relatively fixed, often printed, rite; but for most of the Calvinist churches, which have eschewed liturgical books, these sung texts have functioned very much as the rite itself. In keeping with my experience, therefore, I shall emphasize the psalmody and hymnody of Geneva, Scotland, and England, which formed much of the American Protestant experience of church music.

My basic argument proposes a kind of theological "road map" whereby these traditions weave together ethics and aesthetics with considerable complementarity, especially at the point of sacred song. This relationship has been succinctly explained by Paul Lehmann in a recent article in *Reformed Liturgy and Music*, "Praying and Doing Justly": "What liturgy and its music are all about has to do with what it takes to be fully human."[1] And, he says, when he refers to the word *liturgy:*

As far as Christian faith and obedience are concerned, the focus and context of liturgy are etymologically and theologically political. This is the case whether liturgy is understood in the narrower sense of the musical elements of divine worship, or in the broader sense of the verbal elements of worship which include the Creed, the Prayers, the Proclamation of the Word. *Praying and doing justly are intrinsically reciprocal to the integrity of faith and obedience in both senses of liturgical understanding and action.*[2]

He then identifies the relationship of prayer and faith in its ecclesial and civic contexts by reference to Calvin:

How central politics are to the liturgical calling is instructively confirmed by Calvin's account of the relation between faith and prayer and between prayer and "the external means or supports by which God in Christ invites us into fellowship (*societatem*) with them and preserves us in the same (*in ea retinet*)." Faith, according to Calvin, is the "principal work of the Spirit"; prayer is the principal exercise of faith"; and the external means or supports are "the true church" (*vera ecclesia*) and "civil government" (*administratio politica*). Accordingly, the doing of the Spirit, the doing of faith, and the doing of justice are the marks of the integrity of Christian faith and obedience. They identify the messianic reality and meaning of the presence of Jesus of Nazareth in and over human affairs.[3]

This perspective provides us with a touchstone for analyzing not only the strength, but also the most painful weaknesses, in contemporary Reformed experience as it seeks to relate ethics and aesthetics. That touchstone is the significance and congruence in the Reformed understanding of the church as ordered congregation, with the civic, political order. In Calvin's Geneva, Knox's Scotland, Puritan New England, *and* Wesleyan "meetings" and "societies," the phenomenon of corporate song was symbolically central to the ordering of human life, personally and socially.

So let us look at that song in these historically interrelated traditions for further and more detailed clues to the current social stance of these communities. The place of liturgical song in these traditions is most clearly expressed by that eminent divine and theologian, the late Karl Barth of Basel. In volume 4 of his *Church Dogmatics,* wherein he undertakes to define and describe the various ministries of the Christian community, he identifies as first and foremost, "our office to praise God."[4] He describes praise this way:

> The praise of God which constitutes the community and its assemblies seeks to bind and commit and therefore to be expressed, to well up and be sung in concert. The Christian community sings. It is not a choral society. Its singing is not a concert. But from inner, material necessity it sings. Singing is the highest form of human expression. It is to such supreme expression that the *vox humana* is devoted in the ministry of the Christian community. It is for this that it is liberated in this ministry. . . .
>
> What we can and must say quite confidently is that the community which does not sing is not the community. And where it cannot sing in living speech, or only archaically in repetition of the modes and texts of the past; where it does not really sing but sighs and mumbles spasmodically, shamefacedly and with an ill grace, it can be at best only a troubled community which is not sure of its cause and of whose ministry and witness there can be no great expectation. In these circumstances it has every reason to pray that this gift which is obviously lacking or enjoyed only in sparing measure will be granted afresh and more generously lest all the other members suffer. The praise of God which finds its concrete culmination in the singing of the community is one of the indispensable basic forms of the ministry of the community.[5]

Clearly then, if Lehmann, Barth, and Calvin can be relied on to represent the Reformed tradition, it can hardly be maintained (as has been done) that this community of faith is antiaesthetic. Its severity and conscientiousness at this point must be read as sincere attempts to preserve, not to reject, the personal and corporate power of communal song.

The only further point of detail that needs mention by way of explicating the aesthetic conservatism of this tradition is to note the source of the texts for that song: that ancient collection of prayer and praise which has been so central to both Jewish and Christian worship, the psalter (as well as certain New Testament canticles in Christian churches), which Eric Werner describes as "the greatest legacy of the Synagogue to Jewish Christianity and then to the Gentile Church."[6] So says Calvin, in his "Articles Concerning the Organization of the Church and of Worship at Geneva" (1537):

> On the other hand there are the psalms which we desire to be sung in the Church, as we have it exemplified in the ancient Church and in the evidence of Paul himself, who says it is good to sing in the congregation with mouth and heart. We are unable to compute the profit and edification which will arise from this, except after having experimented. Certainly as things are, the prayers of the faithful are so cold, that we ought to be ashamed and dismayed. The psalms can incite us to lift our hearts to God and move us to an ardour in invoking and exalting with praises the glory of his Name. Moreover it will be thus appreciated of what benefit and consolation the pope and those that belong to him have deprived the Church; for he has reduced the psalms, which ought to be true spiritual songs, to a murmuring among themselves without any understanding.
>
> This manner of proceeding seemed specially good to us, that children, who beforehand have practised some modest church song, sing in a loud distinct voice, the people listening with all attention and following heartily what is sung with the mouth, till all become accustomed to sing communally.[7]

James Hastings Nichols, Princeton's able chronicler of Reformed worship, perceptively notes that

> in classical Reformed worship the "liturgy" in the strict sense, the people's part, was all *sung*. It is not the spoken prayers, taken by the minister, but the sung liturgy of the people which must be studied in the first instance to comprehend the meaning of early Reformed worship.[8]

Nichols suggests that the power and enduring shape of this metrical psalmody related to its simplicity as song, its comprehensiveness as psalter, and its particular hermeneutical assumptions about the Hebrew Scriptures by Calvinism:

The Old Testament and the psalms were to be read Christologically and as prophetic of the life of the church. Political and cultic references in the psalms that to a modern congregation seem archaic and irrelevant were at once understood by the 16th-century Reformed Church to be metaphorical prophetic allusion to her own life. . . . The Reformed sense of the church was particularly close of course, to the Hebraic view of an elect people. . . . As the staple of private and family worship as well as of the services of the church, the psalms became known to many by heart. No other book of the Old Testament, at least, could rival the psalms in the affections and knowledge of Reformed [laity]. Ministers frequently preached from the psalms also; the psalter was the only Old Testament book on which Calvin preached on Sundays.[9]

In conclusion, says Nichols, "to know and love the psalms was the mark of a [Reformed] Protestant."[10]

It certainly was also the mark of that extraordinary Calvinist, Congregationalist exercise in political theology which was Puritan New England. A Unitarian pastor in Chestnut Hill, Massachusetts, in his 1980 Minns Lecture, "The New England Way and Vatican II," reminded his audience at the First and Second Church, Boston, that

In New England we have one of the richest, if not the richest, heritages of psalmody in this land. Putting the tunes and translations of Plymouth and Massachusetts Bay together, we have the very best of metrical psalmody. But the Psalms have been suppressed in our worship to an appalling degree. . . . That is the crying shame not only when you consider the way the Psalms were sung . . . but when you consider the revival of psalmody that the *Liturgical Constitution* of Vatican II sparked.[11]

Joseph Bassett concludes:

For these New Englanders the Biblical Word was the language the People of God spoke. Thus, when they faced an issue in their personal or religious life, they didn't read the Bible as a law book. They read it for the wisdom which their forebears passed on to them out of their experience. The seventeenth-century New Englander's ability to range over Biblical texts and tie into the earlier experiences of God's People is based on their sensitivity to Scripture as first and foremost the language of their community. I would hope that we might learn to take up the melody of the Biblical Word from them.[12]

Now finally, as we assemble these bits and pieces of Reformed experience, let us welcome the Methodists aboard. For them, as for Calvinists and Puritans, the creation of a body of corporate song, biblically based, became the critical step in shaping piety *and* in energizing a serious measure of social change. The commitment of the Methodists in England to address the corruptions and injustices of the establishment and of the developing industrial revolution, was quickly matched by an equally impressive and extensive program of evangelizing and "humanizing" (to come back to Paul Lehmann's word) the American frontier. For this latter purpose Wesley's 1784 prayer book was seen to be useless, but he himself, perhaps unwittingly, provided a replacement for it: his own body of biblical song, which in intention and practice breathed the same air as the older psalmody, as did the Watts' oeuvre, which became a matter of considerable controversy among the Calvinists.

With this much of a historical picture before us, and taking due notice of the obvious fact that the corporate song of these traditions became their "prayer book," we may now turn to current Reformed experience to analyze the present configuration of ethics and aesthetics, that is, the congruence, if there be any, between "praying and doing justly."

That congruence was perhaps most succinctly stated by John Calvin when, in book 4 of the *Institutes* he summarized the Reformed cult in terms of four stages: "the Word, prayer, the dispensation of the Supper and alms."[13] Not only is there a balance of word and sacrament, but also the balance of proclamation and response as in the pairings of word and prayer; sacrament and alms. This is the cultic secret that is essential to the larger balance of praying and doing justly, or, to use the word-play much favored by George MacLeod of the Iona Community, the connection between *cult* and *culture*. However well or poorly the Puritans, Presbyterians, and Methodists endeavored to shape

their respective societies by reference to their cultic song, they
were committed to such an enterprise. Cultic song and cultural
shape were meant to interpenetrate one another, even though
the models might be as disparate as theocracy on the one hand
or counterculture on the other. The question is: What has
happened to this conviction on the way to the twentieth century?
And, of course: What is next?

Returning to Calvin's description of faith and prayer we may
observe that in several ways, for these Reformed communities
we have identified, crucial shifts have occurred in the content
of that faith and prayer, and at the same time, certain aspects
of the so-called external supports for that prayer have been overtaken by alien traditions of piety and praise that have robbed
the traditions of their distinctive cultic patterns, thus opening
them to cultural accommodation rather than to witness. What
are those shifts and alien patterns of prayer? And what resources
are available to Reformed churches today to equip them for a
genuinely evangelical encounter with a culture that, if anything,
is more violently post-Christian and secularist than ever before
on the American continent?

The most important theological shift that happened in these
Reformed communities was the loss of a commitment to the
ordering of society's life in favor of an increasing concern for
individual salvation. The whole pattern of the Calvinist Great
Awakening (mid–eighteenth century), the Methodist frontier
evangelism (late eighteenth century into the nineteenth century)
and the nineteenth-century revivals (beginning in New York
state) all contributed to the kind of individualistic understanding
of redemption that stripped much of Reformed Christianity of
its social agenda except in narrowly defined areas such as
temperance and Sabbath observance. Interestingly, some forceful
figures on the scene saw what was happening. Such a person
was the Presbyterian, Lyman Beecher, who, in the early nineteenth century found himself deeply suspicious of his evangelistic
friends Finney and the Methodists, for this very reason. One
of Beecher's biographers, James Fraser, puts it this way:

> The Methodists accused Beecher of meddling in politics. But
> Beecher and the northern evangelists like him could not keep out

of politics. They were attempting to build the kingdom, and that was a political proposition.

And probably more than Beecher realized, the real problem was that he continued to the end to view the coming kingdom as the New England town purified and refined and spread across the continent.[14]

Whether or not our social vision requires the pure New England Commonwealth, we may be able to understand, especially from the standpoint of a Calvinist reading of the Hebrew Scriptures (as previously noted), that a messianic reading of history (whether eschatological or not) includes social and political history. Surely a measure of how far Calvinist churches have fallen from such a vision is the widespread astonishment among their members today that those churches should, from time to time, make ethical pronouncements on such national and international subjects as nuclear war, the economy, apartheid, abortion, sexuality, and other issues of public concern. The same might be said of the Methodist churches, while noting also that they are still trying to recover that unique symbol and source of social, political ecclesial reality, the local disciplinary, class meeting.

In short, "doing justly" came to be very narrowly defined so that the churches involved were increasingly subject to acculturation and cooptation by the prevailing preoccupations of society. An American "established religion" was being formed that only dimly recognized its social and political conscience.

Further, a chaplaincy-like relation to culture blunted the religion's ability to critique national and political idolatries. Some Presbyterians will recall the astonishment with which their church greeted the prophetic challenge to McCarthyism in the early 1950s as expressed in their (then) Moderator's "Letter to Presbyterians" (President John A. Mackay of Princeton Seminary).

And it is now clear in the 1990s that these churches' constituencies by no means approved or supported the commitment of the leadership, bureaucratic or elected, to the various social challenges of the Civil Rights or anti–Vietnam War movements.

Thus these churches are increasingly being encouraged by conservative elements within, and by their own declining numbers,
to resort to that antipole of corporate ethical and aesthetic
expression: *evangelism* (as having to do not with corporate worship or social witness but with the salvation of individual souls).
This late twentieth-century development, however, may be seen
to have significant *liturgical* roots in the nineteenth century when
the churches lost their unique liturgy, that powerful corpus of
psalter and biblical song, with its distinctive music. Unlike
Roman Catholics, Anglicans, Orthodox, or Lutherans, this was
their liturgy *and* their systematic and almost sacramental connection to the Bible. They had neither lectionary nor fixed liturgy
to keep the biblical language, metaphors, and assumptions
resonating among them. With the ascendancy of pietistic "hymns
of human composure" and the adoption of ever more sentimental
music, the reformist and messianic spirit evaporated. What was
left was a religion of personal feelings and occasional attempts
to modify public behavior. For that enterprise one needs ardor,
to be sure, but not order. Furthermore, with the loss of the
Reformed churches' moorings in the Hebrew Scriptures and
its psalmody, even Jews became estranged sinners, fit subjects
for evangelization along with the rest of non-Christian humanity,
in the eyes of these communities. Happily, Karl Barth has
challenged that arrogance with his tart observation that

> in relation to the Synagogue there can be no real question of
> "mission" or of bringing the Gospel. It is thus unfortunate to speak
> of Jewish mission. The Jew who is conscious of his Judaism and
> takes it seriously can only think that he is misunderstood and
> insulted when he hears this term. And the community has to see
> that he is materially right.[15]

This whole point is reinforced when we recall that however much
Reformed churches have been enriched by their greatly expanded
hymnody, it has unfortunately been at the expense of their
commitment to psalmody. That loss is nowhere so clearly and
pathetically illustrated than in the epidemic among us these days
of greeting the people of God at the beginning of their Lord's
Day assembly, not with a sentence from the Scriptures or a full

Psalm-introit, but with the sad, weak, and culturally bound expression, "Good morning."

The argument here is not to renounce hymns and modern music but to recover the psalms and their appropriate music, of various styles. Happily, this is beginning to happen. The new hymnals of the Presbyterian Church (USA), the United Methodist Church, the Christian Reformed Church, and the Reformed Church of America all include definable sections of psalmody: metrical, responsorial, antiphonal, and responsive (spoken). Further, the renewed use, by the churches that have published these books, of a comprehensive Lord's Day lectionary, usually the *Common Lectionary,*[16] provides a systematic way of using the psalms, week by week.

This development, the widespread use by non–prayer book churches of a lectionary system, is perhaps the most important single result of at least three decades of ecumenical liturgical renewal, triggered largely by the impact of the liturgical reforms of the Second Vatican Council as mandated in its document, *Sacrosanctum Concilium.*[17] That the churches of the Reformations of the sixteenth, seventeenth, and eighteenth centuries should turn to a lectionary table that is based largely on the Roman church's *Ordo Lectionum Missae* (1969),[18] like *Common Lectionary,* is the most astonishing and hopeful ecumenical manifestation that could be imagined. Because of this revolution, how Scriptures are being used, liturgically and homiletically, Protestant preaching is becoming more exegetical, more ecumenical, and more integrally related to the Christian calendar than has been so for centuries. And in terms of the subject of this essay, with this shift in the use of the Scriptures in public worship it is now possible for parish minister and musician to work well ahead in planning instrumental music, choral music, and hymns. At last it is possible for Protestant worship to be truly and fully based in the scriptural material for the day according to an essentially christological calendar comprising a sequence of Sundays during whch the synoptic Gospels are read "in course" (ordinary time, being the Sundays after Epiphany and Pentecost), and two cycles of Sundays revolving around, respectively, Christmas and Easter. This, too, has

become an important agendum for the new hymnals that have
been appearing in the last decade. Perhaps these two movements
of psalmody and calendar/lectionary-based hymnody represent
an effective reversal of the process whereby the Reformed
churches lost the peculiar body of song which was for them
the liturgical-aesthetic opening to social ethics.

A broader liturgical question opens up at this point. Just as
Paul Lehmann suggested that in Reformed churches, *liturgy* can
be understood in a narrow sense as referring only to "the musical
elements" or in a broader sense that includes creed, prayers,
and proclamation, we might, in concluding this essay, propose
an even wider definition that includes ritual gesture, ceremony,
action, space, and atmosphere. This might, on the face of it,
sound strange in a strictly Reformed context. Nevertheless, it
is precisely the cultural context of North American Christianity
that should give some pause for thought to the Calvinist churches
with their inherited liturgical austerity. Whether or not the increasing popularity of so-called charismatic churches, with their
simple but compelling liturgies of song, gesture, and participation, is to be regarded as an important cultural-ecclesial
phenomenon, the increasingly powerful, violent, and virulent
secularism of our day surely beckon "mainline Protestant"
churches to forms of religious and pious expression that they
had, for all sorts of historical reasons, rejected. I cannot possibly
express this better than has a colleague, Bruce Rigdon, just a
few years ago in a conference on worship at Lindenwood College, St. Charles, Missouri; his remarks were reported in the
pages of the Presbyterian journal, *Reformed Liturgy and Music:*

> Let's talk about culture for a moment. Calvin lived and worked
> in a religious culture. He was surrounded by symbols, too many
> symbols he thought, that informed everything everybody did and
> thought. It was the enormous accomplishment of medieval culture,
> like the cathedral. And in this mass of religious influences and
> movements, Calvin discerned that it was necessary to purify.
> Hence, he pushed aside all kinds of things, took all sorts of things
> out of the church in order to focus the eyes of the people of God
> on what Calvin believed to be the central symbols, the powerful
> symbols of the Gospel.

My dear friends, you and I live not in a religious culture, but in the most secular culture the world has ever seen. Our problem is *not* that the atmosphere in our culture is loaded with powerful religious symbols that need to be cleansed. Our problem is that it is a desert out there. Thus, for the same reason that Calvin had to purify symbolic life in order to empower it, we must do the opposite in order to be as faithful as Calvin was. Ours is the task of allowing religious symbols to be born and to stir us and to become powerful among us and, in the long run, to recognize that the task given us is overwhelming. It is the conversion of a violent and pagan culture in which our children are called to grow up. We live in a culture which powerfully tells everybody moment by moment in all forms of media that God is absent from the world, that the world is not God's but belongs to us, and we are entitled to do anything with it that we deem suitable. So secularization, if that is the right word for it, creates for us a very different context than the one in which Calvin had to work and his community had to live.[19]

If this be prophecy, then maybe even the Reformed churches, with their cautious approach to all matters musical, aesthetic, ceremonial, and ritual, may be on the way *back* to forms of praying that will better support the "doing justly" which is essential to serious social change in our secularized, consumerized, and competitive culture. Then, maybe, even the Reformed churches will find a way to celebrate, on a weekly basis, not only the word (and prayer) but also the sacrament (with alms) such that the eucharist, that bread and "cup of blessing," might be experienced again as what Paul Lehmann has described as "a laboratory of maturity."[20]

NOTES

1. Paul L. Lehmann, "Praying and Doing Justly," *Reformed Liturgy and Music* 19/2 (1985):78.

2. Ibid.

3. Ibid.

4. Karl Barth, *Church Dogmatics*, vol. 4, part 3/2: *The Doctrine of Reconciliation*, trans. G. W. Bromiley (Edinburgh, 1961), p. 865.

5. Ibid., p. 866–67.

6. Eric Werner, *The Sacred Bridge* (New York, 1970), p. 145.

7. John Calvin, *Theological Treatises,* trans. J. D. S. Reid, Library of Christian Classics 22 (Philadelphia, 1954), pp. 53–54.

8. James Hastings Nichols, *Corporate Worship in the Reformed Tradition* (Philadelphia, 1968), pp. 34–35.

9. Ibid., pp. 37–38.

10. Ibid., p. 40.

11. Joseph Bassett, "The New England Way and Vatican II," *The Unitarian Universalist Christian* 36/3–4 (1981): 59.

12. Ibid., p. 60.

13. John Calvin, *Institutes of the Christian Religion,* vol. 2, trans. Henry Beveridge (Grand Rapids, Mich., 1953), p. 601.

14. James Fraser, *Pedagogue for God's Kingdom: Lyman Beecher and the Second Great Awakening* (Lanham, Md., 1985), p. 41.

15. Barth, *Reconciliation,* p. 877.

16. Consultation on Common Texts, *Common Lectionary: The Lectionary Proposed by the Consultation on Common Texts* (New York, 1983).

17. Vatican Council II, Constitution on the Sacred Liturgy (*Sacrosanctum Concilium*), 4 December 1963.

18. Congregation for Divine Worship, *Ordo Lectionum Missae* (Rome, 25 May 1969).

19. V. Bruce Rigdon, "Experiencing the Presence of God in the Desert," *Reformed Liturgy and Music* 19/1 (1987): 54–55.

20. Paul L. Lehmann, *Ethics in a Christian Context* (New York, 1963), p. 101.

The Hymnal as an Index
of Musical Change
in Reform Synagogues

BENJIE-ELLEN SCHILLER

Coming to America

Between the years 1825 and 1875, roughly 250,000 Jews emigrated to the United States.[1] The vast majority came from German-speaking countries where, decades earlier, Jews had gained their rights as citizens. As newly emancipated Europeans, desirous of conducting their lives in a manner befitting their newly acquired status, they had gradually embarked on a process of modernization that soon made its way into their most ancient and venerated customs and traditions, including, of course, their style of worship.

Already in Europe, Jews had sought to readapt their mode of prayer so that it would resemble what they conceived to be the proper German etiquette for a religious service. As early as 1810 they were attempting in Cassel to subdue "unsuitable traditional singing which interrupts the prayer,"[2] and from then on, it was not unusual for individual synagogues to promulgate *Synagogenordnungen,* official pronouncements on order and decorum that prohibited such things as wandering up and down the aisles during prayer, loud kissing of the *tsitsit* (prayer shawl fringes) and swaying to and fro during prayer.[3] Their style of worship until this time had been anything but subdued and reserved. For the most part, Jews had prayed and sung out loud, each at a different pace and volume, a style that must have

187

appeared chaotic to an outsider, even though it did in fact have its own inherent method and cohesive structure.

By the time the German Reform Jews landed in America they had thus successfully discarded the aspects of Jewish ritual that they felt lacked the dignity and decorum reflective of their newly emancipated lives. Their style of worship now incorporated much of the western Protestant tradition. Where traditional Jewish law had governed the entirety of the Jew's way of life until this century, now a new governing principle of non-Jewish aesthetics and decorum dictated their decisions in fashioning their new style of worship. They were "passing" into the west, "not with civil rights but with bourgeois rites" borrowed from the non-Jewish society round about them.[4]

Formerly, the cantor had led the service by chanting the Hebrew prayers in the *nusach* (melodic formulas determined by liturgical time and regional style),[1] while the congregation responded in a prescribed, albeit apparently cacophonous, manner. Now a rabbi, who was seen as functioning akin to a Protestant minister, *read* the service that centered on his sermon. A four-part choir rendered the newly notated music of the prayers, which themselves were often translated into German, while the congregation prayed silently. Whereas formerly the chanting of the liturgy for a Sabbath service had taken several hours, now the reformers abbreviated the service both for theological and aesthetic purposes, so that a tasteful, appropriate, and "tolerable" service in the modern, non-Jewish sense would result. "Even synagogue architecture was affected by the decorum movement. . . . [R]eformers wanted to tidy up visual irregularities, just as they wanted to replace individual cantillation with uniform prayers."[5]

Though these modifications in worship had already occurred in Europe, yet to be seen was how they would fit into an American mold, and what norms of American culture reformers would appropriate, now that they were becoming respectable American citizens. By the mid–nineteenth century the governing principle in America was individualism: "As propagated by Ralph Waldo Emerson, this doctrine meant a willingness to break sharply with the past, to rely on the sovereign self and almost never on tradition. . . . [Religion] would have to be more the product of individual experience than inherited law."[6] The American individualism that Emerson celebrated became fertile ground for Reform Jews seeking to readapt their religious way of life in the new world. Their religion could now be practiced out of individual choice because for the first time in Jewish memory, Jews were free to change the shape and scope of their religion, and as individuals, to choose their own desired level of observance rather than to be governed by the mandates of the community at large.

Many Jews took advantage of their new freedom and abandoned Judaism completely. Those who remained steered their individual courses toward the model prescribed by the predominant religion of the American upper class. "Everywhere, absolutely everywhere, we see how deeply the American model of mainline Protestantism governed what Jews did, from the fetish for decorum, to the passion for preaching, and even the adoption of family pews. . . . Americanized religion for Americanized Jews."[7] The yearning to be part of the American religious landscape was particularly evident in the modernization of synagogue music.

The First Union Hymnal *(1897):*
Defining Musical Taste

By the 1870s, musical sophistication increased as congregations amassed sufficient wealth to hire prestigious choirs and to acquire organs. At the same time, the choral repertory expanded to include abundant hymns, the texts of which were English translations of Hebrew prayers or adaptations of Protestant favorites. Rearrangements of European classical music were used as musical settings. The cantor, the embodiment of Jewish musical tradition, became a relic of the past and was replaced by professional musicians, usually a choir director and an organist who were not necessarily Jewish but who, in conjunction with the rabbi, chose the music for the synagogue.

Thus the style of worship had slowly but surely become

tasteful and proper by the standards of the American bourgeoisie. For example, the Reform service's preference for hymns betrays its "Protestantization": "In denominations that concentrate more on preaching, on the spoken word, hymn singing is the predominant congregational contribution to the music."[8]

Just as classical Reform Judaism was establishing its dominance in American life, another part of the equation that was to shape synagogue music entered the American Jewish scene: the arrival of eastern European Jews. Their numbers, unprecedented in Jewish history—2.3 million men, women, and children between the years 1882 and 1924—greatly reduced the impact that Reform synagogues would ultimately have. Eastern European Jewish culture differed sufficiently from the German Jews' that a schism inevitably developed between the two groups. The *reform* of religion was itself an alien concept to Jews from Russia, Lithuania, or Poland, who were either Orthodox (bound strictly to Jewish law), or had abandoned religion altogether in favor of an ethnic and cultural display of their Jewish identity combined frequently with socialism or even atheism as well. They barely spoke English; instead, they preferred Yiddish, the very Judeo-German dialect from the Middle Ages that German Jews had emphatically replaced with High German and then English in their rush to become emancipated. Following the railroads and the industrial expansion of the Midwest, German Jews had boldly spread themselves throughout America, thus successfully acculturating as merchants and entrepreneurs even in tiny cities all over the country. By contrast, eastern European newcomers constituted the cheap labor of large cities, where they clustered in tightly knit neighborhoods and preserved a culture all their own.

The influx of eastern European Jews precipitated an identity crisis for Reform Judaism in America. It is surely not mere coincidence that at the height of new immigration, Reform leaders, hitherto sharply divided, finally came together. In 1885, a platform of Reform principles was adopted at a conference in Pittsburgh, and five years later the first meeting of the Central Conference of American Rabbis (CCAR) was held. Our study of Reform music from this time forward will be largely based on the proceedings of the Committee on Synagogue Music whose discussions have been preserved in the yearbooks of the CCAR.

Given the wide divergence of practice typical of Reform's highly decentralized structure and its dependence on individual rabbinic whim, the CCAR turned immediately to the need for uniform standards in worship. A *Union Prayer Book* was projected, and, already in 1890, "several motions were made by members to the effect that a means be devised for establishing uniformity in the mode of public and private worship of congregations and individuals adhering to the Reform principles of Judaism."[10]

Toward this end, a committee on hymns was established. To achieve uniformity, it published a hymnal from which every Reform congregation in America would choose its music.

Published in 1897 by the CCAR and the Society of American Cantors, *The Union Hymnal* contains 129 English hymns for four-part choir, many of them taken from smaller hymn collections of individual Reform congregations from Europe and the United States. Dominating the collection are works by secular composers, such as Mendelssohn, Beethoven, and Haydn, combined with those of the Jewish composer and cantor Alois Kaiser (1842–1908), a major figure of synagogue music of this time. The musical style is European romantic, borrowed directly from the Protestant chorale tradition. The few Jewish motifs that do exist are successfully hidden harmonizations thoroughly embedded in nineteenth-century secular music.

The book features also an appendix of twenty Hebrew musical settings, fourteen of which are prayers within the body of the liturgy, while the remaining six are closing and opening hymns. Fully half of the Hebrew settings are composed by Kaiser, who was known for adhering to the sophisticated musical taste that was lauded so highly by his congregation, Oheb Shalom of Baltimore, in the last decades of the nineteenth century. The remaining Hebrew settings were written by Jewish composers from Europe who, like Kaiser, adapted western romantic music to fit the Hebrew texts of the prayers. The music was majestic and glorious, well-suited to the Hebrew texts, all of which praise God. The same majesty, however, seems less appropriate when set to texts such as this one:

> Speak gently of the erring one,
> And let us not forget
> However darkly stained by sin,
> He is our brother yet.[11]

Preoccupied with praise and glory of God and humanity as the sole themes, the editors did not concern themselves with presenting a varied repertory that would allow for the musical celebration of the entire Jewish calendar, with its variation of mood and tone—from the solemnity of Yom Kippur to the carnival-like festivity of Purim.

Clearly the *Union Hymnal* was designed for use by the professional choir and rabbi alone, and was not to be circulated among the congregation, which was still viewed as a passive assembly rather than the active traditional individualists of the premodern synagogue. Since the Reform service centered around the rabbi's discourse, the hymns were arranged by themes, so that the rabbi could choose from one hundred "anthem texts" (i.e., scriptural readings in English in the back of the hymnal), and then select the hymns that best suited the theme of his sermon.

The editors adopted extreme measures to ignore Jewish music, even modern Jewish music of their time. Salomon Sulzer, often called today the "father of modern synagogue music," is hardly represented here. Sulzer, like Kaiser, utilized the same European classical styles. His fame rests, however, on his skillful preservation of many traditional Ashkenazi motives. Even though he wove these into the rest of his romantic style, they were too noticeable for the tastes of the editors of the 1897 hymnal!

Uniformity, the intended goal of the hymnal, was achieved, but at the cost of congregational participation. The repertory was uniformly upgraded to meet the highest western standards. Each service was designed to be intellectually and musically sophisticated, with the result that "the congregation's role, already restricted to docile, decorous hymn-singing in early German modernism, was cut back so far that by 1892 the CCAR began to worry that the spirit was going out of congregational worship by comparison to Christian practice.''[12] The hymnal only made the problem worse.

The Second Hymnal (1914): Adding Devotion to Aesthetics

Already in 1904, Kaiser himself recognized that this lack of active congregational involvement was deadening the spirit of his congregation's worship, but he was ahead of his time.[13] Only in the second decade of this century did Reform Jews catch up to him and express the need for emotional as well as intellectual involvement within their worship.

In 1913, for example, Rabbi Kaufman Kohler, the convener of the Pittsburgh platform meeting twenty-eight years earlier and chief architect of its very rationalistic contents, conceded to his colleagues:

> We have been too intellectual and too little emotional . . . [W]e should touch the soul more. I heartily endorse the idea of giving greater care and attention to a hymn-book, and such a hymn-book as is offered to us whenever we enter any church where over the text the notes are given to make the people sing.[14]

These rabbis sensed that music could potentially provide spiritual nourishment, but they did not know exactly what kind of music they were looking for. One participant expressed the frustration that many rabbis shared:

> Few of our congregations are alive to the need of music which serves a devotional end. We are not all clear about the kind of music we ought to hear in our synagogues and too many look upon music as an external decoration rather than a fervent outburst of an inward God-seeking spirit. And owing to the indefiniteness of imagery conjured up by music, many songs have entered the synagogue which disturb and stifle rather than stimulate the spirit of devotion.[15]

With the accent now on "devotion," we see some development in the rabbis' aesthetic theory. The music's purpose is presumed to relate to the worship itself. Should a song be superior according to the standards of classical music but still not be conducive to prayer, then, according to the ideals set for the second *Union Hymnal* (1914), the song is inappropriate for prayer.

The *Union Hymnal* of 1914 contains 246 hymns, almost twice as many as in the 1897 hymnal. However, the new hymnal's significance goes beyond its impressive size.

First, a substantial increase in arrangements are cited as "TRAD," denoting a Jewish source. Forty musical settings are harmonized to suit western harmonic practice, but even here, a quote of Ashkenazi *nusach,* or a traditional prayer motif can be heard in the melody line.

Second, even though the majority of the pieces are still composed by, or readapted from, the works of non-Jewish composers like Mendelssohn, Mozart, and Beethoven, there is a marked increase in Jewish composers. On the other hand, the section of twenty-four Hebrew hymns and responses hardly changed from the 1897 book.

Third, we note a great difference in the section entitled "Children's Services." While the 1897 hymnal contained only twelve hymns for religious school, the 1914 hymnal has expanded to include eight separate children's services.

Fourth, this hymnal is designed to be used by the congregation instead of by the professionals alone. The music is therefore slightly more singable, even though all but one of the settings remain scored for four vocal parts. Where the musical strength of the 1897 hymnal lay in its harmonic richness, the focus has begun to shift toward the melodic line in order that each hymn text be clearly and convincingly expressed by the worshiper.

Fifth, whereas the hymns of the 1897 hymnal were selected with the rabbi's sermon in mind, the 1914 themes correspond to Jewish holy days and rites of passage. The early reformers "had exalted reason and denigrated ritual, identified most strongly with the larger community of humankind and pressed toward the boundary of Jewish identity. In retrospect, one can see signs of the new trend, to look inward and backward as much as forward. . . . More than one rabbi called for a new emphasis on what Rabbi Louis Wolsey called the 'specially Jewish aspect of our religion.''"[16]

The response to the 1914 hymnal varied. Because of their ambivalence toward musical traditions from their Ashkenazi roots, Reform rabbis were not unanimously in support of the hymnal's underlying philosophy. In their report to the 1918 conference the Committee on Synagogue Music referred to this music as "sickly ghetto wailings and the fantastic chazzanut,"[17] by which they had in mind traditional cantorial fantasia, melismatic and often improvisatory in style. They cited specifically traditional renditions of liturgy that the Reform rabbis had eliminated on theological grounds, namely, petitions for the return from exile, and the subsequent reestablishment of the sacrificial cult.

On the other hand were those aspects of the tradition that the Reform rabbis sought to restore: an increase in the amount of Hebrew in the children's services, for example, which went hand in hand with their congregational participation in the central prayers of the service. As time went on, the committee proposed simplifying the musical arrangements of these traditional hymns, in order further to facilitate congregational participation. By 1921, transposition to a lower key was suggested to achieve the same goal.

The Union Hymnal *(1932):*
Jewish Identity for Second-Generation Families

Already by the 1920s rabbis were unabashedly looking inward, as they tried to evaluate their music and consider its future.

> Before we can have Jewish music, we must know what Jewish music is. And to know it in spirit we must not only busy ourselves with historical and aesthetic questions, but we must free the devotional song spirit so that it blooms again and creates new forms. We must not only promote investigation and teach the leaders of Jewish congregations our liturgical song but efforts must be made to induce the gifted musicians to turn their talents to glorifying the religious life of the Jew.[18]

By this time the chasm separating Germans from eastern Europeans was narrowing. Eastern Europeans were becoming Americanized while, simultaneously, German reformers now felt secure enough as Americans to reassert a distinctively Jewish orientation. Jewish musicians were thus encouraged to compose new music rooted in Jewish sources rather than borrowed ones. The motto of the twenties could have been: "Music that speaks to the Jewish spirit within us."

But sacred music never changes overnight. As World War I ended, the synagogue itself had begun to change. It was "no longer the spiritual home just for immigrant men; it was now meant to serve families as a rallying point of identity."[19] The second-generation Jews, born in America, acculturated from birth, were moving with their families to new areas, where an altered agenda for synagogue music included the following goals:

1. to stimulate congregational singing;
2. to inspire Jewish devotion;
3. to revive values of Jewish melody;
4. to exclude, as far as possible, non-Jewish music and poetry;
5. to provoke in the children of our religious schools a love for Jewish poetry and song;
6. to encourage an earnest study of Jewish music in the religious schools.[20]

Note the preponderance of the word *Jewish* in this list. The 1914 hymnal had admitted a little traditional Jewish melody and incorporated the talents of several old and new Jewish composers—a big leap from the preceding hymnal—but the majority of its musical settings were still written by secular composers. By 1930, however, Reform rabbis spoke of a yearning for their own uniquely Jewish sound expressing the soul and the heart of Judaism. They had a musical problem, however. On the one hand, they said they wanted Jewish-sounding singable music for worship. But they did not realize just how deeply immersed in non-Jewish melodies they were; it would not be easy for them to get used to a musical sound so different from what they were accustomed to. In the preface of the 1932 *Union Hymnal,* the Committee on Synagogue Music thus states clearly, "It has been our aim to combine Jewish and general musical values."[21] But western music and Jewish *nusach* do not easily complement each other. Furthermore, these Jews no longer were acquainted with Jewish congregational singing. Decades of effort and patience would be needed to find ways to help congregations feel comfortable enough to sing aloud together.

Only ten years after the 1914 hymnal was published, work on its revision began—for the first time with a professional musical editor, the well-known composer, author, and teacher Abraham Wolf Binder. One of Binder's lifelong concerns (his students sometimes called it an obsession!) was the utilization of the proper *nusach* in accordance with the corresponding prayer representing a particular season. Certain tunes, or motives, or both, had long been crystallized into Ashkenazi tradition so that they were inextricably linked with the particular holy day on which they were sung. Binder resurrected some of these most well-known *misinai* tunes and motifs (as they are known—that is, tunes that ostensibly go back all the way to Sinai), using them again in the flow of sacred time.

In pursuit of this and similar traditionalizing ends, Binder assembled a committee of outstanding cantors and composers. Behind the inclusion of cantors was the sociological fact that by the late 1920s, the role of cantor was gradually emerging anew in Reform synagogue life—a result, certainly, of the integration of eastern European Jews into the ranks of Reform leadership.[22] To be sure, the majority of Reform congregations still employed a choir director and an organist, not a cantor. But the more Reform Jews would search for authentically Jewish sounds (as opposed to a musical style taken from western host cultures), the more relevant the sacred Jewish singer became.

The hymnal of 1932 thus incorporated the works of more than twenty Jewish composers, including the great masters such as Sulzer, Lewandowski, and Naumbourg, as well as contemporary composers. Fully 209 of its 292 offerings were written by Jews, many of whom worked directly with Binder, such as the cantors Beimel and Jassinowsky, Samuel Alman, Joseph Achron, Jacob Weinberg, and Rabbi Jacob Singer. Binder saw his own dramatic breakthrough as not simply recovering the past but making it "artistically worthy."[23]

> It was also the purpose of the Committee to blaze a new path in the musical style of hymnology. Up to this time hymn tunes were in the old Lutheran chorale style. From this we have entirely departed and have substituted instead melodies which are, first of all, melodious; easy to teach; delightful to sing; within the range of the average human voice; inspiring and uplifting. . . . [T]his arrangement will also be suitable for unison singing.[24]

Binder's appraisal was accurate. Every musical setting is in a realistic range for the average voice. Upon hearing any of these pieces one is immediately drawn to a singable melody.

Binder took Reform music in a second new direction, too. As mentioned earlier, the predominant expressive tendency in the previous two hymnals had been one of majestic praise and joy. Of the 1914 hymnal, it was said, "All melodies for the Sabbath [should] be in joyous strain, in major rather than in a minor key. . . . If 214 tunes are in major and twelve in minor, it was because of a very definite conviction that the Jew has come down to a modern day in a spirit of victory, and that the atmosphere of the American Reform congregation should be a reflection of the position, the culture, and the attainments of the Jew in this free and joyous land."[25] By contrast, representing his committee in 1930, Binder reversed the Reform obsession with major keys, explaining, "Many traditional Jewish melodies . . . are in major and the minor ones are not necessarily sad and wailing, as is commonly misunderstood. Melodies in minor very often reflect the deep and subtle religious spirit of the traditional synagogue."[26]

Already in the 1914 hymnal, the education of children had been prominent. Reflecting the continued shift of focus to education, the 1932 hymnal expanded its "Children's Services" to nineteen! The children's services of this hymnal thus became part and parcel of an increasingly child-centered Judaism designed above all to ensure that the next generation would become dedicated members of the Jewish people.

Typical of the seriousness with which the rabbis made musico-liturgical decisions is the heated debate from the 1930 CCAR convention over the inclusion of *Kol Nidre* in the hymnal. On the one hand this "plea for absolution from enforced vows, born of Jewish persecution, continued to move worshippers with its strange words and haunting melody."[27] But many of the rabbis associated *Kol Nidre*'s exoneration of unfulfilled vows with the old attestation of "Jews' duplicity in making promises."[28] Binder was one of many present who recalled the power of its emotional impact upon the congregation when he sang it on Yom Kippur. "Everybody was enthusiastic about it. It was not a question of words, it was simply the feeling that at this particular moment throughout world Jewry, all are united in one song."[29] The committee eventually voted to publish *Kol Nidre*—but only as a song without a text, thus getting around their reservations about its traditional lyrics.

Another philosophical discussion revolved about *Hatikvah* (later to become the Israeli national anthem), the song expressing hope for a homeland. Reform Jewish leaders were divided over Zionism, but, nonetheless, even many of the non-Zionists resonated with the underlying message of *Hatikvah*, as expressed by a leading proponent of Zionism, Rabbi Stephen S. Wise: "We are a living people, and this represents the aspiration and the dreams of a living people. If you omit *Hatikvah*, it is as though you are saying to Jewish people: we are a church and nothing more."[30]

The twin cases of *Kol Nidre* and *Hatikvah*—especially the latter—demonstrate the crucial role of music in the expression of heart and soul. Rabbis who objected on theological grounds to the lyrics of both works nonetheless heard in the music an underlying symbolic message that transcended theology. There had been no argument concerning the inclusion of the "Star Spangled Banner" because American patriotism was not in question for American Jews of the 1930s. The Zionist theme, however, was another story. But by the end of the heated discussion on *Hatikvah,* the committee voted to include it.

Through Depression and Holocaust

The 1932 hymnal was issued just as Americans were entering the Great Depression. Ideological concerns took second place to economic ones. Looking back, however, we can see that throughout the 1930s the recovery of tradition in song and ritual was moving Reform Judaism closer to the other branches of American Judaism. As Michael Meyer puts it: "The interwar period did witness a progressive diminution of differences between Reform Jews and their coreligionists. The rapprochement appeared in the broadening sense of Jewish identity, the progressive reappropriation of traditions, and the turn toward Zion."[31]

The reclamation of an authentic Jewish sound was to continue from then on. The desire to present such music inevitably threw into question also the decision by earlier generations to abandon the cantorate. Once again, this traditional transmitter of Jewish song found a place in the American Reform synagogue. Modern cantors, however, would have to master the tradition of the past and to attain the musical capacity to adapt that tradition to modernity. Indeed, the hymnal's success depended on the parallel success of the cantors whose American-style artistry matched the hymnal's blend of tradition and modernity.

At issue was the Reform movement's very deep-seated desire to arrive at a musical sound that was, on the one hand, undeniably Jewish but, on the other hand, distinctively American. The leading figure, Binder, and cantorial composers like Walter Davidson were now joined by others: Isidore Freed, Hugo Adler, Max Helfman, Herbert Fromm, Heinrich Schalit, and Lazar Weiner. As music directors in large Reform congregations, many of the composers—like Binder himself—could actively implement their new musical styles in the repertory of their congregations' prayer service. These and other outstanding composers not only recovered, but also integrated, traditional melodies into their own work in such a way that they upgraded the standard of synagogue music to a level of artistic excellence beyond compare in all of Jewish history. In 1943, Rabbi Jacob Singer, a leading member of the CCAR Committee on Synagogue Music, was able to evaluate the long-term project that had been undertaken as nothing less than "a gradual emergence of a distinctly American *nusach* or tradition in synagogue music. Out of the many elements of which American Israel is composed, we are shaping a song which is becoming articulate and distinctive, and yet traditional withal. Our effort is stimulated by our new sense of responsibility for *Klal Yisrael* [the totality of the Jewish people] since so many centers of Judaism have been laid low by the despoilers of our times. By discarding the banalities of the ghetto and yet retaining its valuable elements, we shall create a Jewish song in this country worthy of our tradition and our opportunities."[32]

As Singer noted, this "new song" was stimulated by the desire to recognize the Holocaust, which, even as it was happening, was raising Jewish consciousness in ways no one could have predicted. It would soon become commonplace to commission new works for synagogues, often in the form of entire Friday night or Saturday morning services. The great masterpiece that served as a model for this genre was Ernest Bloch's *Avodat Hakodesh* (*Sacred Service*) which had been published in 1933. Although written for cantor, professional choir, and orchestra, it is most often performed with organ, due to the financial constraints of most American synagogues during the thirties but continuing on even now. The new compositions that followed in the decades after Bloch's epic work tried to maintain his own standard, so that they too were designed for choir, cantor, and organ, even though, of necessity, they were composed only with the large "cathedral-style" Reform congregations in mind, the very places, that is, that could afford to commission such a work in the first place.

Had the recovery of tradition been limited to masterworks demanding enormous sanctuaries and musical forces, it would

hardly have survived the postwar years except as a collection
of cherished musical relics to be heard and enjoyed in the great
old synagogue spaces that first-generation German Jews established in the inner core of America's largest cities. By the fifties,
however, post-Holocaust generations were joining Americans
in general in opening up the suburbs. Hardly able to satisfy the
musical demands of the great sacred services such as Bloch's,
they developed a simpler musical style designed for organ and
volunteer choir or cantor, often with the congregation singing
along. "It is high time we break the conspiracy of silence in
the synagogue," urged Reform rabbis at their 1944 convention. "Congregational singing need not and ought not be limited
to hymns alone. We have many occasions when *zemirot* [tradi-
tional Jewish melodies] and folksongs of Jewish origin can be
used by a volunteer adult or junior choir."[33]

Especially during the turmoil of the Second World War,
Jewish leaders cared very deeply about musical participation,
which they associated with the spirituality typical of educated
congregants at home with Jewish identity. Jews were under siege
in Europe, and therefore Jews here in North America were
anxious to borrow from no "folk" other than their own. As
they saw their ancestors' homelands destroyed by the Holocaust,
they yearned to hear and to sing the sounds of their own people,
to add their voices to those of their ancestors.

To take responsibility for the continuity of Jewish culture here,
beyond the reach of Hitler's destructive forces, Reform Jewish
leaders sought educational methods to enlighten their flock to
the task of rediscovering themselves as Jews. They thus devised
an annual synagogue program entitled a "Sabbath of Song."
Reform Jews were urged also to adopt family rituals with traditional music, so as to promote Jewish identity beyond the
synagogue. And in the synagogue, meanwhile, the movement
implemented an annual Jewish Music Week at which Jewish
music, new and old, would be featured.

In addition, in 1945 several leading cantors, musicologists,
and rabbis formed an organization called the Society for the
Advancement of Jewish Liturgical Music, which was designed

"to provide standards for Jewish Liturgical Music; to fix methods for writing authentic Jewish melodies; to publish lists of available music; and to encourage the composition and performance of such music by holding contests, making recordings, and by other means; to further the knowledge and appreciation of Jewish music."[34]

The Professionalization of the North American Cantorate

The recapturing of traditional Jewish music, the growth in new compositions in which *nusach* and traditional motives were utilized, the growing accent on the congregation's singing the music rather than merely listening to complex versions of it, and the emphasis on educating the laity in musical sophistication are all facets of what Mark Slobin calls the "professionalization" of American Jewry, a response to the Holocaust that was characteristic of the 1950s and 1960s.[35] With the death of its parent culture in eastern Europe and in Germany, American Jewry was forced to claim a sense of its own authenticity and was no longer compelled to look toward another, older, Jewish cultural center for legitimacy.[36]

Perhaps the most significant example of this postwar trend toward cultural and religious independence was the Reform movement's decision in 1947 to establish a School of Sacred Music to train cantors. In 1951, the Conservative movement followed suit, as did the Orthodox in 1954.[37] More than any other institution, the new cantorate has shaped the course of Jewish music over the last several decades. The Reform movement's school proved paradigmatic, in that it was built around a core faculty that included musicologist Eric Werner, hymnal editor Abraham Wolf Binder, as well as several of the composers mentioned above—Isidor Freed, Lazar Weiner, and Max Helfman, for instance. Growth was by no means steady, but by the 1980s, the School of Sacred Music had come of age, openly voicing its goal: to train cantors both academically and professionally, and thereby to raise up generations of fully professional cantorial clergy, charged with continuing, developing, and enriching the Jewish musical heritage.[38]

The Union Songster *(1960)*

The impact of the Holocaust and the recognition of the substantive difference between the pre- and the postwar years were recognized as early as 1947, when the CCAR's Committee on Synagogue Music began planning for yet another hymnal. Unlike its predecessor fifty years earlier, which had sought a musical repertory that was inspirational and triumphal, this committee faced the challenge of salvaging the Jewish musical heritage and educating laypeople to appreciate and sing it. The committee aimed, not only at educating children and returning Jewish music to congregational song, but also at developing a Reform theology that went beyond triumph to incorporate the experience of the post-Holocaust years.

By 1954 this committee, which now included Eric Werner, Abraham Wolf Binder, and Malcolm Stern, determined that their future *Union Songster,* as it came to be called, was not to take the place of the 1932 *Union Hymnal*—in fact, it pointedly did not reproduce many of the hymnal's songs.[39] In addition, it eschewed four-part choral music in favor of simple, singable melodies more appropriate for families and religious schools. With the Judaism of the past having gone up in flames, the *Songster*'s architects sought to ensure Jewish survival through their only guarantors: the many children of the baby-boom era.

The distinctiveness of the *Union Songster* was the singability of its music and its inclusion of texts and music for a broader range of holy days within the Jewish and the American calendars. We find here for the first time a *Havdalah* service (the standard ritual marking the end of the Sabbath); services for Purim, Chanukah, and Passover; a Consecration service; and a Mother's Day service.

While a mere thirty years earlier the editorial committee had debated the inclusion of *Hatikvah,* the post-Holocaust (and post-Israeli-statehood) *Union Songster* included an entire religious service honoring the existence of the state of Israel. Deeply committed to the establishment of the state of Israel, postwar Reform Jews did not hesitate to express their pride and support for a Jewish state and, therefore, to pray for it and sing the songs suggestive of it in their worship.

Within a decade, the impact of the state of Israel was to be felt in ways that the *Songster*'s authors could not have predicted. Though the *Songster* openly supported Zionism, it predated the efflorescence of Jewish culture that Zionist theory predicted and that a Jewish state now delivered. An intensely musical culture, enriched moreover by ethnic traditions of Jewish immigrants from all lands, Israeli Judaism has pioneered its own large and varied repertory of songs, not all of them (or even most of them) self-consciously religious, but many of them (like *Hatikvah*) expressive of the religious yearnings of Jews as members of the Jewish people. By the 1970s, particularly after the 1967 Six-Day War, many of these songs were finding their way to the American synagogue, often with Hebrew lyrics that people sang without understanding. The very melody and the existence of Hebrew reminded people of their peoplehood in an age when the Jewish people had almost been destroyed, but now had miraculously been reborn on its age-old biblical soil. Many of the *Songster*'s offerings were systematically overlooked, even deemed irrelevant, as, for better or for worse, American Jews found themselves singing Israeli music born not in the synagogue at all but in song competitions and popular Israeli culture.

Moreover, the preference for Israeli music over the songs of the last several generations of Reform Jews was part of a larger phenomenon yet: a countercultural movement spawned by the sixties and seventies in general in this country, and evident in a new-found critique of the synagogue by the baby-boomers come of age.

Countercultural Judaism of the Sixties and
Seventies: Chavurot and the Youth Movement

As we approach the age of the third-generation American Jew, we come across a continuation of the identity crisis that their parents experienced several years earlier. These American Jews were still recovering from a decade when the monumental events in Jewish history had occurred within a few years of one another: the Holocaust and the establishment of the state of Israel. They had watched from America as one Jewish world died and another was created. In each instance, the American Jewish response was self-examination. Third-generation Jews knew they had survived and prospered here but now had to ponder the dilemma of being a post-Holocaust Jew of the Diaspora.

At first, and in keeping with the early sixties, these young Jews lost interest in institutional Jewish life, seeing its synagogues as typical bourgeois expressions of comfortable living amid the inequities of Vietnam, the enslavement of African-Americans, and third-world poverty. The sixties and seventies therefore began to see a decrease in affiliation among American Jews.[40] But the Six-Day War changed all that, as even young and critical Jews faced the sudden possibility of a second cataclysm that would end the state of Israel as abruptly as it had been born. Turning inward to their own Jewish heritage, they began exploring ways to retain their Judaism, but not in their parents' mode, which they perceived as shallow and without substance.[41]

By 1968 the Chavurah movement was thus born. A *Chavurah* was a countercultural community, usually of young Jews intent on radical democracy, equality, and cultural self-sufficiency. Its members worshiped and celebrated in an informal setting, celebrating smallness of size, personalized relationships, a recovery of tradition, and the importance of participatory worship. Influenced by the Chavurah's critique of large, impersonal, and nonparticipatory worship, more and more synagogues of the seventies and eighties began questioning the musical heritage of the hymnals, especially the elaborate harmonic structure that underpinned standard Reform hymns. Moreover, more and more small Reform congregations that had developed in suburbia faced budgetary restraints that precluded hiring a cantor, thus necessitating that, Chavurah-like, they develop their own brand of "do it yourself" Judaism. Together with the populism of Israeli music, the Chavurah cultural style favored informality, popular culture over high culture, and a certain disdain for the very professionalization that had marked earlier postwar attitudes.

A third tendency of the period, supportive of the other two, was the burgeoning of the Reform Jewish youth movement, known as the National Federation of Temple Youth (NFTY). While older (college-age and beyond) brothers and sisters founded the Chavurah, younger teenagers still at home began attending NFTY summer camps in record numbers. There at camp, with the support of large numbers of their peers, they leveled their own critique at formal synagogue life. To the Israeli melodies and the do-it-yourself traditionalism of the Chavurah, they added their own brand of popular music, namely, the folk-rock sound of simple songs composed by guitar-playing teenagers.

As we have already seen, sacred music reflects cultural, social, and political contexts. Liturgical music of the 1960s and 1970s thus accommodated itself to these three shifts: Israeli consciousness; the Chavurah and its yearning for a populist version of traditional authenticity; and the emergence of the youth movement. The music gradually became simpler, thoroughly democratic in its singability, largely Hebrew, and playable on guitar.

To be sure, established composers, such as Gershon Kingsley and Raymond Smolover, sought to tap the new market with more sophisticated sounds, like jazz or folk-rock, thus capturing the essence of the teenage cultural revolution. This new style was not necessarily simplistic and overly informal; it provided sophisticated rhythms and lyrical melodies where before synagogue music had been more sedate.

In such an era, the *Union Songster* never fully succeeded. Shortly after its publication—and certainly following the 1967 Six-Day War—American synagogue pronunciation of Hebrew changed from Ashkenazi (northern European) to Sephardi the translated lyrics of all the Hebrew songs in the *Union Songster* were quickly unusable.

The Music for Gates of Prayer: *Eclecticism*

By 1975, the Reform movement's new liturgical series was inaugurated. Given the problems of the *Union Songster,* a committee was composed to plan a hymnal. It was to accompany the new prayer book, *Gates of Prayer,* which included an appendix containing seventy Hebrew and English hymns as well as English transliterations for twenty-four worship responses. While deliberating on the final shape of that volume, an interim book called *Shirim Uzemirot* was issued.[42] It contained melodies only for the most basic responses and songs.[43]

The final hymnal, *Sha'arei Shirah: Gates of Song,* was published only in 1987. The makeup of its board of editors bears witness to the successful professionalization of the cantorate in the Reform movement and the growing number of graduates of the School of Sacred Music. Each hymnal since 1897 represents the work of rabbis of the CCAR with musical suggestions from a single music editor such as Binder. By contrast, the editorial committee of *Sha'arei Shirah* was composed of members of the American Conference of Cantors (ACC), the CCAR, a music editor (also a cantor), and a professional Jewish music publications editor.

The 173 selections in *Sha'arei Shira* cover the entire Sabbath liturgy of *Gates of Prayer* and a wide variety of Sabbath hymns and songs. Like the *Union Songster* and *Shirim Uzemirot,* the book was intended from the outset for congregational use. The music is singable, with settings in a moderate vocal range. All the older arrangements reappear in Sephardi Hebrew. There is an alternative to the usual organ arrangement in order to allow an amateur organist, pianist, or guitarist to accompany the cantor, choir, and/or congregation.

Another unique feature is the number of musical settings for Hebrew prayers within the Shabbat service; each major response has three and often four selections from which to choose. *Sha'arei Shirah* contains neither children's services nor liturgical readings; it serves solely as a musical compendium for use by the congregation (aided by cantor and organist) in order to encourage congregational participation in worship. Both the content and form of the book typify Reform synagogue music in the late 1960s and 1970s. Its wealth of musical sources reflects the eclecticism of these times. In a single compendium one finds Israeli melodies, Hasidic tunes, works by nineteenth-century European masters like Lewandowski and Sulzer, Sephardi melodies,Yiddish folk songs, and a wide range of contemporary American compositions.

What we have is the first collection of an expanded musical canon, complete with pipe organ, guitar, and drum; cantor, choir, and congregational singing. Michael Isaacson speaks for many when he talks about the contemporary synagogue as having traveled from the postwar experimentation stage and a free-for-all period of folk settings to the point where we should be "optimistic that the next decade will . . . synthesize the popularism and relevance of today with the classicism and rich heritage that has been handed down to us."[45]

Toward the Twenty-First Century

In the 1980s, the Reform movement estabished a Joint Commission on Synagogue Music, representing cantorate, rabbinate, and laity. Diversity of taste continues to direct the committee's discussions as its members create a myriad of programs designed to educate Reform Jews about Jewish music.

An increasing number of works composed for use in North American synagogues is published each year by Transcontinental Music, the music publishing company of the Union of American Hebrew Congregations. This music represents an array of synagogue composers of our era, such as Ben Steinberg, Simon Sargon, Samuel Adler, Stephen Richards, Michael Isaacson, William Sharlin, Bonia Shur, and Charles Davidson. All of these had established themselves as composers before the time when women cantors, as well as women rabbis, began to make their mark on the Jewish community in the area of liturgical expression. By 1990 the works of Andrea Jill Higgins, Rachelle Nelson, and my own have begun to enter the canon. Composers of the 1980s fuse musical aesthetics with the need for effective congregational worship, sometimes by stressing traditional modes, other times by leaning more or less heavily toward the classical Reform choral genre, or by weaving a simple congregational refrain into a richly textured setting for cantor and choir. Diversity of voice is a concern, too, especially given the rising number of female cantors who require music written in a vocal style appropriate for women.

The popularity of the folk genre of sacred music has not decreased. The influence of Israel is still felt, varying with the repertory in vogue at any given time. American folk composers (Debbie Friedman, Michael Isaacson, Jeffrey Klepper, and Daniel Freelander are names that come to mind) continue to create singable, uplifting songs that gain rapid acceptance.

But people feel strongly about their musical tastes with the result that they argue vehemently over what is an appropriate musical language for synagogue use.[46] Many critics have responded negatively toward the incorporation of the folk idiom within a worship service, seeing the growing popularization of new idioms as threatening to erode centuries' old standards of Jewish music for worship. On the other hand, the popularists have become attached to the warmth and informality of their preferred style, maintaining, in fact, that in some cases, it is this very music that draws them to prayer after years of adult absence from the synagogue; it has become ''their music.''

Perhaps the future of Reform synagogue music will synthesize all these styles. Cantors will continue to expose their congregants to the richness of Jewish musical tradition in an effort to familiarize them with many different musical languages. Recognizing the popular appeal of Israeli and American folk music, as well as its capacity to involve worshipers in an active yet worshipful way, Jewish composers will utilize its rhythmic liveliness to enhance their own melodies. Congregations will grow more and more accustomed to participating in many kinds of Jewish music as they grow to appreciate the more formal styles of the past, the traditionalism of modern solo chazzanut, and the richness of a tradition that goes beyond the moment.

They will become choirs in themselves as their proficiency in singing improves, even as they appreciate the capacity of cantorial presentation that can move them in ways that unison singing does not. In addition to the organ, other musical instruments such as the flute, *tof* (Israeli drum), piano, and guitar will accompany our music. We will strive for a sacred music that is both inclusive and transcendent, ancient yet contemporary, stately yet inviting, practical yet inspired.

NOTES

1. Michael A. Meyer, *Response to Modernity: A History of the Reform Movement in Judaism* (Oxford, 1988), p. 236.

2. Mark Slobin, *Chosen Voices: The Story of the American Cantorate* (Urbana and Chicago, 1989), p. 18.

3. See lists of regulations in Jakob J. Petuchowski, *Prayerbook Reform in Europe* (New York, 1969), pp. 105–27.

4. John Murray Cuddihy, *The Ordeal of Civility* (New York, 1974), p. 38.

5. Slobin, *Chosen Voices,* p. 19.

6. Meyer, *Response to Modernity,* p. 226.

7. Lawrence A. Hoffman, review of Jack Wertheimer, *The American Synagogue: A Sanctuary Transformed,* in *Religion and Intellectual Life* 6/3–4 (Spring/Summer 1989): 241.

8. Slobin, *Chosen Voices,* p. 50.

9. Arthur Goren, *New York Jews and the Quest for Community* (New York, 1970), p. 1.

10. *CCAR Yearbook* 3 (1892): 96.

11. *Union Hymnal* (1877), no. 85.

12. Slobin, *Chosen Voices,* p. 45.

13. *CCAR Yearbook* 14 (1904): 52.

14. *CCAR Yearbook* 23 (1913): 148.

15. *CCAR Yearbook* 28 (1918): 58.

16. Meyer, *Response to Modernity,* p. 295.

17. *CCAR Yearbook* 28 (1918): 58.

18. *CCAR Yearbook* 28 (1918): 59.

19. Slobin, *Chosen Voices,* p. 55.

20. *CCAR Yearbook* 40 (1930): 90.

21. *Union Hymnal* (New York, 1932), p. vii.

22. Cf. Slobin, *Chosen Voices,* pp. 45–46.

23. *CCAR Yearbook* 40 (1930): 91.

24. *CCAR Yearbook* 40 (1930): 97.

25. *CCAR Yearbook* 40 (1930): 91.

26. *CCAR Yearbook* 40 (1930): 91.

27. Meyer, *Response to Modernity,* p. 321.

28. Ibid., p. 321.

29. *CCAR Yearbook* 40 (1930): 101.

30. Report by Committee on Synagogue Music, *CCAR Yearbook* 40 (1930): 101.

31. Meyer, *Response to Modernity,* p. 298.

32. *CCAR Yearbook* 53 (1943): 167–68.

33. *CCAR Yearbook* 54 (1944): pp. 127–28.

34. *CCAR Yearbook* 54 (1946): pp. 92–93.

35. See Slobin's chapter, "Post-War Professionals," in *Chosen Voices,* pp. 94–111.

36. Ibid., pp. 94–95.

37. Ibid., p. 94.

38. See statements in promotional literature designed by Lawrence A. Hoffman in the 1980s, during his tenure as director of the School of Sacred Music.

39. Rabbi Malcolm Stern, chairman's report of the Committee on Synagogue Music of the CCAR, *CCAR Yearbook* 63 (1954): 96.

40. Slobin, *Chosen Voices.*

41. On the Chavurah movement in general, particularly for its contextualization amid countercultural, generational conflict, see Riv-Ellen Prell, *Prayer and Community: The Havurah in American Judaism* (Detroit, 1990).

42. Jack Gottlieb, ed., *Shirim Uzemirot: Songs and Hymns for Gates of Prayer* (New York, 1977).

43. These were published in an addendum to the back of *Gates of Prayer.*

44. Charles Davidson, ed., *Sha'arei Shirah: Gates of Song* (New York, 1987).

45. Slobin, *Chosen Voices,* pp. 248–49.

46. See, e.g., the symposium, "The Discussion of Music in Lawrence A. Hoffman's *The Art of Public Prayer,*" *CCAR Journal* 38/3 (Summer 1991): 1–23.

PART 3

Composing Sacred Sounds: Four New Settings of Psalm 136

Introduction

We have already heard from two prominent composers—Miriam Therese Winter and Benjie-Ellen Schiller. We turn now, however, to composers who discuss their own music, rather than the music of church and synagogue in general. At the original conference on which much of this book is based, four composers from different liturgical traditions were commissioned to set Psalm 136, newly translated in inclusive language. Each was asked also to write program notes about her or his composition for the audience. Here, we reproduce the music they provided, as well as a written version of their annotations, in which the composers explain what they have attempted to do in bringing Psalm 136 to song.

Nansi Carroll has studied at the Royal Academy of Music in London and at Yale University's School of Sacred Music. A Roman Catholic, she serves as Artist-in-Residence at St. Augustine Parish and the Catholic Student Center in Gainesville, Florida.

The Methodist tradition is represented by Don E. Saliers, Professor of Theology and Liturgics at Candler School of Theology, Emory University, in Atlanta. A scholar too, Saliers has contributed several well-known books and articles, particularly in the field of spirituality. As a composer, he contributed to the formation of the *United Methodist Hymnal* (1989).

Exposed as a child to Jewish music by his father, who was a cantor, Ben Steinberg went on to become an internationally known composer, with commissioned works ranging from cantatas for chorus and orchestra to complete synagogue services. Describing his work as "preserving the best of the traditional past while remaining true to the contemporary present," Steinberg works as Music Director of Temple Sinai, Toronto, and lectures widely on synagogue music and current composition.

Finally, Alec Wyton, an ASCAP award-winning composer of over 150 works, is currently Minister of Music at St. Stephen's Church in Ridgefield, Connecticut. From 1954 to 1973, he served as Director of Music at the Cathedral of St. John the Divine; from 1974 to 1986, he held the post of coordinator of the revision of the Episcopal Hymnal, and he taught and worked at the Manhattan School of Music.

INSTRUCTIONS FOR COMPOSERS

The following remarks are taken from the instructions sent to each composer as preparation for the work of composition. The text of Psalm 136, as it was sent to them, is also included.

The last page of these instructions contains the text for your composition. Before working with it, please read the following instructions carefully, as they explain why the text is as it is, and why you should feel free to deviate from it in certain ways.

The text is a translation of Psalm 136, but it differs from others you will have seen. It is suggested, though not mandated, for your work. The next several paragraphs explain why it appears as it does, and how you may change it, if you wish, in order to accomplish your musical goals, or to accord with your theological concerns.

Please note first that the text has been altered so as to utilize only gender-inclusive language regarding God. We ask you please not to restore terms like *he* and *him* to refer to God.

The text has also been shortened, primarily through the omission of parallel verses whenever those verses seemed redundant and when, in addition to their redundancy, they contained sexist language, or they proved difficult to understand in the light of twentieth-century sensitivities, or both. A guiding principle here was the axiom that liturgy, unlike classroom instruction, is to be celebrated publicly without a cognitive concern for reinterpretation getting in the way. Classical liturgy has regularly proved selective in its citation of Scripture (see, for example, the inclusion of Exodus 34:6-7, the thirteen attributes of God, in the Jewish service for festivals, where the final two words of the second verse are deliberately omitted so as to transform the biblical original, ''God will surely not forgive,'' into ''God will forgive''—the very opposite of the biblical intent.) So, here, the specifics of God's vengeance on Pharaoh's Egypt (verses 10b, 15) and the various kings Israel encountered on the way to the Land of Israel (verses 18–20) are omitted, even though God's central covenantal act of salvation against those biblical foes is retained.

You may feel constrained to put back some or all of the missing verses, on the grounds that, as Holy Writ, psalms have their own integrity that insists on their being recited without the omission of verses, even in liturgical settings. If you feel that way, we will, naturally, honor your sensitivity, but we ask you, please, to alter sexist references in any verses that you retain.

Perhaps most obvious to you will be the retranslation of several words in ways you will not have seen. Most noticeably, the Hebrew *chasdo,* usually translated as ''his mercy'' occurs here as ''God's covenant.'' Inclusive language demanded ''God's,'' but why do we say ''covenant''? Here we follow scholarship on the meaning of *chesed;* clearly it becomes difficult to conceive of God's mercy in the same breath as God's slaying the Egyptian first-born (verse 10) or drowning the Egyptian army (verse 15); so long ago, scholars recognized that *chesed* does not mean ''mercy'' in the universal sense, so much as it means ''covenantal mercy,'' the grace with which God acts towards those to whom God is linked in covenantal promise. ''Covenantal mercy'' was a mouthful, however, so how the language sounded suggested the simple metonymic shortening to ''covenant.''

Regularly, the words of this version of the psalm are phrased to accord with aural considerations of the words' sound. Please feel free to change the text when your music demands lyrics with a different rhythm, syllabification, or accent, as long as you are convinced that the essential meaning remains the same.

We ask only that any proposed changes be cleared through our translation committee first, normally a pro forma process entailing your filing your proposed text with us, and our sending you a letter accepting your textual emendations. You may use the original Hebrew in place of, or along with the English, in any combination you desire.

Please remember throughout that you are being asked to compose for actual use in synagogue or church. What that commission entails, we would rather leave to you, as we do not wish to curtail your artistic freedom by being too restrictive. The approach to translation—as outlined above—has left you considerable latitude in rendering the lyrics, precisely because we do not want the music to be necessarily limited by chance accents that happen to fall in a given word, when you might well find an acceptable synonym that does greater justice to your composition. You will have to decide also just how much of the psalm to use and how to use it, and here, too, we hope you will exercise your discretion. Assume a normal church or synagogue context with which you are familiar. At the outside, in terms of musical forces, plan for one soloist or cantor, and, if you like, a reasonably small backup ensemble, not more than a quartet; or for a duet, perhaps, or a trio. Assume the use of an organ or piano, and/or one other instrument, say, a flute or a cello. You may wish to write a part for the congregation or not, to use the refrain as a congregational response, or not; to use the refrain regularly, or sometimes, or not at all; and you may use the entire psalm as it is sent to you, or only some of it, or even add back in some of the lines we have left out (subject to the considerations outlined above.) In other words, you should feel free to do exactly what you want with the music, without feeling unduly hampered by the textual version in front of you. Though the text is obviously not beside the point, we have done our best to leave you free to overcome the accidental restrictions of those aspects of the text that are not of central concern, and we ask you to exercise textual logic as well as musical judgment at every step along the way. We want to free you for your greatest possible musical creativity, not to impede your creative energies with detailed specifications.

Our choice of Psalm 136 was not accidental. Known early in Jewish tradition as an example of "the great *Hallel,*" it rapidly found an honorable place in the calendrical cycle of both church and synagogue. We hope you will investigate your own liturgical traditions for this psalm, so that what results from your creative efforts will be a combination of your musical sensitivity (for which you have become justly known) wed to the appropriate liturgical considerations that will make your setting a desirable choice for worship.

As you know, this letter is going to four composers in all, each representing a different musical and liturgical tradition. We look to the four of you to demonstrate simply by what you do and the reasons why you do it how social change and sacred musical traditions reflect each other. We will premier all four works at the Hebrew Union College as our climactic session of the conference, at which time we will ask you to discuss your composition briefly, highlighting your musical choices and the ways in which your own musical and liturgical traditions have influenced the piece.

Our goal is to cast some light on the creative process that lies behind musical composition in a time of change. Your own experience is exactly what we wish to feature. Far from its being an unimportant side product of this conference, your own role in shaping musical taste should be seen as primary. We hope that, along with your music, you will freely share with us how the music came into being.

FROM PSALM 136

1. Give thanks to God, for God is good
   God's covenant lasts forever.
4. To the One who alone performs great wonders.
   God's covenant lasts forever.
   5. Who fashioned the heavens with pattern and plan
      God's covenant lasts forever.
   6. While expanding the earth upon the waters.
      God's covenant lasts forever.

7. To the One who made great lights—
   God's covenant lasts forever.
   8. The sun to rule by day,
      God's covenant lasts forever.
   9. The moon and stars by night—
      God's covenant lasts forever.
10. To the One who struck down Pharaoh.
    God's covenant lasts forever.
11. But brought Israel out of Egypt.
    God's covenant lasts forever.
    12. With a strong hand and an outstretched arm,
        God's covenant lasts forever.
13. To the One who split the Red Sea.
    God's covenant lasts forever.
    14. And let Israel pass through it.
        God's covenant lasts forever.
16. To the One who led our people through the wilderness.
    God's covenant lasts forever.
17. To the One who defeated mighty monarchs.
    God's covenant lasts forever.
    21. And gave us their land as a heritage,
        God's covenant lasts forever.
23. Who remembered us when we were low,
    God's covenant lasts forever.
    24. And delivered us from our tormentors.
        God's covenant lasts forever.
25. The One who provides for all that live.
    God's covenant lasts forever.
26. Give thanks to the God of heaven.
    God's covenant lasts forever.

The Roman Catholic Tradition

A Psalm of Thanksgiving:
Psalm 136
For Cantor, SATB Choir, Assembly, and Keyboard

NANSI CARROLL

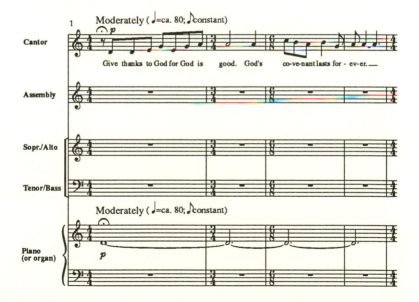

I am rediscovering composition. Though developing compositional skills had been a significant part of my early musical training, I practically ceased writing music for a number of years in order to concentrate on performing. I have returned to composing mainly as a result of my involvement in church music.

As a Roman Catholic working in a parish, I inhabit a rather lively musical environment. Liturgical evolution since the close of the Second Vatican Council not only mandated structural changes in the mass but also, and perhaps more critical to radical renewal, called for a deepened understanding of the role of the full assembly as actors in liturgical celebration. Though these factors have meant the loss of some music, such as polyphonic settings of the Kyrie, Creed, and Sanctus, they have also called for the composition of new music. They have compelled musicians to search through the Roman Catholic tradition, and other traditions as well, for music that is usable in our contemporary liturgical practice. We are involved in establishing and recovering musical traditions.

In this atmosphere of change, the singing of psalms, essential to our renewed worship, is an important link with our earliest Jewish and Christian traditions. Ordinarily, psalms are sung responsorially, that is, verses alternate with a refrain. This body of music is written in a variety of styles: the verses may be chanted by a cantor on a simple melodic formula with the congregation singing the refrain; they may be chanted freely or metrically by a choir, again on a simple formula; they may require a trained soloist to sing the verses; or, in still other cases, they may feature a more songlike type of writing for both verses and refrains, such as settings in the folk idiom.

My own settings of psalms are responsorial and usually follow a pattern of two or more verses sung to the same formula with a final contrasting verse. The dialogue takes place between choir and congregation as if they were two choirs.

I have followed this pattern in my setting of Psalm 136 here ("A Psalm of Thanksgiving," as I prefer to entitle it). The first two verses adhere to the same formula. The choir responds to the cantor, who sings the refrain as it occurs in the psalm. Verse 3 uses the same formula harmonized simply, with the upper voices taking on the cantor's role. The fourth and final verse is sung by the choir in a different mode, extending and building up the entire setting to a climax in which the final words of the verse are sung more slowly than in the previous verses.

As I wrote "A Psalm of Thanksgiving," I tried to imagine a parish with a fairly strong music program—with a music director and a volunteer choir that might prepare a piece such as this over the course of two or three weekly rehearsals. With this in mind, I worked within fairly strict limitations of tonality and vocal range. I varied the instrumental and choral articulation as well as the texture to create changing degrees of intensity.

In returning to composing after an extended absence and attempting to make connections with my early work as I develop technically, I find congregational song to be a good and exacting teacher. A congregation has certain vocal limits and is further restricted by the need to perform with little or no rehearsal. Yet, the congregation has extensive emotional power. To my mind, the congregational music that is most affective invites the congregation to feel this power without manipulation. I look to ethnic music, chorales, and plainsong as examples of music that are idiomatic for the congregational vocal "instrument." This form of music springs from a deep human rootedness. It achieves maximum effect with a minimum number of notes.

Both the refrain and the first three verses of "A Psalm of Thanksgiving" are plainsong inspired, though they do not follow its strict patterns. I wished to contrast the congregation's and the choir's music by making the refrain more lyrical. Therefore, I used the entire first line of the psalm for the refrain and let it determine the instrumental writing and the structure of the setting as a whole.

The commission to set Psalm 136 posed a number of challenges for me. The first was the litany structure inherent in the psalm as each new phrase is answered by "God's covenant lasts forever." In my composition, the sameness of the response's persistent presence is mitigated by the fact that the refrain sung by the congregation is extended with additional words by the choir. Second, the word *covenant,* which suggests to me a kind of gentleness and patience, appeared to be at odds with the violence of later verses, e.g., "the One who struck down Pharaoh." I chose to ignore these violent expressions. In retrospect, I think what I gained in expressive unity, I may have lost in an essential humanness. Third, the repetition of the word *God* to avoid pronouns that implied male or female gender was difficult. I find my own setting to be somewhat boxed in by the repetition of the word *God.* The challenge for all of us is to find God-language that is lyrical as well as inclusive.

Finally, I am continually challenged by my own church's liturgy. Where would this setting of Psalm 136 fit? The mass is a large whole with many constituent parts. There are therefore a number of ways of combining sung and spoken word, sound and silence. More important, however, than any individual part of the mass, is its overall structure—its direction, its moments of greater and lesser emphasis. I wonder if I would have set this text the same way had I done a full eucharistic setting, and thus would have had to consider all the other parts with which this one would have had to blend. I had originally thought that "A Psalm of Thanksgiving" might possibly be a response to the first reading during the Easter season. Now, I'm not entirely sure that it is appropriate there because the piece feels more like an anthem and would overemphasize this section of the liturgy.

In my work as a Roman Catholic church musician, I experience social change within the context of liturgical change. The two seem to catalyze each other. Together, they have a strong impact not only on my work but also on my musical development. One of the first things I notice is the high mobility of people, a particularly telling characteristic of my parish, which serves primarily a university population. Most of the community has not lived here long. The people come from parishes with differing attitudes toward liturgy. They may, in effect, not only be strangers in town but strangers to the liturgy and music as well. Since Vatican II, there is no universal expression of the mass for Roman Catholics. Rather, it is significantly influenced by local resources, desires, and needs. We make up a church that is moving from perceiving itself as a refuge from the world to seeing itself as involved in the world. In addition, we are a diverse people. We are neither monochromatic, nor monocultural, nor monogendered, nor monolingual. Our diversity is reflected not only in the languages in which we sing but also in the proliferation of musical styles we prefer.

Social change as I define it calls for a body of music that is hospitable and eclectic: music that challenges our assumptions. When I think of hospitality in my own music, I think of finding a common ground—elements in my music that transcend specific differences and speak to a common musical experience. Specifically, I refer to tonal and melodic patterns modeled on folk elements and plainsong. Of course, along with the people with whom I work, I am committed to eclecticism in musical choice; but I have not yet attempted to write in a variety of styles. Rather, I write in a style that benefits from the influences of a variety of cultures. As I long for a greater degree of creative stability, I look forward to tapping these resources continually.

Finally, as I am stretched in word and sound I see evidence that increased awareness of and involvement in the world is being expressed in a renewed purposefulness in the work of musicians—performers and composers who work in both religious and more secular arenas. I sense a continued social concern being expressed in liturgical texts. The need for inclusive language is one manifestation of inclusiveness on a larger scale. This witness, however, stretches; it is not comfortable. Church music is growing, and I hope it will continue to grow in openness to what is uncomfortable. I wish this openness to inhere in my own work: I want to develop a wider music vocabulary that may give voice to a broader spectrum of human experience.

The Methodist Tradition

Psalm 136

For Choir, Congregation, Organ, and Optional Percussion

DON E. SALIERS

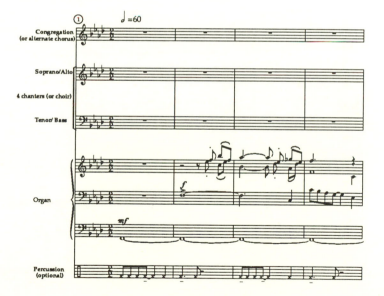

235

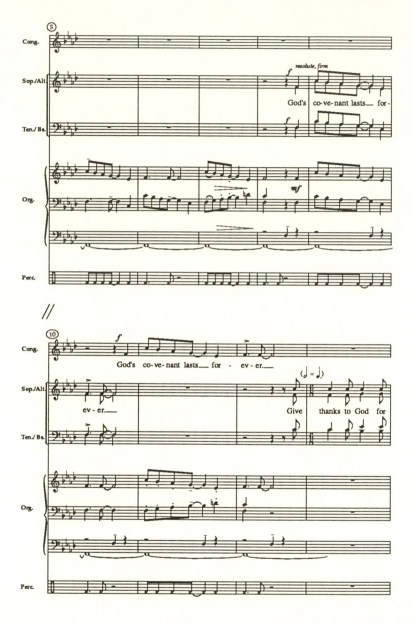

co-ve-nant lasts___ for - ev - er.___

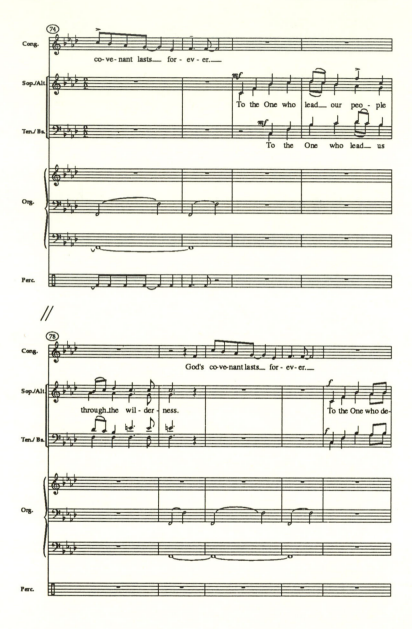

co - ve - nant lasts___ for - ev - er.___

co - ve - nant lasts___ for - ev - er.___

The rediscovery of psalms as sung prayer is one of the liturgical revolutions of our day. There is no doubt in my mind that this is an intrinsically ecumenical event as well, for it draws various Christian traditions back to a common source in Hebrew Scripture and permits us to share prayer forms more deeply than we have for centuries. For some time now I have found myself composing psalm settings each week for use by a specific Christian ecumenical community. Sunday liturgy at Cannon Chapel at Emory University, of Methodist origin, gathers a wide range of worshipers from different racial, ethnic, and denominational backgrounds. We have two choirs, one employing an African-American Gospel style, and the other a twelve-voice chamber choir that often presents anthems based on psalm texts. Thus the context for which this setting of Psalm 136 is conceived is itself a sign of considerable social and liturgical change.

Most of the time we use relatively simple forms of responsorial and antiphonal psalm singing, with an occasional metrical version drawn from the Genevan or Scottish traditions. I find myself also employing an improvisational cantillation of the texts. But there are several occasions that call for a more extended and more festive setting. So the opportunity to set Psalm 136 has provided a chance to move toward a "through-composed" form that incorporates a cantor (or a group in unison) with a small choir and organ (with optional percussion) to be in dialogue with the congregation's refrain. In this psalm, of course, we have perfect litany form.

While not appearing often in the Common Lectionary, Psalm 136 speaks powerfully of God's mighty acts and suits a number of festive occasions, particularly in the season from Easter to Pentecost. Interestingly enough, the psalm is appointed in a regular cycle: at evening prayer in the *Book of Common Prayer* for Saturday (vigil of Sunday morning), beginning with week 5 of Epiphany. Thus, the opportunity to use this kind of setting of a psalm in anthem style for choir and congregation occurs frequently. United Methodists, for whose recently published hymnal I wrote several antiphons, are now, as a denomination, in the process of learning to sing the psalms in public worship. This process itself has already begun to generate a new level of liturgical sharing across traditions and is generating new musical interests as well, particularly for the use of the choir to enable congregational song.

The translation of this psalm text struck me immediately as strong, even rough-hewn, with rhythmic complexity. I began my work by reading the text several times aloud until a basic treatment of the refrain began to emerge. Since we composers were urged to conceive our settings for actual liturgical celebration rather than for choral or solo recital, the refrain, "God's covenant lasts forever," would obviously anchor the assembly's participation. In fact, structurally speaking, this psalm's strongly litanic form is rare. But its very uniqueness left very open the relationship to be forged between singers, other musicians, and the congregation. The refrain had to be both clear enough for ease of entry in singing, and interesting enough not to become dull by repetition; accumulative force is the hallmark of litanies.

The text is not the vocative; rather, it is a declaration—a recital of God's wonderful works. In my tradition the recently recovered eucharistic prayers, while addressed to God, contain this same pattern of active remembrance and declaration of God's relations to creation throughout salvation history. The prayers invite petition and end in doxology. Psalm 136, then, has a very similar thematic structure: creation; redemptive history; universal providence; doxology. So I set about articulating the four-part thematic structure in musical terms. First, it occurred to me to have choral extensions or expansions at the four points of the form as in a concertato style. But my context called for something simpler. Thus the similar organ interludes, or comments, between the sections emerged, with an eight-measure carol-like section leading to the doxological ending.

The four-part setting of the verses for four or eight chanters (or chamber choir) emerges in 6/8 meter in dialogue with the 2/2 of the refrain. In order to keep a tight unity and a secure relationship between choir and congregation, 2/2 becomes 6/8, with a half-note becoming a dotted quarter, maintaining throughout a steady, even relentless, pulse. The cantor's role becomes one of mediator, as well as animator, between the congregation and the musicians. Additional percussion would strengthen the basic rhythm of the refrain and provide a richer texture over the organ pedal point F and the alternating F octave skips on the two principal beats of the measure. This reinforcement of the pulse is reminiscent of the rhythms found in some of Heinz Werner Zimmermann's psalm settings.

When we think about the shift from passivity to the "full, active, and conscious participation" of the people, many of us are gravitating toward through-composed musical forms for liturgical use. This particular example gathers the whole assembly with its diverse gifts and roles into one complex, but mutually involving, act of praise. This new stress in worship, actively being present to one another, manifests both recent ecclesiological and theological shifts. Such shifts in self-awareness on the part of worshiping congregations assuredly reflects social change filtered through recent liturgical reforms. At the same time, distinctive Protestant forms of music, such as *alternatum praxis* among Lutherans, are being discovered ecumenically. For many Protestants, especially those of the broad middle "mainline," worship still remains relatively static and even passive in its musical forms, save hymnody. Even with respect to hymns, the repertory remains relatively small. For most Protestants, until recently, choral, solo, and instrumental music were basically added on or inserted in as special music in worship. This situation is changing dramatically; at the heart of the change is the correlation of the recovery of psalm and canticle alongside the well-known "explosion" of hymnody in the past two decades.

One of the most profound aspects of social change in American culture is, quite obviously, the ecumenical mutuality and cross-pollenization that is now taking place. Borrowings of idiom and form across traditions occur in my setting of Psalm 136. One example is found in what emerged as I settled into F-minor (with A-flat major implied and other slight harmonic excursions). I kept hearing the opening bars of a tune called the Leoni *Yigdal* (*Yigdal* is the name of a morning hymn in the daily Jewish service. Set to music by an eighteenth-century British cantor, Myer Leoni, the work was overheard by Thomas

Oliver, a Methodist minister, who thereupon borrowed it and altered the words for his own use). The tune is quite well known among most Protestant denominations, who use it for the text "The God of Abraham Praise," or "Praise to the Living God." In my setting of Psalm 136, references to the old Jewish melody appear in the pedal part of the organ interlude and open up in the last two verses by the chanters—the concluding verse being a fughette on the first line of the tune. Thus, when a Protestant congregation prays this psalm in song, the Jewish references become heightened, creating more depth and complexity in the activity of psalm-singing, as well as engendering a proper tension between the standard Christianization of psalm texts (via the older use of Gloria patri) and the original historical referents embedded in the psalm text itself.

A further reflection came to me in working with the strong center section: salvation, represented by the occupation of the land, requires displacement of others, and here another tension emerges. In history, God's covenant has implications (not always happy ones!) for relationships between nations. The translators of this text have purposely omitted the slaying of kings—Og the king of Bashan, for example. At one point I considered returning these specific references and creating more turbulence underneath the praise of God who rescues us from our enemies. Yet this psalm finally holds the specific revelatory acts of God *and* the universal providence of God in dialogue. These become focused in the intensification of the word *covenant* as the psalm unfolds. So the refrain of the whole litany: "God's covenant lasts forever." By the end, this range of covenantal faithfulness has accumulated several meanings as well as musical textures. The universality of God's particular choices and saving acts toward specific people shines through.

An afterword: My choir found the setting a bit difficult to learn and had some fear about its holding together in actual performance in the liturgy. Nevertheless, they did well; the congregation also held their own. All said: "This is a psalm translation that we won't forget."

The Jewish Tradition

Psalm 136
For Cantor, SATB Choir, and Organ

BEN STEINBERG

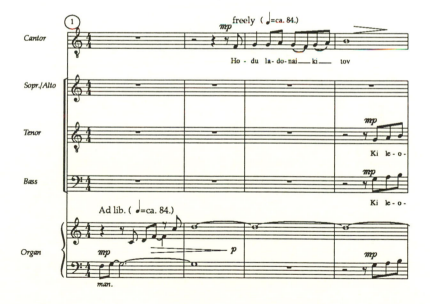

255

* Take breath only if necessary here.

*In quartet, alto sing larger notes.

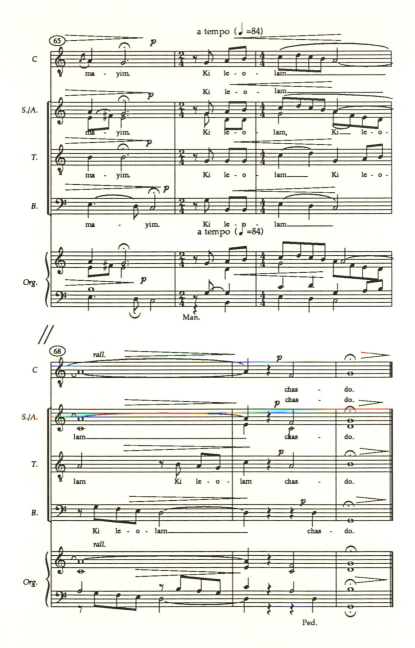

As a Jewish composer living and working in the late twentieth century, I am heir to an ancient musical tradition with a seemingly endless variety of modes, rhythms, melodic motifs, and structural ideas. At the same time, I am influenced by contemporary compositional techniques that admit a range of musical freedoms and sound-concepts unheard of during previous centuries. The fusion of these two possibilities—ancient Jewish and contemporary western—intrigues me: the combination of their musical languages offers me the unique opportunity to express my faith and sense of peoplehood through the artistic accents of my own time. The challenge for me is to write as a twentieth-century composer but with respect towards my forebears who bequeathed to me such a rich musical past. Thus, my Jewish compositions encompass simple *gebraucht* pieces, that is, necessary standbys that encourage congregational participation through easily singable, recurrent choruses; to pieces for cantor and choir that are designed for congregational listening; to more sophisticated, musically complex works for performance by chamber groups or chorus plus orchestra. While only a portion of my Jewish music is designed for use during religious services, all of it is to a certain extent liturgical, in the broad concept of the word *liturgy* as an expression of public worship. Indeed, I have often sensed a greater feeling of communal prayer during concert presentations of my cantata *The Crown of Torah* (for narrator, soloist, choir, children's chorus, and instrumental ensemble) than in many more formal worship services. My own compositions reflect this experience and contain a variety of musical approaches.

No composer anywhere can be oblivious to social change, for life's pace, its events, and its resultant resonances determine the sounds about us, the sounds of today, to which we all respond and which echo in our writings. Somehow, to study a work with a text written by a medieval poet or a biblical psalmist is to be confronted with the concepts of another time—a seeming contradiction in styles and an apparent confusion of incompatible mind-sets to which a composer must play matchmaker. Actually, they wed beautifully. The intelligent and careful introduction of contemporary musical techniques expands a good text, increases the effectiveness of its message, and illuminates its depths. This is no less true for composers today than in earlier centuries, when great composers like Palestrina, Bach, and Mozart set biblical or liturgical words to music.

Worshipers in synagogues or churches cannot disengage their twentieth-century ears as they enter a sanctuary for a worship service. The music they encounter in concert halls, or cannot escape in elevators, supermarkets, and television commercials, reflects their society's sonorities, values, and technologies. What they hear also shapes their musical expectations and triggers involuntary responses to certain rhythms, harmonies, and tempi. The composer of commercial jingles knows this psychological dimension of music well and uses it effectively. The serious composer of religious music, no less aware, writes music that resonates accordingly. Artistic response to social change is not a choice—it is inevitable.

My setting of Psalm 136 offers an example. The people who commissioned the work requested that composers retain their documentation in order to "reconstruct the decision-making process" used during composition. Being a cooperative type, I did as I was told. I kept a few notes as I went along, and that was a mistake; trying to write music while looking over my own shoulder, as it were, became difficult for me. Still, I tried to follow the guidelines, which invited composers to write a usable and accessible choral piece that reflected not only some modern musical techniques but also Jewish tradition, perhaps through modes, *nusach,* chant, and so on.

As I looked at this text, therefore, what did I hear? An atonal setting for large chorus and symphony orchestra. But I finally stopped monitoring myself, quit taking notes, and pretended I was just writing something for a cantor, a good synagogue choir, and an organist. Then, later, I analyzed what I had written. Now I can say, as Bela Bartok once said when shown an analysis of one of his compositions, "I had no idea how clever I was."

Four concerns became important to me in writing this piece:

First, the music should reflect the text closely, then be capable of assuming a wordless musical life of its own.

Second, the piece should be readily and quickly understood by a congregation. The form had to be recognizable, and if the piece was not actually easily singable for all, at least part of it had to be adaptable for congregational singing (I resisted the temptation to expand the music, and so, with the exception of a small bit of choral business in the third section, I kept it simple).

Third, both soloist and choir should have a characteristic role and express themselves with dignity.

Fourth, the traditional melodic theme customarily assigned to this text should be respected. This expectation, however, was problematic because of the confusion of *nusach* melodies for this text. In Jewish tradition, a *nusach* is a specific melodic pattern used by Ashkenazi, or northern and eastern European, cantors as a basis for improvisational chant. The particular *nusach* varies from service to service, from one holy day to another, and, indeed, from one community to another. Psalm 136 occurs liturgically as a Sabbath morning staple in a section of the service called *pesukei dezimrah* (the early morning rubric known as "verses of song"). The *nusach* for *pesukei dezimrah* is suggestive of a minor key for weekday mornings but is a kind of modified major for Sabbath mornings; this is further complicated by the fact that in the new Reform prayer book, this text is used not only in its original placement (mornings) but in the afternoon as well, where another *nusach* is the norm. I was thus confronted with three different models of *nusach* from which to choose. But Psalm 136 also turned up as part of the Passover seder liturgy, where yet another *nusach* governs liturgical chant, so the Passover model added to the possibilities. Not wishing to self-destruct like an overloaded computer, I elected therefore, to use a freer harmonic treatment. Perhaps my decision can be viewed as a composer adapting sacred sound to social change because of a desire for self-preservation. The traditional components I used were these: (1) a cantorial line in which musical accentuation is often achieved by melismatic embellishment; (2) an antiphonal approach, in part; (3) a modal treatment, in part; (4) the Hebrew language because, most importantly, I have always believed that both rhythm and melody are influenced by language.

For this setting of Psalm 136 I used the Hebrew version from the *Gates of Prayer* prayer book. The text divided itself neatly into four sections, an invocation followed by three sections dealing with the three subjects that would probably be considered mandatory religious reading for any Jew marooned on a desert island: Creation; Exodus as the paradigmatic act of God's Redemption; and the final Redemption that we expect at the end of time. Specifically, the organization took this shape: invocation, verses 1–3; Creation, verses 5, 8, and 9; Exodus, verses 11, 12, 16, and 21; Redemption, verses 23–26.

A compositional problem was, of course, the recurrent refrain *Ki le'olam chasdo* (God's mercy endures forever). The very phrase that gave the original text much of its strength, unity, and rhythm threatened musical redundancy, or even dullness. I decided to use the refrain in a number of ways. It appears in the first section (the invocation) traditionally, as an antiphonal response. In the second section (Creation) it was not used, because I was anxious for this part of the text to be presented in a flowing, uncluttered way. Then the refrain was clustered, chorally, as a bridge from the second to the third section (from Creation to Exodus). In the fourth section (Redemption), it was used antiphonally again, as in the first section. Initially, I had planned the total number of statements of "mercy enduring forever" to be the same as if the phrase had been retained as an antiphonal response (i.e., fourteen repetitions of *Ki le'olam chasdo* throughout the piece), but I decided that no one was capable of counting them anyway, so I changed my mind.

The musical decisions for this setting emerged from the text itself. The first section (the invocation) is a simple antiphony, musically quite symmetrical, except for a small extension in the last response. In the second section (Creation), I felt that the text should be clearly presented, especially the fifth verse, praising the God "who made the heavens with understanding." Accordingly, the cantor sings this phrase, the choir joins in to explain the mechanics of creation ("the sun to rule by day, the moon and stars by night"), then the choir repeats the cantor's initial phrase to emphasize that it was God "who made the heavens" and that they were "made with wisdom and understanding." The third section (Exodus) begins with a choral

272 BEN STEINBERG

bridge consisting only of the words *Ki le'olam chasdo,* since these words seem to provide the raison d'être for the reference to the Exodus. This leads to a cantorial solo (a traditional touch). Believing that we adorn the things we love and embellish the words we believe, the Ashkenazi cantorial tradition lingers lovingly over important phrases. In this tradition, improvisation plays a significant role. For this reason, these brief, free cantorial phrases are designed to sound improvisational, even to lend themselves to possible further improvisation. (Of course, as a synagogue composer I expect a cantor to recognize when this is possible and to perform the phrases with dignity.) The Exodus from Egypt is then described by the choir, with both rhythmic and harmonic movement, again punctuated by the use of the phrase *Ki le'olam chasdo,* especially surrounding the words (from Deuteronomy) that refer to God's strong hand and outstretched arm. The part of the Exodus section that exhorts us to thank the God "who led the people through the wilderness" and "gave their land for a heritage" is to me so central to Judaic belief that it needs no shouting. The music, therefore, becomes subdued here, expresses gratitude rather than excitement, and functions as a few chord progressions to begin the modulation back to the original key.

Finally, in the last section (Redemption) is a universalist component in Judaism, beautifully expressed. Verse 23, quiet and respectful, refers to God's remembering us at times of Egyptian bondage and Babylonian exile. Verse 24 describes deliverance, and just as the phrase resonates with hope and gratitude, so too the music rises. The phrase in both text and music that provides the climax in this section is the universalist statement in verse 25 that speaks of God's giving sustenance to all people. This transition from God's gift to the Jewish people to God's gifts for all humankind seemed to me to represent the fulcrum of this section. From here, where does one go but to words of gratitude to the name of God as God was addressed by other nations—the God of Heaven? The final reference to God's mercy enduring forever is not shouted with enthusiasm but spoken softly with respect.

Over many synagogue arks, which house the holy scrolls of

Torah, there is printed the phrase *Da lifnei mi atah omed* (Know before Whom you stand). Traditionally, the cantor led the service, representing the people before God, while facing those words! That sense of reverence and even awe prompted the musical treatment of the piece's final phrase. I attended a cantorial concert recently and to my surprise heard one soloist apologize to the audience for the fact that the piece he was about to sing had a quiet conclusion. He said he hoped he would get as much applause as his colleagues, whose pieces all had *fortissimo* endings. That questionable compositional approach notwithstanding, the last musical phrase in this piece quietly echoes the first, just as the final words themselves almost exactly duplicate the beginning of the psalm . . . and I hope no apology is necessary for the lack of a theatrical, *fortissimo* ending.

The Episcopal Tradition

Psalm 136

For Unison Voices with Congregational
Refrain and Organ or Piano

ALEC WYTON

ev - er. 5. Who fash - ioned the heav - ens with pat - tern and plan 6.while ex -

pand - ing the earth up - on the wa - ters. God's cov - e - nant lasts for - ev - er. 7. To the

One who made, who made great lights - God's cov - e - nant lasts for - ev - er. 8. The

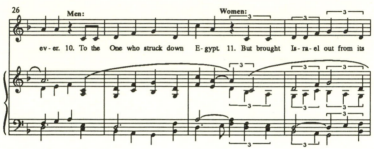

wil-der-ness. 17. To the One— who de-feat-ed migh-ty mon-archs. God's

cov-e-nant lasts for-ev-er. 21. And gave us their land as a her-i-tage. 23. Who re-

mem-bered us when we were low. 24. And de-liv-ered us from our tor-men-tors. God's

A lifetime of work as a composer, performer, and director of music is an extraordinary gift. It offers a remarkable breadth of involvement from which to create and evaluate music for use in the church as well as to envision sacred music's future possibilities.

My development as a church musician continues to this day. Membership in the Church of England offered early and lasting influences. As a young chorister I was exposed to the beauty of Anglican chants and hymns as well as other forms of English church music dating from the sixteenth to the early twentieth century. My first teacher trained me well in counterpoint and conventional harmony as well as in the discipline required for the performance of music on the piano and organ. Study at the Royal Academy of Music in London and at Oxford University brought exposure to the music of Vaughan Williams and Herbert Howells, with whom I enjoyed a lifelong friendship. My first job as an organist and choirmaster put me in contact with Benjamin Britten, C. S. Lewis, W. H. Auden, Henry Moore, and Graham Sutherland. I was in the midst of incredible creativity and artistic possibility. Especially Britten opened new doors that led to an expanded awareness of rhythmic, melodic, and harmonic variety.

Thus it is that my own compositions utilize a wide range of techniques: the harmonic freedom of modes, the resilience of counterpoint, and sometimes more conventional patterns. For the most part, texts suggest the appropriate choice for a musical setting. I read and reread the words until I hear music that will express their meaning. I follow the same process, whether I am composing a formal setting of the music for a eucharist, or an anthem, or a hymn, or an opera.

In my setting of Psalm 136, I used rhythmic patterns and key changes to provide a fresh access to the text. Triplets and duplets accommodate the irregular flow of the words. The repetitive motif throughout the psalm enables a congregation to be comfortable enough with the music to hear the text clearly. To this repetition, however, I added key changes in order to guard against monotony. The sudden change of key (verse 13) expresses what I consider to be an extraordinary moment in the text; I wanted people to sit up and take notice. I wrote this psalm with an ordinary congregation in mind, that is, a nonprofessional choir and a congregation of moderate musical ability that would enjoy the variety inherent in men's and women's voices.

Over the years of composing for the church, I have moved from emphasizing the choir as the most significant musical resource to developing a singing congregation. There's nothing quite as transforming as a whole church singing together. I believe with Martin Luther that when people sing together they open themselves to the gospel in an unparalleled way. So every occasion of worship should offer a variety of musical expressions, some that are immediately accessible to all the people and some that the congregation must work at and grow with. This belief guides my composition. I write for a choir that will support the liturgical expression of the congregation, often in alternation with it.

My style of writing is influenced by a concern for word painting and the appropriateness of music for particular liturgical contexts. For example, in a composition for the celebration of Epiphany called "We Three Kings," I wanted the music to convey the journey of these monarchs, so I wrote music that unmistakably conveyed such movement. But since a liturgical setting demands more, I thought carefully as well about the theological meaning inherent in this feast. The first goal was measurable: people will comment about whether the music expresses the journey of the Magi. But one can only hope that listeners will listen deeply enough to perceive the disclosure of God as well.

The season of Pentecost offers a different kind of challenge. Traditionally in the Episcopal eucharistic ritual, we sing a glorious plainsong sequence after the first reading assigned for the day. However, such sound seemed inappropriate as an answer to Acts 2:1–11, a text that describes the disciples' response to the sudden presence of the Spirit among them. How could we presume such comfort, such security (inherent in the plainsong), after hearing a text that expressed surprise, fear, amazement, confusion? The liturgical context demanded music that matched the emotions of the reading. We moved the singing of the Pentecost sequence to another place in the service and substituted music that offered a similar expression to what had been felt by the disciples.

The breadth of musical tradition in the Episcopal church supports such choices. Neither the doctrine nor the practice of the church imposes restrictions on the use of any style, from the earliest chants to rock, pop, and jazz. A galaxy of sound makes room for a very inclusive community. If God created everything and everyone, then everything and everyone has the right and duty to praise God with the talents they were given. When I was organist and master of choristers at the Cathedral of St. John the Divine in New York, we initiated an afternoon happening every Sunday in conjunction with evensong. We invited musicians and dancers from the Julliard School of Music to contribute what they were learning and imagining. The creativity they offered stretched us all and broadened our vision for Sunday mornings as well. Guiding our efforts to be open to new liturgical expressions was not so much a ''worship free-for-all'' where anybody who could strum three chords on a guitar or bang aimlessly on a drum was welcome to lead us. Rather, as the Rev. Walter Hussey, vicar of St. Matthew's Church in Northhampton, said, ''Only the best is good enough for God.'' This belief remains with me even as I know that ''the best'' will vary from community to community.

Each community dictates its own possibilities. For example, from the sixties onward, influenced by the spirit of the times, people demanded simpler music that was accessible to everyone rather than appealing primarily to a musical elite. My own music at that time, especially in the late sixties and seventies, was rooted in a vivid tonality. Since then it has shifted to more conventional harmonies, all in an effort to make it possible for people to feel at home in church.

In addition to the influence of social demands on composition, practical considerations are also significant. My work at the Cathedral of St. John the Divine is an example. On any Sunday morning, 60 percent of the congregation was probably there for only a single time. To offer a genuine invitation for the people to participate fully was quite a challenge. What was required were familiar hymns and simple settings for the Creed, the Gloria, and the Lord's Prayer with the choir's four parts based upon a monotone that the congregation could sing without rehearsal.

Throughout my life I have been both intrigued and compelled by the power of music to create an ambience through which all people, no matter what degree of musical or theological sophistication they enjoy, would know something more about themselves and God. Music breaks barriers; music honors differences; music predicts possibility. Convinced that music has this power, I am committed to making it available to every congregation.

PART 4

Critiquing Sacred Sound:
Perspectives on the
Sacred and the Secular

Introduction

Finally, to round out this book, we have asked three commentators to consider musical composition in American churches and synagogues today: composers Samuel Adler and Jon Michael Spencer, and liturgist Virgil Funk. Adler chairs the composition department at the Eastman School of Music. He has published over 320 works in all media, including operas, orchestral compositions, band pieces, chamber music, songs, and much liturgical choral music. Schooled from his youth in the Jewish musical tradition of western Europe, he is a respected commentator on the role of the composer in today's religious milieux. Spencer, Associate Professor of Popular Culture at Bowling Green University, has done extensive research in black sacred music; he has published five books and numerous articles on this topic. In addition, he has composed hymns, cantatas, dramatic poems, and an opera. For these works he has won national compositional awards. Spencer is founder and editor of the semiannual periodical, *Black Sacred Music: A Journal of Theomusicology*. Funk is a Roman Catholic priest whose interest in music led him to found the National Association of Pastoral Musicians and the Pastoral Press. In the latter capacity, he has spearheaded the publication of a vast number of liturgical and musical works by many authors and composers. As president of the association, he travels regularly throughout North America to assess the state of religious music at this critical point in our history.

Adler warns against secularity and wonders whether sacred music is possible at all in our time. Funk underscores the diversity in taste that characterizes our age, and he seeks to concep-

287

tualize it according to certain schools of thought, liturgical theory, and musical goals. Spencer raises questions about the "liberative lag" in African-American hymnody, suggesting that the Eurocentric biblical analysis on which much of this hymnody relies is itself captive and promotes racism, sexism, and classism.

Sacred Music in a Secular Age

SAMUEL ADLER

Music as Scapegoat in Modern Times

Writing in 1932, T. S. Eliot observed:

> One of the consequences of our failure to grasp the proper rela-
> tion of the Eternal and Transient, is our over-estimation of the
> importance of our time. We are still dominated by the doctrine
> of progress, we ask whether any particular past age has done
> anything for us; if not, it is regarded as pure waste. The notion
> that a past age of civilization might be great in itself, precious in
> the eyes of God, because it succeeded in adjusting the delicate rela-
> tion of the Eternal and the Transient is completely alien to us. A
> just perception of the permanent relations of the Enduring and the
> Changing should make us realize our own time in better propor-
> tion to times past and times to come.

This is certainly a significant admonition for those of us who
are concerned with creating and appreciating sacred sound, for
it challenges the view that we today are in an essentially different
situation from the ages that preceded us. Secularity has always
challenged and influenced sacred sound, whether in the form
of the aesthetic wishes of royalty or by way of the impinge-
ment on the liturgical status quo by the musical tastes of the
bourgeoisie. Changes for the better have resulted from these
pressures, so that one would have to admit that the nagging
conscience from outside the religious establishment can be quite
beneficial to sacred sound, not only in the past, but in the present

as well. To name but one such benefit, it is largely advances in compositional techniques and in secular music skills that lead composers to create great liturgical music masterpieces. The competition between church and state, musically speaking, is therefore not necessarily detrimental to sacred music; on the contrary, religion's response to challenges from outside itself has often raised the musical standards of church and synagogue higher and higher.

The problem today, however, is that rather than meeting the challenge by enlisting our very finest talents in the creation of new religious sounds and then educating the sensibilities of our congregants, we have succumbed to the voice of ease and surrendered to the spirit of populism. Thus our time does indeed differ from similar periods of the past, precisely in the fact that sacred sound has buckled under the stress of the secular challenge, producing the melting down or congealing of two sounds into one single musical entity that we might affectionately call *spiritual entertainment,* and that sounds suspiciously like Broadway musicals or television sound tracks.

Musicians, especially, face yet another, even more serious, problem unique to our time: sacred music or the music for our worship has been cast in the role of convenient scapegoat for all maladies afflicting the attendance at, participation in, and comprehension of worship services. Rather than highlighting the fact that communal prayer is foreign to most of our population, or noting that theology and especially the authority of both church and synagogue are not at all primary in the lives of today's congregants, clerics who are critical of what goes wrong in worship take the easy way out by ascribing the problem to music. Why is attendance down? People don't like the music! The kind of music sung by the choir is too much like concert music. The music does not "warm" the service. People cannot relate to the music or sing along with it. From such critiques, it quickly follows that we ought to change the music so it will sound like what the average person is used to hearing on radio and television. Even though the words of the prayers may not mean very much to them, worshipers will at least love the tunes and have a good time singing along. Our clergy and liturgical planners will have to be convinced of the deceptive folly of such oversimplified scapegoating of music and musicians before we can begin to hope for any fundamental change in our present situation.

The Synagogue

The issues raised in this book are surely central, in that they affect everyone with an interest in contemporary sacred music—indeed, everyone for whom worship is an essential part of life. The dilemmas that my Catholic and Protestant colleagues describe are not altogether unlike what I observe in the synagogue, except that—as in many things Jewish—difficulties are compounded in Jewish worship by a multitude of other problems specific to the Jewish experience on these shores.

A brief glance at the history of liturgical music demonstrates the first paradox unique to Judaism: the dissonance between the exceptionally rich Jewish contribution to sacred music over the years on the one hand, and the low popular esteem such music now enjoys in the Jewish community, on the other. Undeniably, the music of the synagogue is at the same time the oldest and the newest liturgical music of our western liturgies. By that I mean that Jewish music has long-standing traditions, yet very little that is traditional to all Jews everywhere. In fewer than two hundred years of modern existence, it has produced some of what may well be considered the worst and, only more recently (within the past sixty years), some of the loftiest musical creations.

The result is that despite a musical heritage going back beyond historical memory, liturgical music in Judaism has never enjoyed the high status that has been accorded the classical musical heritage of the church. Moreover, liturgical music is treated differently in each branch of Judaism, so that Jews bring at least three major perspectives to their musical heritage.

First, in the Orthodox tradition, liturgical music means a cantor improvising on very loosely agreed-to formulas. This includes the reading of Scripture (both the Torah as well as the Prophets—the *Haftarah*) according to formalized chants that

vary with the holy day cycle. Congregational melodies inter-
rupt the cantorial chant from time to time, but these are generally
predictable old tunes that people may or may not choose to sing.
There are no musical instruments other than the human voice.
The strictly Orthodox tradition usually features no choir and,
in any event, only men's voices are heard in this service that
exists officially and actually for men alone. Outside of these
traditional musical forms, there is not now, and possibly never
will be, any significant creative musical activity at all in this
denomination. As a matter of fact, novelty is in and of itself
mostly frowned upon.

Second, non-Orthodox denominations vary considerably and
can be arranged on a continuum ranging from those very similar
to Orthodoxy with regard to worship style and musical practice to those at the other end of the spectrum, who have
developed a long history of openness and receptivity to the music
of the post-Enlightenment west. The right wing of the Conservative movement thus leans toward Orthodox traditions, while
the left wing tries to combine some of the traditions of Orthodoxy
with other traditions that were derivative of the European culture
of the nineteenth-century, when liberal alternatives to Orthodoxy
first surfaced.

Third, further still to the left are those congregations who
consider themselves Reform, and who, early on, developed
services that were very much like their Christian neighbors.
Culture was the key word in their deliberations. They loved
music—the concert as well as the Christian sacred music
performed in their time—and they felt that just as the music
of the church lent dignity to Christian worship, so too could
the choir, the organ, the hymn, and beautiful music composed
in the style of the time add a great new cultural dimension to
Jewish spirituality.

The reformers' positive attitude toward European culture thus
spawned considerable musical activity from the very beginning
and continues to inspire Jewish composers to this day. If musical
creativity beyond the traditional cantorial role with its standardized chants and recitatives is to occur, it will therefore come
from within the ranks of Reform worship, where musical instru-

ments, choirs, and musical innovation have been the norm for over a century.

The secular challenge will hardly affect Orthodoxy to the same extent as Reform Judaism. Orthodoxy established itself directly in opposition to the modern world and by definition holds fast to the traditional prayer experience regardless of popular cultural trends. Reform Judaism, on the other hand, arose precisely in dialogue with modernity, so that the same positive relationship with the surrounding culture that produced synagogue art music at one time in its history now threatens to do the very reverse; insofar as the surrounding culture with which Reform claims to be in dialogue is merely a heightened form of secularism, Reform synagogues face the threat of destroying their own musical heritage that goes back now over 150 years.

We should pause to consider how monumental are the changes that have affected Jewish worship in the twentieth century. At the top of the list are the Holocaust and the establishment of the state of Israel, both of which now loom large as new empirical data to be integrated not only theologically but musically into the modern Jew's spiritual repertory. The demographic makeup of our congregations has changed also, in that great numbers of Orthodox and Conservative Jews have joined Reform congregations. Once, the average gathering of assembled worshipers was entirely of recent German origin and was trained simultaneously to appreciate the western European musical heritage and to devalue traditional eastern European Jewish music; the very reverse may often be encountered today —a congregation intent on reclaiming tradition, including traditional music, but not particularly interested in modern compositions. The musical forces available to congregations have changed, too. In the early years, Reform congregations threw out the cantorate with the traditional music associated with it and installed instead professional choirs and soloists. With the successful flourishing of the Hebrew Union College's School of Sacred Music as an official educational institution for the training of Reform cantors, the cantorate has returned in force. But for many reasons, both economic and cultural, professional choirs have virtually disappeared, except for major holy days

and special liturgical events, when the music budget expands
to allow the hiring of extra voices. But above all, America today
is marked by this phenomenon: the growing secularization that
deemphasizes attendance at worship in general as a sacred obligation. All of these overwhelming problems that influence the
development of our sacred sound require careful consideration
as we seek new directions.

I believe that no careful attention has been given to most of
the problems I mention, with the result that the status of liturgical
music in the American Reform synagogue today (and I include
here also the handful of large Conservative congregations that
emphasize composed music as part of the worship experience)
is best described as confused, even chaotic, fueled by ignorance,
misinformation, and simple neglect. Let me discuss briefly some
of the trends I have mentioned, in the hope of initiating the
dialogue whence some kind of direction may emerge.

The Return to Tradition

Above all, since the 1960s we have seen a frantic return to
tradition, fueled by a revival of ethnicity and a new accent on
Jewish peoplehood. This has been a natural result both of history
(the Holocaust and American Jews' identification with the state
of Israel) and of sociology (the demographic influence of eastern
European Jews and their cultural offspring). The ironic result
has been that while American Jews enjoy the greatest economic
and intellectual freedom ever possessed by any Jewish community, they have celebrated this affluence by driving the
practice of the Reform synagogue back into the womb of the
eternally hated ghetto, romanticizing its ways and practices—
and especially its music—for fear of losing "Jewish identity,"
as if only in the *shtetl*'s parochial atmosphere could Judaism
truly exist.

Our educational programs have therefore focused more and
more on "tradition," not necessarily tradition as it was, but
tradition as we imagine it to have been. We have, however,
established no choral organizations and no instructional forums
for the appreciation of Jewish music. Ignorant about the entire

field of sacred music and lacking any avenue by which to be exposed to it, the great majority of synagogue goers criticize the musical traditions of Europe and North America as either "untraditional" or simply not to their taste.

Similar criticism is often directed toward the organ, an instrument introduced into Reform temples only after much debate during the nineteenth century. Several myths exist regarding this important innovation, particularly the charge that the organ is too "untraditional," or even Christian, in its essence. To be sure, the organ was the instrument of the church before it came into the synagogue. We can no longer claim with any certainty that there was once a proto-organ (what the Mishnah calls a *magrefah*) in the ancient Temple in Jerusalem. We really do not know exactly what the *magrefah* was, although scholars these days are more and more hesitant to identify it as an organ. These facts, however, do not make the organ a "Christian" instrument. (On the organ, see the discussion of nineteenth-century musical history by Goldberg, above; on the *magrefah,* see the remarks by Schleifer.) Similarly, the mixed chorus—another innovation—is hardly non-Jewish in its essence. Both the organ and the mixed choir remain the legacy of our Reform forebears who insisted that Judaism need not be inconsistent with the best of contemporary culture and who therefore struggled mightily to perpetuate organ and choir, just as they did the equality of women, the use of the vernacular in worship, and theological emendations of the liturgy. Are we to give any of these features up because of a romanticized notion of a ghetto that, truth be told, our ancestors were rightly delighted to leave behind?

I do not mean to imply that all reforming innovations of the past 150 years should be automatically retained. But they should not all be automatically dropped either, certainly not merely because we believe them, falsely, to be alien to traditional Judaism. The truth is, after all, that even so-called traditional music idioms have been affected by the surrounding cultural, temporal, and local contexts as well. The vaunted chazzanut of most eastern European Orthodox cantors, for example, though loosely derived from several kinds of mostly synthetic modes, are actually performed in such a way that they display the influence of early nineteenth-century Italian opera. And traditional melodies beloved by Orthodox congregations are as apt to derive from Viennese waltzes and Polish mazurkas as from some putatively pure Jewish musical heritage.

Given our recent disdain for the Reform experience of the past, we have found it convenient in recent years simply to treat its liturgical music with benign neglect. We have taught our children that the only music worth singing is the "happy music" they learn in youth groups in summer camps. In many cases, we have even found it expedient to eliminate the weekly Friday evening late service, because it is "too formal." Instead, we relegate such worship to a once-a-month get-together and advertise the other weeks as family services, "tot-Shabbat," and the like. Who wants to hear a choir perform when the congregation can get its religious experience from singing the same nostalgic tunes week after week?

Discovery of the Banal in Synagogue and Church

Even as we have recovered so-called tradition, we have discovered genuine banality. We have determined that contemporary sounds in music are anathema to most congregations, as to most concert-goers who prefer, at best, baroque or romantic favorites. Armed with this determination, cantors now feel free to do their own thing, even if their own thing is purely the music they themselves compose, regardless of its quality. Of course even Bach nearly invariably performed only his own music—or arranged music that was traditional in the same way that many cantors and music directors in our synagogues arrogate to themselves the position of composer and change a few chords or make up a new tune which is like many well-known tunes that they have heard, and then call it their own. Nonetheless, we ought to need no reminder that there is a difference between Johann Sebastian Bach and this kind of a pseudo-composer. Synagogue music today has thus fallen largely into the hands of the "new traditional composers" who write in a popular style that is pseudo-Jewish, pseudo–pop-American, and pseudo-Israeli. These composers are believed because their style offends no one, challenges no one, and is easy to perform. If this state of affairs continues, the more challenging musical works composed for the synagogue since the nineteenth-century—already rarely heard today—will become museum pieces to be resurrected only for special occasions.

Composers who write banal liturgical music are certainly not limited to the synagogue. They exist also in every church. Like their Jewish counterparts, they are readily recognizable in that they write music merely to please. The difference is that, untouched by the romantic notion of a pseudo-Jewish heritage to be rediscovered in the sounds of the *shtetl,* the church's counterparts do not sound like the pseudo-Hasidic or Israeli tunes that have become the trademark of the Jewish commercial sacred music norm.

Ironically, despite all of this, we have in creative music today the largest body of active composers who happen to be Jews. Many of these are our leading American composers who would gladly write liturgical music, or at least sacred music, were they asked to. The music they write will not be Jewish music but music written by Jews—in the same way that Christian composers write, not Christian music, but sacred settings composed by people who profess Christianity. If our best composers are to come to the aid of the sacred, however, we will have to address our situation honestly, divest ourselves of the mythology that scapegoats music for the ills of worship in general, and convince those charged with planning worship that good music is not only possible but desirable.

Rescuing the Situation

Lately, the American Reform movement has realized that it is extremely important at least to take stock of its musical situation. With that end in mind, it has established a Commission on Synagogue Music to study the situation and make some recommendations. (Details of the role of the commission are provided by Benjie-Ellen Schiller, above.) The commission has itself noted the problems of ignorance, misinformation, and apathy that I describe, and promises to establish a public dialogue about the state of Jewish music. Perhaps, then, we are at a turning point, once again prepared to emphasize the kind of professionally created music that originally inspired the Reform synagogue to break out of the traditions of the ghetto whence it had come.

If now is a turning point, it will just be initiating a long process of change. Much needs to be done, especially if we reconsider my opening observation: the prevailing secularity of our society must be overcome if genuine sacred music is to flourish. Once we recognize the elementary truth that music for the synagogue cannot simply be a pabulum, several steps will move us closer to our goal. With the resurgence of such true musical life here, we would create a music for the synagogue second to none.

First, synagogue music does require easy-to-learn songs, such as it now contains. In addition, it requires challenging works worthy of the great prayers in our liturgy.

Second, we have failed to perpetuate the great choral tradition begun at the dawn of the Reform synagogue and brought to great heights of excellence in Germany by the early 1930s. In fact, the creation of an American equivalent was actually begun in the 1920s and 1930s by immigrants fleeing from the Holocaust, as well as by such American composers as Jacobi, Binder, and Freed (see Benjie-Ellen Schiller's essay, above). Further, this movement continued at a feverish pitch through the fifties and sixties. Now, however, it has been replaced by the search for authentic Jewish tradition.

Third, though changing with the times is necessary (a message inherent in Reform Judaism), the last thing we should expect is a *return* to just anything, including the reestablishment of the music of German or French classical Reform, or even the American classical Reform tradition. However, we can and should move forward to a new musical synthesis that builds on, and makes selective use of, these traditions of the past.

Fourth, musicians must remain true to their own calling, committed to the proposition that through music, possibly more than through any other art, the sacred may be reintroduced into people's lives. While the need—perhaps even the ability—to pray regularly in our temples is no longer of the utmost importance to congregants, if indeed it ever was, it does not follow that committed musicians, loyal to their field as well as to their religious convictions, must be as neglectful of the sacred as the congregants are.

Who more than the composers among us should take up the task of differentiating the sacred from the profane? Of course, we are living in a secular society, yet people, young and old, yearn for a more meaningful spiritual experience. Concerned musicians must seize the moment and formulate a sacred sound that is at once rooted in the several genuine traditions that constitute our religious past and fashioned, not for some other time and place, but for the contexts in which we ourselves live.

"Sing a New Song": A Petition for a Visionary Black Hymnody

Jon Michael Spencer

In my book, *Black Hymnody: A Hymnological History of the African-American Church,*[1] I give a historical reading of the black church through a study of the hymns in the hymn books of ten denominations. Because the hymns sung in the black church are an essential aspect of our religious worldview, my study provided me with information regarding the status of our theological and doctrinal beliefs as well as our social perspectives over the last two centuries. The book closes with a postscript that makes explicit some of the underlying implications in this hymnological history; I conclude that the black church and its hymnody are caught in a liberative lag with regard to the self-identity and self-determination of African Americans who are Christians. That postscript is essentially the prologue of the present paper, in which I identify three primary aspects of this liberative lag. I claim that a Eurocentric biblical analysis, interpretation, and doctrinal guardianship hold black hymnody by and large captive to the subordinationist traditions of racism, sexism, and classism.

Examples that reinforce racism and sexism set a context for my discussion. In Reginald Heber's "From Greenland's Icy Mountains," we sing:

Can men, whose souls are lighted with wisdom from on high,
Can they to men benighted the lamp of light deny.

Or again, as in John H. Stockton's hymn, "Come Every Soul by Sin Oppressed":

For Jesus shed His precious blood rich blessings to bestow;
Plunge now into the crimson flood that washes white as snow.

All too frequently, references to sin use images of darkness; to goodness, light or whiteness.

The popular hymnic language of the church is certainly as problematic with regard to sexism, not because the texts explicitly degrade women but because they exclude or subordinate women through the preponderance of male images and pronouns for God as well as through masculine nouns and pronouns even in reference to women. Among such hymns, too numerous to list, are Frederic Faber's "Faith of Our Fathers," Charles Wesley's "Come, Father, Son, and Holy Ghost," and the hymns of the patriarchal social gospel movement, such as William Merrill's "Rise Up, O Men of God." Hence, the notion that Christ can make a woman "male" and therefore suitable for entrance into God's "*king*dom" is not simply an extraneous idea found in the apocryphal Gospel according to Thomas (99:18–26); Christian hymnody implies the same idea, along with the notion that blacks, albeit allegedly "cursed," can be washed "white."

In challenging African American hymnists to be sensitive to contemporary currents of social change, I am responding in part to the challenge of visionary black scholars, among them some African American biblical scholars; these Scripture scholars are leading us to examine one of the black church's principal "near-canonical sources" that reinforces subordinationist boundaries.[2] Vincent Wimbush notes that the various scholarly approaches to the African American religious tradition—history, sociology, theology—have neglected to examine the role that the Bible has played in shaping that tradition.[3] Therefore, as these scholars raise our consciousness about an adoption and dissemination of a liberationist rather than a precritical literalist interpretation of Scripture,[4] I hear them challenging as well the African American hymnist. "A primary responsibility of the African

American biblical scholar,'' says William Meyers, ''is to aid
the African American believing community in understanding,
surviving, and altering its present socio-political situation
through accurate and appropriate interpretation and application
of Holy Scripture.''[5] One of my goals as an African American
hymnologist is to clarify the relationship between the biblical
text and the wider canon that is our hymnody. Hymnologist Benjamin Crawford says the development and future of religious
ideals rest on the hymns people sing: ''For the average
churchman [sic] the hymn book is more a book of religion than
his Bible. More religious interest is brought him by song than
by the Scriptures. In fact much of scriptural truth is conveyed
to him through hymns.''[6] If this measurement of the role of
hymnody in the religious life of the laity is accurate, then a
revised hymnody is a prerequisite in order to help African
American congregations ''live into a new way of thinking'' (see
Janet R. Walton, introduction).

My reading of the research of black church scholars suggests
that the black church is captive to the theological and doctrinal
hegemony of Eurocentric biblical Christianity that emphasizes
an overly dogmatic devotion to the Bible. This perspective keeps
our theological way of thinking bound, to a substantial degree,
to the Greco-Roman metaphysical worldview as regards
divinity;[7] and it forces modern marginalized readers—the victims
of sexism, racism, and classism—to side against the marginalized
groups in the Bible.[8] Thus, there is something very suspect about
the black church maintaining Christian orthodoxy when in fact
that orthodoxy looks patronizingly upon traditions that at best
supplement and never alter Eurocentric cultural preferences.
This is especially so when the Eurocentric preferences require
(as is usual) the suppression of worldviews that, say, value the
experiences of being a woman, or a person of color, or poor.

Quite aware of this dilemma, African American biblical
scholar Clarice Martin asks why black men and ministers reject
the subordinationist ethos of master-over-slave while essentially
accepting the kindred ethos of male-over-female.[9] ''Orthodoxy''
of this kind of hierarchical ''body politic''—a European head
over an African foot, a male head over a female foot, a wealthy

head over an impoverished foot—has resulted in the sickness in the Christian "body." To continue with this tradition that has split up the black church and cut us off from the root of our African history, identity, and potentiality is to participate in the tradition's sickness. What African American Christians ought to be endorsing is not uniformity and conformity but an ever-emerging church that is permitted to mature into an institution of liberty (a community of redemptively free people), equality (a community of individuals with equal rights and opportunities), and family (a community of siblings free from patriarchy, race prejudice, and class divisiveness).

History has proved that the so-called orthodoxy of "let the church be the church" is part and parcel of what has been called *Christendom*. In his *Attack upon "Christendom"* (1855), Søren Kierkegaard defined *Christendom* as religion that stands diametrically opposed to New Testament Christianity; as religion that plays at faith and worship, at liturgical "pomp and circumstance," rather than demanding theological substance.[10] In Christian hymnody, *Christendom* reflects such images: Christ is a royal potentate surrounded by white angels that worship "him" upon a mighty throne.

> All hail the power of Jesus' name!
> Let angels prostrate fall;
> Bring forth the royal diadem,
> And crown him Lord of all.

Where Christ is protrayed as male rather than as female (or feminine), as white rather than as a woman or man of color (or oppressed), as master rather than as servant (or poor), what results is the hymnic tradition of gender, race, and class hierarchism rooted in Greco-Roman societal conventions and philosophical sanctionings.

Let me say that the intent of this critical assessment is not to denigrate the black church, which historically has been the most important institution owned and operated by African Americans. I understand all who resonate with what the esteemed preacher from Los Angeles, E. V. Hill, once said in a wonderful sermon: "As for me, church still fulfills my heart's desire. I love thy church, oh God. I'm still coming as an empty pitcher before a full fountain. In my heart, I still have an itchin' that only the gospel can help me."[11] Neither is the intent of the challenge I put forth to denigrate the black hymnists whose songs have sustained us over the last century—the gospel hymns of Charles Albert Tindley (Methodist), Charles Price Jones (Holiness), and Lucie E. Campbell (Baptist). But these gospel hymns are so anticultural—Jesus Christ is portrayed as *everything* and the world as *nothing*—that even the value and beauty of African American and African culture are left unaffirmed. Jones's "I Am Happy with Jesus Alone" illustrates the point:

> Should father and mother forsake me alone,
> My bed upon earth be a stone,
> I'll cling to my Savior, He loves me I know,
> I'm happy with Jesus alone.

In search of a solution to this sort of dilemma I looked to Africa. Haki Madhubuti, the African American poet and cultural critic, suggests that a study of the work of Cheikh Anta Diop and kindred African and African-diaspora Africologists takes a requisite initial step for recapturing the minds of African Americans.[12] As my essay attests, I did turn to Diop, as well as to John Henrik Clarke and others, for information and inspiration. These Africologists see an Egyptian anteriority as the basis of a reconceived and renewed African American culture. Thus, it is upon such scholars' shoulders that I stand in calling for a renaissance in the black church that is to begin with a revised black hymnody. Hymns such as my own "Our God Who Reigns Lord before Us" and "Gird Our Loins and Guide Our Lives," illustrate beginning possibilities (see examples 1 and 2). From a church that cherishes its origins, the renaissance can overflow into the community. "Without the full participation of the church," says Molefi Asante, "we cannot have a genuine re-creation. In fact, our history shows, that the church, sooner or later, establishes itself as transmitter of the new visions within our community."[13]

Where the black church is captive to the theological, doc-

Example 1. Jon Michael Spencer's setting of *Our God Who Reigns Lord before Us.*

Example 2. Jon Michael Spencer's setting of *Gird Our Loins and Guide Our Lives.*

trinal, and social hegemony of Eurocentrism, African Americans
are limited in their development of self-identity and self-determination, inwardly as well as in the larger social milieu. Religion
works like an opiate in our societal bloodstream: We are
divesting ourselves of personal power by investing the God
presented us by the guardians of orthodoxy with all power. We
are left marginalized and, worse, submissive or indifferent to
the subordinationist practices of that guarded tradition. Religion
itself is not necessarily responsible for this opiate effect; religion
need not limit human aspiration and achievement. African
American self-identity and self-determination can be achieved
in and through religious and theological growth. An appropriate
religious dictum for African Americans to remember is "Know
thyself," the inscription Socrates found outside the temples in
Egypt where Egyptian priests taught him philosophy.[14] This kind
of African anteriority can be the basis of a renewed sense of
self-identity and a resulting self-determination.

By what means, then, can we alleviate the problems reflected
in black hymnody and progress more rapidly, via the vehicle
of our religion, toward gender, race, and class liberation? Songs
that recover the best of our African heritage, while also
remembering past struggles African Americans have overcome
and future hurdles we must overcome, would certainly help
launch us toward the alleviation of problems of gender, race,
and class. Such a new corpus of hymnody would build upon
the base of spirituals and include modern expressions of faith
that recoup the best of our African anteriority, such as in
W. E. B. Du Bois's poem of 1899:

I am the smoke king
I am black
I am darkening with song;
I am hearkening to wrong;
I will be black as blackness can . . .

I am carving God in night,
I am painting hell in white,
I am smoke king
I am black.[15]

Preventing the possibility of such an anteriority is a silent
concensus among us (and among outsiders who observe us) that
we cannot comprehend or practice Christianity without European interpretation, without European hymns, without the
"Caucasian Jesus" sanctioning the validity of our religion.
Madhubuti says, "We in our search for meaning generally go
the way of European-American 'correctness,' not realizing that
what is 'normal' for others may be deadly for us."[16] African
American historian Asa Hilliard affirms in his foreword to the
1976 reprint of George G. M. James's *Stolen Legacy* (1954):
"Mental bondage is invisible violence."[17] Therefore, I am
calling for a reformation and a renaissance comprised of a
renewed look at history, culture, and cosmology in the ancient
African civilization of Egypt in order to create a hymnody that,
somewhat like the poetic and narrative literature of the Hebrew
Bible,[18] esteems Africa. As African American historian John
Henrik Clarke put it, "If we have to change tomorrow we are
going to have to look back in order to look forward. We will
have to look back with some courage, warm our hands on the
revolutionary fires of those who came before us and understand
that we have within ourselves, nationally and internationally,
the ability to regain what we lost and to build a new humanity
for ourselves, first and foremost, and for the whole world
ultimately."[19]

Given my suggestion that we engage in an Egyptian anteriority
for the purpose of engendering a hymnic renaissance, the critical
reader of this essay might ask how I can, without contradiction, draw on the thought of Eurocentric scholars, particularly
since I am critical of their historical record. Chancellor Williams
says, and I concur, that even the most racist writers usually
prove the opposite of what they intended to assert. "Indeed,
it is doubtful whether anyone, even a devil, could write a book
completely devoid of truth."[20] I also agree with Cheikh Diop
that Egypt is the root and basis of Western cultures, so that most
of the ideas that appear foreign to African peoples are but the
modified, reversed, or misconstrued thought of Africa.[21] "Consequently, no thought, no ideology is, in essence, foreign to
Africa, which was their birthplace," says Diop. "It is therefore

with total liberty that Africans can draw from the common intellectual heritage of humanity, letting themselves be guided only by the notions of utility and efficiency.''[22] I believe this to be axiomatic but insist on—as with our choice of hymnody—selectivity, critical review, and frequent revision. As regards our hymnody, these review processes must be based on the legitimizing and systematizing of measurements (values, cosmology) of an Egyptian anteriority. If we choose to maintain some aspect of orthodoxy as regards our hymnody, it should be as a result of our having reviewed it in light of Egyptian thought or of having rediscovered its meaning in the context of our natural African cosmology. The precedent is in Eurocentric hymnologists' and hymnists' customary dependence on a Greco-Roman philosophical anteriority.

I understand fully that my petition is a progressive step that at present seems even to be an impossibility. Black Christians are too deeply entrenched in tradition, too attached to the old ''songs of Zion,'' to accept suddenly more compelling expressions of self-identity and self-determination rooted in an African anteriority. That our hymns have functioned at a ''tertiary level of canonicity'' makes change difficult.[23] Far less extreme and as a beginning is to do what the moral abolitionists, social gospelers, and civil rights' freedom fighters did to help give momentum to their movements: We can choose selectively from extant hymnody and revise it so that it resonates with the specific ethos and needs of our own time. Omitting or revising hymns containing negative sexist, racist, and classist language and imagery for the purpose of restoring our self-identity and self-determination will require the dispensation of a biblical hermeneutic and exegetical criticism that seeks to liberate our minds from perceiving the biblical canon and its cognate canon of hymnody as completed entities whose meanings are static for all time.

As regards the dilemma surrounding gender and hymnody, hymnologist Helen Pearson suggests that her colleagues engage in ''hymnic exegesis,'' asking certain critical questions about the text, just as biblical scholars engage in scriptural exegesis.[24] In order to carry out such ''hymnic exegesis'' to the necessary degree, so that we get at the very mythological root of these dilemmas, I contend that hymnologists must also engage in biblical exegesis, since scriptural myths and writings have been (mis)used to perpetuate problems surrounding gender and race. Two examples of myths that have thus found their way into our hymnody claim that women are depraved and inferior because of the disobedience of Eve in the Garden of Eden (Gen. 3:1-6) and that blacks are cursed and natural slaves because of the transgression of Ham (Gen. 9:18-27). These misinterpretations must be corrected by African American biblical scholars as preludes to a revised black hymnody.

The problem of classism requires a similar scrutiny. Jesus' defense of the poor, as documented in Scripture, hints at the extraordinary witness of the poor. Jesus' birth in a stable, his riding into Jerusalem on a donkey, and his depiction of wealth as an impediment to salvation suggest a reversal of prevalent social values. The "poor and needy" are called "blessed." Even Paul is implored by the apostles of the Jerusalem church to remember the poor in his mission to the Greeks—"which very thing" Paul "was eager to do" (Gal. 2:10). In spite of these passages (frequently cited by some systematic theologians to support liberation theology) history repeatedly implies that poverty is a curse. Although no biblical myth defends the bias, the master–slave dialectic in Paul's letter to Philemon (Phil. 8-21) can help us understand the dynamics of classism in modern times.

The need for African American scholars to engage in biblical exegesis and for our hymnists to consider their findings seriously is based on the fact that the scriptures have been used by the guardians of orthodoxy to perpetuate sexism, racism, and classism. The Bible and its interpretation have been, as African American biblical scholar Charles Copher says, sources of blessings to millions of people; but they have also been sources of some of the most solemn curses humankind has ever known.[25] I believe that part of the reason why Christian hymnody perpetuates these curses and why we have been hesitant to make appropriate revisions is that we still read the scriptures literally

and maintain outmoded interpretations that have been perpetuated through the traditional Eurocentric subordinationist reading.
I urge African American hymnists to give serious attention
to African American biblical scholarship that applies the
historical-critical method of exegesis. As African American
biblical scholar Thomas Hoyt says, the historical-critical method
serves as a defense against the problems of biblicism (dogmatic
literalist interpretation) and fundamentalism.[26] The historical-
critical method will help our hymnists recognize Scripture as
embodying a history of writing, editing, canonization, translation, and commercial publishing that have contributed to the
perpetuation of gender, race, and class hierarchism and oppression. By helping our hymnists understand original contexts,
meanings, and intents, we will begin to rid our church hymnody
of sexist, racist, and classist language, even though hierarchism
pervades the scriptures. If we can move beyond the point of
simply reading the Bible to the point of studying it critically,
I believe we can begin to progress uninhibitedly toward a
postpatriarchal, postracialist, post classist hymnody.

NOTES

1. Jon Michael Spencer, *Black Hymnody: A Hymnological History
of the African American Church* (Knoxville, Tenn., 1992).
2. William H. Myers, "The Hermeneutical Dilemma of the
African American Biblical Student," in Cain Hope Felder, ed., *Stony
the Road We Trod: African American Biblical Interpretation* (Minneapolis, 1991), 51, 53, 54.
3. Vincent L. Wimbush, "The Bible and African Americans: An
Outline of an Interpretative History," in Cain Hope Felder, ed., *Stony
the Road We Trod* (Minneapolis, 1991), 81–82.
4. Clarice J. Martin, "The *Haustafeln* (Household Codes) in
African American Biblical Interpretation: 'Free Slaves' and 'Subordinate Women'," in Cain Hope Felder, ed., *Stony the Road We Trod*,
(Minneapolis, 1991), 228.
5. Myers, "Hermeneutical Dilemma," 44.
6. Benjamin F. Crawford, *Religious Trends in a Century of Hymns*
(Carnegie, Pa., 1938), 24.

312 JON MICHAEL SPENCER

7. Robert E. Hood, *Must God Remain Greek? Afro Cultures and God-Talk* (Minneapolis, 1990), 110–11.
8. Renita J. Weems, "Reading *Her Way* through the Struggle: African American Women and the Bible," in Cain Hope Felder, ed., *Stony the Road We Trod* (Minneapolis, 1991), 72–73.
9. Martin, *"Haustafeln,"* 225.
10. Sören Kierkegaard, *Attack upon "Christendom"*, trans. Walter Lowrie (Princeton, 1968), 121, 191, 212.
11. Cited in Jon Michael Spencer, *Sacred Symphony: The Chanted Sermon of the Black Preacher* (Westport, Conn., 1987), 60.
12. Haki R. Madhubuti, *Enemies: The Clash of Races* (Chicago, 1978), 49.
13. Molefi Kete Asante, *Afrocentricity*, rev. ed. (Trenton, 1988), 71.
14. George G. M. James, *Stolen Legacy: Greek Philosophy Is Stolen Egyptian Philosophy* (New York, 1954), 3, 88.
15. "The Song of the Smoke," in W. E. B. Du Bois, *Selected Poems* (Accra, Ghana, 1964), 12.
16. Madhubuti, *Enemies,* 117.
17. Cited in John A. Williams, "The Stolen Legacy," in Ivan Van Sertima, ed., *African Presence in Early Europe,* (New Brunswick, N.J., 1985), 84.
18. See Randall C. Bailey, "Beyond Identification: The Use of Africans in Old Testament Poetry and Narratives," in Cain Hope Felder, ed., *Stony the Road We Trod* (Minneapolis, 1991), 183.
19. John Henrik Clarke, "African Resistance and Colonial Dominance: The Africans in the Americas," in John Henrik Clarke, ed., *New Dimensions in African History: The London Lectures of Dr. Yosef ben-Jochannan and Dr. John Henrik Clarke* (Trenton, 1991), 33–34.
20. Cited in Runoko Rashidi, "Blacks in Early Britain," in Ivan Van Sertima, ed., *African Presence in Early Europe* (New Brunswick, N.J., 1985), 252.
21. Cheikh Anta Diop, *Civilization or Barbarism: An Authentic Anthropology*, trans. Yaa-Lengi Meema Ngemi, Harold J. Salemson and Marjolijn de Jager, ed. (New York, 1991), 3.
22. Ibid., 4.
23. James A. Sanders, *Canon and Community* (Phildelphia, 1984), 14–15. Cited in Myers, "Hermeneutical Dilemma," 53.
24. Helen Bruch Pearson, "The Battered Bartered Bride," *The Hymn* 34 (Oct. 1983): 216.

25. Charles B. Copher, "Three Thousand Years of Biblical Interpretation with Reference to Black Peoples," in Gayraud S. Wilmore, ed., *African American Religious Studies: An Interdisciplinary Anthology* (Durham, N.C., 1989), 105.

26. Thomas Hoyt, Jr., "Interpreting Biblical Scholarship for the Black Church Tradition," in Cain Hope Felder, ed., *Stony the Road We Trod* (Minneapolis, 1991), 24.

Enculturation, Style, and the Sacred-Secular Debate

Virgil C. Funk

Five Worship Programs, Five Styles of Music

My work takes me into Roman Catholic parishes around the country as well as to worship services in other traditions and in other nations. My observations of liturgical renewal over the last twenty years have convinced me that North American Catholics, in particular, now use at least five discernible styles of liturgical celebration, each of which can be associated with a particular goal and a musical form that best expresses its style and purpose. I call these styles *monastic, ritualistic, communicative, dramatic,* and *action–small group.*

The widespread use of these various styles has not been mandated by any central organization, although the development and diffusion of certain styles have been strongly encouraged by the fact that they were modeled at one or another liturgical center, or by one or another key individual who was influential in liturgical or musical circles. Each of the styles cannot be associated with a particular region, but they have all been "showcased" in pastoral settings, as local ways of implementing liturgical renewal. Because of the influence of different seminaries and other institutions on the formation of liturgical ministers (including priests), neighboring parishes may display different styles, or several styles all at once; and because the priests on the staff of any particular parish may have attended different seminaries, the music in a single parish may on any

314

given day encompass diverse styles that may even compete with each other and with the worship program as a whole. But each of the styles responds to the officially directed liturgical renewal and to the articulated needs of congregations (which are certainly influenced by social change). The advocates of each style claim fidelity to the text or to the spirit—usually both—of the official liturgical directions.

My brief description of the five styles is followed by some general comments on their strengths, weaknesses, and proponents. That leads both to an analysis of what the development of these styles suggests for the category *sacred music* and to some suggestions as to where they may take North American Roman Catholic worship in the future.

The *monastic style,* somewhat like worship in the Eastern churches, presents liturgy as entry into another world. But while the liturgies of the East attempt to evoke heaven through the use of gold and bright colors, iconography, age-old chants, incense, and the like, monastic liturgy offers a different approach to the same goal. It tends to strip away distractions and cultural affiliations in order to leave people free to focus on the "mystery."[1] It emphasizes countercultural experiences and gathers the assembly into buildings designed with starkness and clarity of line to suggest otherworldly experiences. The music that best fits this style is plainchant and Gregorian chant, and the goal of worship in this style is to call the assembly to holiness.[2]

The *ritualistic style* reflects the common approach to liturgy in Roman Catholic churches worldwide, especially in Europe and North America, before Vatican II. It stresses form, repetition, and stability; its goal is to perform the rite correctly. The interpretation of *correctly,* however, varies from circle to circle. Before Vatican II, it normally meant "according to the rubrics," and in some places recently that interpretation has returned as a guiding norm. Generally, however, *correctly* these days means "according to the general norms," i.e., with an eye to the functional description of what is supposed to happen during the ritual and within the options and accommodations officially permitted in the rites. The concern with correct performance is intended to create a sense of order that, in turn, evokes perennial truth. This experience of order provides security and comfort to the assembly.[3] People gather in neo-Gothic or neo–Greco-Roman classical buildings for this kind of worship and are best served musically by the Germanic hymn with its measured beat. Such familiar and regular hymnody, even a once-taboo hymn like "A Mighty Fortress Is Our God," provides the assembly with sounds and words of certainty and security.

The *communicative style* stresses understanding. It favors plain speech: "Make sure the assembly knows what you are saying. Be clear. No pretense. No magic. What you see is what you get."[4] Some of the theatrical theories of Bertolt Brecht apply here—not so much to Brecht's attempts through epic theater to create a psychic distance between the audience and the performance, but his goal of influencing through theater the consciousness of the audience. The architecture for this worship features confrontational seating in plain buildings with highlights (banners, plants, color, lights) placed where the action is—e.g., at ambo, altar, and music center. The music's self-conscious contemporary sound makes it immediately understandable as a cultural phenomenon. It stresses a clear, straightforward text and tune, e.g., Suzanne Toolan's "I am the Bread of Life."[5] The goal of such worship is to communicate with the assembly without any need of cultural translation.

The *dramatic style* stresses engagement with the rite as presently enacted, especially through delight. Techniques of dramatic delight in this form range from the use of bishops' miters, triumphant trumpets, and medieval plays to contemporary sacred dance and made-for-television liturgies.[6] The most effective dramatic liturgies fall between the two extremes of updating older dramatic elements and the invention of liturgical thirty-second sound-bites. The musical style is drawn without apology from the more developed dramatic elements of secular culture, e.g., Brubeck's "Mass in Time of Hope." The goal of this worship style is to engage the assembly in the event.

The fifth style, *action–small group,* is more diverse, harder to describe. In some ways it is similar to the communicative style of worship, for some of the groups may be interested in heightened consciousness, particularly for action directed at social change. In other small groups, however, the liturgy may more closely resemble the dramatic style because it embraces dramatic elements from the group's ethnic origins. In either case, this fifth grouping embraces what happens in small groups that are significantly influenced by their distinctive makeup. Such groups include small ethnic communities of African-American, Hispanic, Korean, or Vietnamese worshipers who see themselves as preserving a minority identity in the midst of a larger culture, and groups gathered in the name of a social cause or group of causes, such as social justice groups—for example, feminists.[7] Influenced by the group's identity factor, the environment can range from the intricate, bold, colorful patterns of the Hispanic tradition to a room chosen for its undecorated starkness. The music may be chosen primarily to affirm ethnic traditions or the radical demands of justice, e.g., the music of Black Gospel, Holly Near's "We Are a Gentle, Angry People," or Tom Conry's song about the dawning of social justice, "I Will Not Die."[8] The goal is to invite the assembly to pray through symbols that honor particularity rather than demean it.

Strengths, Weaknesses, and Proponents of Each Style

None of these styles is necessarily better than any other; each is equally valid for the expression of worship, offering a different way of looking at how celebrants, space, and music interact in worship. In fact, each style reflects one or another aspect of the goals of the liturgical renewal as described in the *General Instruction of the Roman Missal* and other texts. The monastic style, for instance, reflects the church's belief that its worship, because centered on the unchanging God, is transcultural and transtemporal (an argument often used for preserving a sacred language like Latin and a sacred music like Gregorian chant and polyphony for use in liturgy).[9] The ritualistic style emphasizes the common roots of Roman Catholic worship and its role as a stabilizing force in the church and in society.[10] The communicative style originates from, and expresses, the catechetical and pastoral aspects of worship, its "horizontal" dimension of speaking to the assembly.[11] The dramatic style places its emphasis on the sacramental nature of worship—the rich use of the external signs of the liturgy's inner reality.[12] The small group model helps to stress the importance of the local assembly.[13]

Each of the styles, of course, has its extremes and abuses which are likely to be noticed by average parishioners as well as professionals. The monastic style, for instance, might be described as "nice, but unreal," while the ritualistic style is sometimes considered "boring, too much the same, too many smells and bells." Someone unfamiliar with the communicative style might ask, "Is that all there is? It's too plain, not enough poetry."[14] The dramatic style, on the other hand, is sometimes called "too secular, too tinselly": entertainment, really, rather than worship. And depending on their origins and purpose, the liturgy celebrated by small groups might be considered "too foreign" and the group "too closed." Or such liturgy might evoke the comment, "They're only interested in good works, not prayer; it's a social gathering, and that's all." Such comments caricature the worst extremes of each style but also contain an element of truth about each one's weaknesses.

Studies of medieval liturgy show a diversity of liturgical expression from region to region: not only a difference of rites and uses, but variations also within those larger ritual divisions.[15] I am fascinated by what I take to be clear evidence for the same urge toward local diversity during this present developmental period in North America. As in the medieval period, when various rites and usages influenced one another, so too now, as these various styles develop, they begin to square off against one another in a process of mutual correction. In fact, I believe that these various North American styles may even have originated in the first place as necessary correctives for one another.

Each style had, and still has, its own defenders and promoters.

In the Midwest, for instance, the liturgical movement had its roots at St. John's, Collegeville; as a Benedictine center, it exercised a strong influence in spreading the monastic style. At another Midwest location, however, the University of Notre Dame and its Center for Pastoral Liturgy, emphasis was placed on correct ritual style. On the East Coast, meanwhile, Eugene Walsh at the Theological College of The Catholic University in Washington, D.C., stressed a directly communicative style of worship that was simple, straightforward, and with no show.[16] On the West Coast, The Institute for Spirituality and Worship at Berkeley emphasized the use of the arts, including dance, at a high dramatic level. (Donald Osuna used this style in the widely imitated liturgies that he prepared and presided over at the Cathedral of St. Francis de Sales in Oakland.) The action-small group model developed all around North America with no identifiable center, though it has been mostly an urban phenomenon; the style took root where there were small ethnic pockets or where like-minded people gathered for support, and it was influenced by the American drive for cohesiveness in small communities.

Diversity of Style and the Category "Sacred Music"

In my opinion there is no such thing as *sacred music,* if by that term you mean a particular series of notes or chord progressions sacred in and of themselves. There are such notes and progressions attached to certain words that particular cultures have learned to identify with religious experiences, but these notes and even the words vary from culture to culture. Through a similar process of learning and memory we have come to identify other notes and chords and words with popular culture, but these also vary among cultures.

Liturgies of the monastic and ritual models draw clear distinctions between popular cultural sounds and religiously associated sounds; the distinctions begin to blur in the communicative, dramatic, and small group or action-oriented models. The way each model relates to the surrounding culture's music, in fact, indicates a progressive interaction with the culture itself, for music carries cultural values at a very high level.

Monastic liturgy, for instance, is deliberately countercultural; it excludes, as best it can, all contemporary or easily identifiable cultural sounds. Ritualistic worship is less countercultural, for it includes harmonization and popular forms of music, though it does not draw these from the current culture. The communicative model embraces elements of all cultures, drawing from current and historical cultures those sounds that best carry the message. The dramatic model uses the music of the popular culture willingly, with no apologies. Small group liturgy, finally, completes the circle by being countercultural in a confrontational way. It takes seriously the traditions and experiences of the gathered group, freely choosing its own music but often excluding that of the surrounding culture; alternatively, action-oriented groups may be critical of all music and texts, especially those that do not serve their cause.

The Future of These Styles

Celebration style does make a difference in the perceived and experienced meaning of our worship, for how we worship influences what we think our worship is about. For instance, the music we sing reflects the kind of God in whom we believe.

In the Christendom of medieval Europe, liturgical cultures intermixed with others. Travel among cultural, educational, commercial, and liturgical centers guaranteed that members of any single subculture knew something about the others as well. The patterns of worship in those centuries became interactive, influencing and developing one another. In our culture, even more so, the worship patterns of any single style do not remain in isolation. Hence, the five varieties of worship that I have outlined can be expected to influence each other, and not just at random: this interactive and developmental pattern is instinctively corrective.

Such interactive patterns are a phenomenon not just of medieval Europe or of our own time, however, because there are relationships in the styles I have outlined to other, deeper patterns, inherent, in Catholicism at least, in ecclesiological and liturgical considerations. I do not mean to argue here that the five styles are unique only to Catholicism, though I leave it to Protestants and Jews to determine the extent to which the styles I outline can be found in their own worship. For Catholics, however, the common cultural currency of the five styles can be linked as well to internal developments in their church. For instance, there are similarities here to Avery Dulles's models of the church, though they are not exact equations, at least in part because the styles I have described are drawn directly from living experience, while his models are derived from theory. Similarly, the models and their accompanying musical expressions can be related to various aspects of official Roman documents but also to the basic elements of the eucharistic liturgy drawn from the Lima eucharistic studies: thanks, memorial, epiclesis, communion, and eschatology.

I know that I have oversimplified the picture, but I believe that this preliminary description of present practice is helpful for our continuing discussion of music in worship. I happen to believe that church and synagogue alike need all of these approaches. The assembly needs (1) to be called to holiness (2) through a stable ritual that (3) communicates clearly and simply but (4) in a way that is entertaining and exciting, and (5) that moves the assembly, finally, to action in the wider world.

In fact, some recent musical styles seem to be responding to this diversity of approach, in that they attempt to bridge the gaps and become inclusive of several styles of worship simultaneously. For instance, the compositions written by Jacques Berthier for the Taizé community fall into this unifying category. On the pastoral scene, some musicians are striving to unify their parish's worship styles or the sometimes conflicting expectations of the community by drawing their selections from a variety of musical resources, beginning perhaps with a "foursquare" hymn as the gathering song, using a plainsong Kyrie, a psalm in the communicative style of David Haas or Michael Joncas, a dramatic choral piece at the preparation of gifts, and a Tom Conry "send-'em-out-armed-for-justice" social gospel song at the closing. At the moment, I grant, such a mixture may only confuse the expectations of the gathered assembly, but perhaps it is the first step in a long march to a new fusion of styles, expectations, and repertories.

NOTES

1. Monastic style reflects a statement like this from the General Instruction of the Roman Missal (hereafter GIRM), introduction, no. 3: "The celebration of the Mass . . . proclaims the sublime mystery of the Lord's real presence under the eucharistic elements. . . . The Mass does this not only by means of the very words of consecration . . . but also by that *spirit and expression of reverence and adoration* in which the eucharistic liturgy is carried out" (emphasis added). The translation of the Latin text is from *Documents on the Liturgy 1963–1979: Conciliar, Papal, and Curial Texts* (hereafter *DOL*), International Commission on English in the Liturgy, ed. (Collegeville, Minn., 1982), no. 1378.

2. "These people are holy by their origin, but becoming ever more holy by conscious, active, and fruitful participation in the mystery of the eucharist" (GIRM, introduction, no. 5; *DOL,* no. 1380).

3. "The current norms . . . are fresh evidence of the great care, faith, and unchanged love that the Church shows toward the eucharist. They attest as well *to its coherent tradition,* continuing amid the introduction of some new elements" (GIRM, introduction, no. 1, emphasis added; *DOL,* no. 1376).

4. "The celebration of the . . . entire liturgy involves the use of outward signs that foster, strengthen, and express faith. There must be the utmost care therefore to choose and to make wise use of those forms and elements provided . . . that . . . will best foster active and full participation and serve the spiritual well-being of the faithful" (GIRM, no. 5; *DOL,* no. 1395).

5. Suzanne Toolan, "I Am the Bread of Life," copyright 1970, GIA Publications, Inc.

6. "After due regard for the nature and circumstances of each assembly, the celebration is planned in such a way that it brings about in the faithful a *participation in body and spirit* that is conscious, active, full, and motivated by faith, hope, and charity. The Church desires this kind of celebration" (GIRM, no. 3, emphasis added; *DOL,* no. 1393).

7. "The 'tradition of the Fathers' does not require merely the preservation of what our immediate predecessors have passed on to us. . . . This broader view shows us how the Holy Spirit endows the people of God with a marvelous fidelity in preserving the deposit of faith unchanged, even though prayers and rites differ so greatly" (GIRM, introduction, no. 9; *DOL,* no. 1384).

8. Tom Conry, "I Will Not Die," copyright 1984, TEAM Publications. The third and fourth verses, in particular, sing of God's promise of a "mighty wind of justice" and of special divine care for the "poor and the needy," the "lost and the desp'rate."

9. See GIRM, no. 1; *DOL,* no. 1391. On the preservation of a particular style and repertory of music, see the Constitution on the Liturgy, no. 116 (*DOL,* no. 116).

10. See the comments on the relation between the Tridentine missal and the missal of Paul VI in GIRM, introduction, nos. 6–9 (*DOL,* nos. 1381–84).

11. See GIRM, introduction, nos. 11–13; *DOL,* nos. 1386–88.

12. See GIRM, no. 5; *DOL,* no. 1395.

13. See GIRM, no. 3; *DOL,* no. 1393.

14. That reaction might be what underlay the negative comments particularly by writers in the United Kingdom about the translation of *Et cum spiritu tuo* as "And also with you."

15. The most familiar criticism of such diversity—and therefore evidence that it existed—is probably from the preface to the first *Book of Common Prayer* (1549): "Heretofore, there hath been great diversity in saying and singing in churches within this realm: some following Salisbury use, some Hereford use, some the use of Bangor, some of York, and some of Lincoln."

16. For a description of Eugene Walsh's influence on liturgical renewal through his seminary work as well as his participation with the Liturgical Conference and other renewal efforts, see Timothy Leonard, *Geno: A Biography of Eugene Walsh, S.S.* (Washington, D.C., 1988).

Conclusion

On Swimming Holes, Sound Pools, and Expanding Canons

LAWRENCE A. HOFFMAN

Retrospect

The essays in this book have issued from people with various points of view. Musicologists, composers, and liturgists; Catholics, Protestants, and Jews; men and women: all have cooperated in producing a volume that might, perhaps, in retrospect, be subtitled with questions—*Sacred Music: Is There Such a Thing Anymore? If So, What Is It?* To be sure, not every Jewish or Christian tradition in America is represented here. Echoes of ethnic churches go unexamined. We have no chapters on Pentecostals, Catholic Charismatics, or Evangelicals (neither the storefront variety, nor the TV ministries, whose massive Billy Graham style crusades depend so heavily on choirs). And a book on sacred music with no mention of the Mormon Tabernacle Choir? Omitted too is Orthodoxy, both Christian and Jewish. The chavurah, womenchurch, new age, and other manifestations of what were once, and sometimes still are, countercultural religious phenomena are also missing except in passing. Given these and other lacunae, we can hardly claim to have considered the whole phenomenon of sacred sound in our time.

Adopting a metaphor that is in keeping with our book's topic, we might conclude that we have captured only part of the contemporary orchestra of American sacred sound. What we do have, however, is hardly random, and not at all insignificant. We have the orchestral ensemble that has played center stage in the churches normally going by the name *mainstream* through the last century of Christian life; and within Jewish life we have focused on Reform Judaism, which is to say, the movement that has most appreciated the "mainstream" musical heritage.

The term *mainstream* is hardly descriptive of the way things are—indeed the bulk of Americans belong these days to ethnic, storefront, evangelical, new age, nonwhite, and other alternatives. *Mainstream* is a cultural holdover from an earlier imperial era, when it was assumed that the European religious migrants come to roost in the New World would do for North America what they had done for Europe, namely, "civilize" it; holdout enclaves of colonial culture were not to be taken seriously. Nonetheless, I use *mainstream* throughout this essay as a term designed to remind us all of two presuppositions: first, the peculiar delusion by which we who inhabit "mainstream" religious institutions imagine that we are central to history; second, the parallel assumption that our cultural constructs, from cathedral spires to organ preludes, must enjoy a privileged status in the evolution of the species. As I proceed, my very high regard for these things will become evident. I do not want to see them come to an end. But I do not on that account imagine myself to be a curator of my culture, to be charged with ringing it 'round with barbed wire fences to keep out the philistine predators of the surrounding wilderness. We are not the Roman Empire, and those "others" out there are not barbarians. The purpose of this conclusion is not to discuss good music over against bad, but to help us think about change, particularly as we prepare to welcome the twenty-first century. I want to suggest some metaphors that will function productively, not destructively, for us, in order that debates on music can be recast in a way other than "Us against Them."

So this book is about the ensemble of sacred music apt to be sung, played, and heard in "mainstream" churches and synagogues. More than a survey, however, it reads like a report by a team of physicians called upon to diagnose the ensemble's health. Like any good medical team performing an examination, we have prefaced our report with a statement of the patient's history, in this case, the musical strains out of which our current ensemble's repertory and style have developed (part 1). Part 2 gave us a recent etiology of the patient's condition, explaining how the sixties to the nineties have differed so markedly from the period prior to the Second World War. Part 3 presented a sampling of sacred sound as it is being composed today—as if we had invited our music in the form of those who write it to amble around the examination room while we listen for signs of musical health. The three essays in part 4 provide somewhat conflicting reports by attending physicians: a generally despairing outlook by Samuel Adler, who emphasizes the corrosive effect of secular culture in general, and its pervasive entertainment industry in particular; a more sanguine diagnosis by Virgil Funk, who classifies the changing sounds of the sacred in our time without negating the spiritual health of those who use them; and a call from Jon Michael Spencer to take seriously the connection between sacred music and that other sacred item we call *justice*.

Patients come to their physician for all sorts of reasons, not necessarily because they think they are sick. Quite commonly, they arrive in the doctor's office with no particular complaints in mind but are drawn there by the recognition of how much has transpired since they paid their last visit. Change may be good or bad, but by definition it is not uneventful—neither for human beings nor for human culture. The one starting point from which the analysis of our musical state begins, then, is the recognition that change has been endemic to our century and has accelerated steadily, particularly from the sixties on, such that the most apt way to sum up the rapid succession of sounds through which North Americans have passed, in both their secular and their religious life, is with the label popularized by Alvin Toffler: *future shock*. Hence our title: *Sacred Sound and Social Change,* with an accent on social change.

Swimming Holes and Sound Pools

We do not even recognize the phenomenon of change, unless we first have experienced equilibrium. Molecules of air continually shaken, heated, and otherwise randomly disturbed in a paper bag cannot be said to undergo recognizable change if the bag is turned upside down, just as human rollercoaster riders overtaken by vertigo will have little sensation of change when the train they are on dips one way rather than the other. What has prompted worshipers in the "mainstream" churches and synagogues here to recognize significant social change, therefore, is the fact that we had achieved musical equilibrium. A colleague of mine speaks of us as inhabiting a sound pool, akin to the local swimming hole.[1] For as long as we or our parents can remember, we have gone there daily to float languorously on our backs, the sun shining warmly on our faces in the hot afternoons. Swimming about in a sound pool with its soothing notes hallowed by tradition is not all that different. Who can blame the people who frequent the swimming hole for imagining that this body of water has always been here, perhaps even planned for our comfort from the ice age on, when mountains reared up just so that cool streams of sparkling water made from melting snow could annually flow to this very spot? And who can blame us for imagining that the same is true of our music? Streams of sound have watered our consciousness for centuries, coming together in a pool of familiar sounds that flow over us and through us whenever we go to pray. The swimming hole on one hand and the music pool on the other are two of a kind: comfortable fixtures of daily life, taken for granted as having always been there.

That is bad geology, of course, and even worse musicology. Expert scientists, whether of rock formations or of music, know that time and change are far more complex than that. Generalizations are appealing, however. We like to think of our sound pool as having been formulated through the centuries by the harmonious happenstance of a single musical chain running vertically through time, stretching as if with some teleological end in mind to our own era, which, in and of itself, must be the right way to sing. Christian church-goers therefore dimly imagine an ancient monastic chant becoming appropriately Gregorian somehow; the introduction of polyphony and then hymns; and a classical heritage spanning the gamut from Lutheran chorales to grand Anglican anthems. Go the old and stable churches like York Minster and that is what you hear—selections from what is loosely called the Western musical heritage, all "good stuff" demanding an educated ear, triumphal pride, and the lurking suspicion that there really is such a thing as destiny.

On the New York Stock Exchange, different investors amass different portfolios; so too, different "mainstream" churches feature different aspects of Christianity's common musical heritage. But from the perspective of a stock broker, a thousand shares of CBS, Coca Cola, and General Electric differ little from a thousand shares of ABC, Pepsi Cola, and General Motors. Whatever shares people actually buy, they are purchasing stock in the same system and the same market rather than (for example) frequenting art auctions or betting on horses with their investment dollars. So too, the musical portfolios of "mainstream" churches may well vary in their preferences: Catholics have favored chant, Lutherans like hymns, Calvinists went for psalmody. But bluechip is bluechip, whether in stock or in music. Over the years, all "mainstream" Christians have frequented the same sound pool and have learned to recognize sacred music when they heard it.

If the swimming hole is sufficiently surrounded by protective foliage, the swimmers float about in blissful ignorance of other people doing the same thing elsewhere—in a nearby lake, perhaps, or at the beach a few miles away. So too, cultural foliage—the preference for our own way of doing things—successfully prevents our attention from being diverted to alternatives. Swimmers in the "mainstream" sound pools did not

easily notice that other Christians were singing other songs—
Shaker folk melodies, Black spirituals, Blue Grass favorites,
northern city Gospel tunes. Sacred music meant bathing in the
sound pool watered by the coursing melodies of Western church
and Western culture, our end of the "evolutionary" spiral that
included the likes of Mozart, Haydn, Bach, and Brahms.

Something seemed both old and right about it. A sort of
"givenness" to the pool of sound greeted Christian worshipers
every Sunday morning. Until very recently, it was widely held,
if only on an unconscious level, that the "right people" were
rooted in Western church antiquity and that they sang the "right
stuff."

"Wie es christelt sich, so jüdelt es sich" ("What goes for
Christians goes for Jews"). So runs an old and trenchant proverb
attributed to various wags, not the least Heinrich Heine
(1797–1856)—who probably did not say it first, but would no
doubt have wished that he had. Heine was a Jew who opted
for baptism, which he described as his "admission ticket to
European culture." Already in Heine's day, Jewish salon society
was attracting philosophers, aesthetes, and artists of all kinds—
everyone from Schleiermacher to Heine himself. For Jews, this
was a generation of immigrants whose migration was not between countries or even continents but between entire worlds:
the world of the ghetto and the world of Christian society. Moses
Mendelssohn (1729–1786), whose successful foray into Christian cultural circles heralded the move, still lived as a traditional
Jew. His son, Abraham, left Judaism for Christianity; and
Abraham's son, Felix—who was baptized even before his
father—was integral to the sound pool of Christian Europe.
Among other things, Felix Mendelssohn's fame rests on his
successful revival (in 1892) of J. S. Bach's *St. Matthew Passion,* and his own oratorio (six years later) entitled *St. Paul.*
On a very grand scale, grandfather Moses and grandson Felix
personify the Jewish transition from their own traditional sound
pool, to the pool of Western culture.

Between the two extremes were those "enlightened" Jews
of taste who reformed their synagogue's sacred sound rather
than abandon it. They had come from a parochial milieu, half

enforced from without, half chosen from within, in which educated worshipers had come to adopt their own Jewish version of the myth of musical correctitude. They posited some ancient chant, some very old melodies labeled *misinai* (from Sinai); and some moderately old but very traditional ways of singing things, cantorial favorites perhaps, or old-time melodies parents had got from grandparents and then handed on. No less than Christians, these Ashkenazi Jews cultivated their own cultural foliage to block out musical accomplishments elsewhere. Knowing that they themselves had not made it to the guild that churned out the great Christian music, they assumed no Jew had, whereas, in fact, a long line of Jews in seventeenth- and eighteenth-century Mantua (best exemplified by Salamone de Rossi, c. 1589–1628) had successfully adapted the sound of the court to synagogue melodies. Ashkenazi Jews ignored the existence of Rossi, as they did Sephardi chant and any number of Ashkenazi localisms as well, preferring the comfort of their own official sound pool, which was, of course, their own "right stuff" rather than the "wrong stuff" that some other Jews may have been singing in Turkey or in Egypt.

The point is we are unhappy with an untidy picture of cultural accomplishment. We like the mythic metaphor of sacred streams coursing carefully together into a neat pool of sound that is our own and is intended as such from the very beginning. We enjoy the construct of musical homogeny through time; it gives us equilibrium. When Jews were ushered into the modern world of Western culture, so that their musical equilibrium was unbalanced, they did exactly what every Jewish author of this book has emphasized: they diverted the stream of Western cultural sounds into the Jewish sound pool, altered their myth to include the newly admitted foreign culture, and paraded on the sidewalks of Vienna or Berlin, New York or Chicago, secure in the knowledge that Jews, too, could have the "right stuff."

An Open Canon

How then do we evaluate a claim to having the "right stuff"? Part 1 of this book explodes the myth to some extent, since it demonstrates the incredible variety of music that has filled the annals of church and synagogue. Whatever the "right stuff" is, it did not grow linearly along a single privileged cultural track. It arose here and there, was engaged by a variety of influences, and came only in retrospect to be accepted as inherently connected with what came before. Whatever our official musical heritage may be, it is very much more diverse than we thought, and if we include the unofficial music of our faiths, the sounds blocked out by cultural protective foliage, we encounter the marginal notes that expand the canon of the past even further.

The history of music turns out to be remarkably like the histories of sacred text and sacred space. Once upon a time, we thought we had unidimensional evolution in our prayer texts too; now we know the norm was immense diversity, until authorities canonized one set of texts at the expense of others, and then established the myth that their creation too was the "right stuff," a natural evolution from biblical bases, church fathers, canonical councils, or rabbinic proclamations. So too with architecture—ancient synagogues, for instance, which we once thought had developed naturally from early Galilean to Byzantine models. No such thing! Synagogues sometimes faced Jerusalem, sometimes did not; sometimes were long and narrow, sometimes square, sometimes neither; some had mosaic floors, some had wall paintings, some had inscriptions in Greek, and some had no such ornamentation. There was no singular archeological plan, and there was no single line of development— not, at least, until scholars decided to invent one. Nobody walks out of worship humming an architectural plan, however, so the architectural scholarly hypothesis, now discredited, matters little to anyone but the scholars. By contrast, the parallel musical hypothesis matters a great deal to people who like to hum, who know that what gets hummed are tunes, and who want the tunes they hum to be the "right stuff."

The theory of the "right stuff" however is not altogether without value. You can explode the evolutionary myth and discover long-lost alternatives in history's corners without thereby abandoning the right or even the obligation to maintain whatever it is that you have been doing for as long as memory serves. Take the texts of prayer, for instance. Granted that once upon a time Arian and "Orthodox" texts parried for prominence, and only eventually did the latter win; that after the fact, the Catholic church should now adopt Arian prayers for its liturgy does not follow. Similarly, take the Jewish equivalent. Of late, we have discovered that some precanonical Jewish material now known as Apocrypha and Pseudepigrapha was written by and for Jewish audiences. But eventually, the Hebrew scriptures were put together (for whatever reason) without Jubilees, or Maccabees, or Ecclesiasticus. Discovering Jewish prayers in Maccabees does not necessarily imply that synagogues today ought to feature them in the structure of their service. Once a canon has been agreed upon, it does not go out of business automatically the minute we discover that it was not always the "right stuff." To some extent, a successful authoritative decision to make something the "right stuff" automatically makes it so, even after we unmask the pretensions by which it came into being.

Thinking of music as a canon can be very helpful, therefore, especially since canonical criticism is not a new exercise for us. In the field of biblical studies we find critics reminding us that even the fixed text of the canon is always coming into being, in that "traditions are received and accepted by a later generation for reasons quite different from the original intention."[2] Canonical criticism thus "focuses on the believing communities at every stage along the way."[3] Canonical criticism applied to liturgy watches how accepted canons are treated, what parts are read, attended to, subjected to exegesis, embedded in favorite prayers, proclaimed as lectionary, and singled out as paradigms for action and faith. This will come as no surprise to feminist critics, certainly, who know, on the one hand, that the fixed biblical text has omitted women's voices and, on the other, that the selective liturgical perception of the Bible in both lectionary and prayer corpus has only exacerbated the damage.[4] A more malleable view of *canon* allows us to value our inheritance from our past but at the same time to use it selectively and wisely, so that the past is not some toxic waste endangering our future.

The Bible, however, is a closed canon, in that its actual contents are not open for revision from year to year. Only its utilization varies with user selectivity—Christians who tote their Scofield Bible to church find the future writ large in Daniel and Revelation; those more apt to cite the new Revised Standard Version do not. More germane to our understanding of music as canon are examples where the actual canonical contents vary constantly. The "Great Books" is such an instance, as we recognize from the current debate about the loosely defined canon of literature that cultured people are supposed to recognize (maybe even read?). As with the Bible, we encounter the claim that the literary canon is selectively prejudicial against minorities and women. Where are the women authors, African-American heroes, South American writers, and so forth? I do not advance the radical argument in favor of chucking out the whole corpus: Shakespeare, Melville, Shaw, and all. But I can think of good reasons to ransack the rejection slips of the centuries to locate women and minority authors of substance; and I think too that the concept of *open canon* can be infinitely expanded in the future to include at least a fair sampling of writers plying their trade today and tomorrow.

Another example of an open canon is the liturgy itself—the texts that have evolved and found a place as sacred literature to be proclaimed as prayer. Here too, neither Jew nor Christian has closed the canon. For some it is more pliable than for others, but we all agree that the gold mines of old texts uncovered by historians in liturgical rejection piles may yet find posthumous acceptance. Mark Twain may not be the only one to be able to boast that the story of his death has been greatly exaggerated. Lots of old and buried texts bear silent witness to the truth of resurrection. And lots of contemporary authors who are not white, Christian males have further expanded the mix of what we say when we worship.

Sacred sound is like a literary or liturgical canon. To begin with, some items are widely regarded as central—Shakespeare for literature, the Lord's Prayer or *Shema Yisra'el* for liturgies, Bach's B Minor Mass or Yom Kippur's traditional *Kol Nidre* for music. Other entities in each canon take turns being central and then, as tastes change, they are replaced; I don't think people read Charles Dickens and Emily Brontë as much as they used to, but *Great Expectations* and *Wuthering Heights* do not on that account cease being in the canon—they are just temporarily out of favor. So too there are prayers on which we were raised that are not said with the same relish or frequency as they were; but they are still canonical. And with music, even if Sunday mass or Shabbat services fail to feature the same songs we used to hear fifty years ago, those missing melodies have not necessarily been dropped from the canon.

Of course some things do get dropped. These open canons of literature, liturgy, and music are not like the Bible, which includes books and lessons we might love to drop but cannot. Offended sufficiently by stories, prayers, or hymns, however, we readily let them pass into desuetude. I doubt that we shall read *Little Black Sambo* any more; Christian prayers to convert the Jews will probably not return; I hardly think Reform Judaism will again embrace the daily *Tefillah* prayer's malediction against heretics. The good thing about open canonical decisions is that they are made beyond the whim of any one person or committee. They take generations to be decided. When it comes to open canons, judgments evolve gradually. They are matters of consensus, since that is all an open canon is: a consensual scheme by which people assume that some things matter more than others.

Over time, the canon grows with new material, and more and more, these days, anyone can try her or his hand at adding to it. Once again, only time will tell whether something is or is not canonical. Not all songs admitted into the liturgy will be sung twice, let alone the many, many times over a course of years that it takes to make a work canonical. On the other hand, if a song never gets sung, it surely will fail. In that regard, one conclusion stands out by virtue of its being repeated by one author after another in this book. Nowadays, getting your tune sung as worship is much easier than it used to be. We can predict, therefore, that the canon will expand accordingly, as it makes room for the best of different kinds of music.

Priestly, Prophetic, and Pastoral Worship

Our authors return again and again to the theme of musical diversity, which has become the norm in both church and synagogue—and not just for musical reasons. We sometimes forget that sacred sound is intrinsically bound up with the sacred texts that are our prayers and the sacred drama that is our worship. Liturgical trends thus have musical consequences. It is not without significance, therefore, that liturgists have begun emphasizing a performative theory of what gets done in worship. By *performative,* I do not mean the normal artistic denotation, as in "the performing arts." Rather, liturgists borrow the term from philosophy and mean by it "performing tasks." Emphasis now is on the task or function required of any particular element in a ritual. Music thus plays many functions in our services. It gathers us together as community, develops emotional moods, provides quiet time for meditation, lets us sing in great elation, interprets sacred texts, and so on.[5] Depending on the performative task at hand, music is variously listened to, sung by choirs, chanted, intoned as communal response, belted out by the congregation, performed by a solo voice, and so on. People write in many styles to accommodate many musical tasks. The canon grows to reflect them all.

The second reason for diversity is the growing importance of the assembly or congregation in liturgical theory and practice. Time was when authorities did not much care what the people thought; when, in fact, leaders of worship rarely knew who the people were and did not much care. In Catholic history, the medieval practice of private masses comes to mind. Huge Protestant churches and Reform Temples went through years of American history in which the prince of the pulpit labored all week to give a stirring hour of Sabbath oratory to a crowd of anonymous auditors, whose sole task was to listen and go home. By contrast, M. T. Winter reminds us that current Catholic ecclesiology identifies the gathering of worshipers as the church. And nowadays, pastors are really that, pastors, whose seminary-taught preaching skills are important, but who probably appreciate the art of counseling and caring far more than their ministerial forebears did. Not just people in the abstract but persons in the concrete have become central to American religious experience, and that new-found attention to who is present among us as we seek the presence of God leads eventually to the recognition that not all persons are alike. Hence a second reason for diversity—not just the liturgical function of the music, but the human diversity among the worshipers as well.

We should not take this newly discovered pastoral emphasis for granted. A recent study of liturgies in progressive Jewish congregations worldwide is worth citing in detail; allowing for some deviation based on theological differences, its conclusions are equally descriptive of Christianity as well.

> There are signs that some of us have entered [a new] stage of liturgical creativity, the stage we call Personalism. Classical liturgies left little room for individuals. Everyone did everything together. Worshipers sat together, stood together, read together, and listened together. Moreover, relatively scant attention was given to prayer outside the synagogue walls. And finally, life cycle events were all the same: group confirmation had replaced individual bar mitzvah; weddings and funerals followed stipulated service texts which were not altered for individual needs. Home prayer books were published, but not widely used. . . .
>
> The 1980's have suggested an increasing accent on individual needs. Already in the 1960's of course, one could see this trend—hence the decision to increase optional readings and individual meditations in many of our books. . . . But by personalism, we mean more than having options in our liturgies, and more also than enjoying several alternative prayer books. . . . When we speak of personalism, we mean above all a new accent on persons, individuals—a recognition that not all our worshipers are the same, a sense that the liturgy must not exclude anyone. Our congregations are filled with women and men, children and adults, young and old, sick and well. They are married and unmarried; people with family needs and individuals seeking private consolation or spiritual purpose. There are homosexuals and lesbians, single

parent families, people without children (of necessity or by design), converts to Judaism, the Jewishly educated and the Jewishly naive. Personalism is the genuine desire to enhance personal spirituality for each person in our midst, to say and do nothing liturgically that inhibits their full participation in the Jewish people, and their full identification with the liturgical vision unfurled in the canvas of our prayers. This new liturgical stage emphasizes the personal voice in public prayer, and the responsibility of public prayer to respect the persons who constitute the public.[6]

The shift from corporatism to personalism is the most major breakthrough for worship in our time. And it is new. We can characterize worship as fulfilling two other roles too, but they are older; we are more familiar with them. First, there is the *priestly* model, in which worship is cultic and priests or other worship specialists invoke the presence of God on a largely passive congregation. The old Jerusalem Temple, for instance, called forth God's presence with the priestly benediction from Numbers and the Levitical chanting of psalms. Second, we find a *prophetic* model, where the goal of worship is to move people to action. Preaching is central here; so too is music that delivers a message and unifies the assembly around a common task in the world—recollect the singing of "We Shall Overcome" during the heady days of prophetic worship that accompanied the Civil Rights marches. Now personalism gives us our third model, which we have already designated *pastoral*. Pastoral worship empowers people to find the presence of God in the ordinary activity of life; it identifies God as sitting with the people rather than on high. It emphasizes a tradition common to Jews and Christians: the Mishnah's insistence, "Where two sit together and the words between them are Torah, the divine presence is in their midst."[7] Or, as Matthew puts it, "Where two or three are gathered in my name, I am there in their midst."[8]

Sacred music is asked to perform with all of these three models in mind. Worship cannot be any one alone. Contemporary American musical creativity has emphasized the assembly's singing and the popular sound because those are often what fulfill the third of our three functions, the pastoral. Our inherited pool of sound contains many examples of the priestly, and quite a few hymns that are prophetic as well, but relatively few examples of the pastoral. We are passing through a twofold stage in readjusting our musical canon: first, new causes in the world are drawing our attention to the liberation music of today; and second, pastoral music especially is being written to make up for the relative dearth in compositions that fit this newly discovered liturgical concern. Some of the musical works in both these categories will eventually enter the canon; others will not. Only history will tell.

Prospect

Was the equilibrium of Christian worshipers upset by the invention of composed polyphony? Were Jewish worshipers shocked by the first Hasidic *niggun*? Surely we are not the first generation to find that our sound pool has become turbulent as new compositions enter it. Swimming holes always have room for fresh water dropped by the rain in a sudden summer storm. When the sun comes out again, you run even faster then usual to dive into the water, which is mostly what it was before, but which has been augmented with just a little bit of freshness. Canons grow too, else they lapse into museum relics that only a few throwbacks to the good old days remember how to read. Archibald McLeish writes J. B. and leads me back again with newfound curiosity to the biblical book of Job—Would I have reread Job so quickly without *J. B.*? Who knows? The old favorites of our musical canon are not threatened by new music; they can only be enriched thereby. The sound pool of sacred music is being enriched by the freshness of new compositions. We should stop running for cover and, instead, enjoy the rain.

NOTES

1. My thanks to Cantor Don Gurney for this suggestive metaphor, which I expand in ways that (I hope) are acceptable to him.

2. James A. Sanders, *Canon and Community* (Philadelphia, 1984), p. 38.

3. Ibid., p. 37.

4. Cf., e.g., Elisabeth Schüssler Fiorenza, "Remembering the Past in Creating the Future: Historical-Critical Scholarship and Feminist Biblical Interpretation," in Adela Yarbro Collins, ed., *Feminist Perspectives on Biblical Scholarship*, (Chico, Ca., 1985), pp. 43–63; Marjorie Procter-Smith, *In Her Own Rite: Constructing Feminist Liturgical Tradition* (Nashville, 1990); Marjorie Procter-Smith, "'Reorganizing Victimization': The Intersection between Liturgy and Domestic Violence," *Perkins Journal* (October 1987): 17–27; Janet R. Walton, "The Missing Element of Women's Experience," in Paul F. Bradshaw and Lawrence A. Hoffman, eds., *The Changing Face of Jewish and Christian Worship in North America* (Notre Dame, Ind., 1991), pp. 199–218.

5. For a discussion of performative theory attached to music, see Lawrence A. Hoffman, *The Art of Public Prayer* (Washington, D.C., 1989), pp. 243–66.

6. Lawrence A. Hoffman and Nancy Wiener, "The Liturgical State of the World Union for Progressive Judaism," *European Judaism* 24/1 (1991): 17.

7. M. Avot 3:2; cf. Avot deRabbi Nathan B, ch. 34.

8. Matthew 18:20.

Index